INCHBALD
Celebrating 65 years of Interior and Garden Design Education

INCHBALD
Celebrating 65 years of Interior and Garden Design Education

JACQUELINE DUNCAN

Unicorn Press

First published in 2025
Unicorn Press
60 Bracondale
Norwich NR1 2BE
UK

tradfordhugh@gmail.com
www.unicornpublishing.org

Text Copyright © 2025 Jacqueline Duncan

Illustrations © as credited

All rights reserved. Without limiting the rights under Copyright reserved above, no part of this publication may be reproduced, stored or introduced into a retrieval system, or transmitted in any form or by any means (electronic, mechanical, photocopying, recording or otherwise), without the prior written permission of both the copyright owner and the publisher of this book.

A CIP record of this book can be obtained from the British Library

ISBN 978-1-7391640-6-5

Designed by Karen Wilks

Printed in Malta by Gutenberg Press Ltd

Frontispiece: Jacqueline, 1965, © All rights reserved

CONTENTS

Foreword	i
Preface	iii
Chapter 1	1
Chapter 2	8
Chapter 3	14
Chapter 4	19
Chapter 5	23
Chapter 6	28
Chapter 7	32
Chapter 8	37
Chapter 9	41
Chapter 10	47
Chapter 11	55
Chapter 12	63
Interior Design	158
Garden Design	186
Acknowledgements	202
Index	204
Credits	210

FOREWORD

I was 21 when in 1960 I went to work for Michael and Jacqueline Inchbald; it was my first job after completing a 3-year diploma course at the Division of Decoration, Bartlett School of Architecture, University College, London.

Jacqueline (now Jacqueline Duncan) had established her Interior Design School at about the same time and it was popular right from the start. Courses took place in what had been called the Ballroom, in the Inchbalds' large and elegant house in Milner Street, Chelsea. The rest of the ground floor was the design office. The interior design, decoration and contents of all the rooms was beautiful; at the time there were few private houses in London to equal it.

photograph: Derry Moore

What has happened since has been remarkable and exciting and Jacqueline describes in fascinating detail what English life was like for a young person interested in design and decoration both privately and professionally. Among the designers she identifies as the most talented and successful were Michael Inchbald, David Hicks, Jon Bannenberg, John Siddeley and John Fowler, while others, survivors from the pre-World War 2 years, were doing good, but to a young person, less exciting work. Antique dealers with shop window displays of furniture and stylish textiles showed that they too were practising interior decoration.

Now of course we have Chelsea Harbour Design Centre and many more studios and shops. The magazines have introduced what is possible for all and much more money has been spent as the UK entered a period of unprecedented prosperity. Furthermore, there is now more acceptance of the role of professional designer/decorator thanks to the innovative education provided by such as the Inchbald School. In 1960 interior design was already a respected profession in France and North America; it has taken longer to become established in the UK.

And there has been a major change in styling. I remember when the basic principle of a successful set of rooms was that they should 'answer the architecture'. Also that elements should respond to each other. Now people expect the elements to work in contrast, so anything goes. The art historian, John Cornforth, called this effect 'A bumpy ride'. He was very interested in what he described as 'The rise in decoration'. Just as with clothes, tastes change and will again.

Over the years, I have met, employed and talked to many students from the Inchbald School. All have been complimentary of their courses, and I quote: 'I enjoyed every minute of it'; 'Happiest time of my life'; 'I found the work addictive'; 'It was too short'; 'I would do it all over again'.

Jacqueline has a gift for putting people together. She introduced me to some of my first clients and I know she has done the same for others. She is also extremely capable of 'turning people on', to use a 1960's expression, and continues to do so with great generosity and enthusiasm.

David Mlinaric CBE
April 2025

PREFACE

WHY and HOW

In 1949 I was 18, convent educated and the reluctant survivor of two finishing schools, establishments which no longer exist. The first taught me a modicum of French but such limitation was entirely my fault.

The second one, the House of Citizenship, was founded and run by a daunting feminist called Miss Dorothy Neville-Rolfe, who wanted all her students to embark on meaningful careers. This was in direct contrast to maternal ambitions then prevalent, guiding daughters to the idylls of marriage and children, cooking and flower arranging, and of course elegant living. On balance I suspect Miss Neville-Rolfe died a disappointed disciple of birth control, womens' rights, and above all, womens' potential in current affairs.

I was a cause of irritation in my final leaving interview with her:

'Now what are you going to do with your life?' she asked hopefully. But hope was ill founded. 'Get married, I suppose', was the muttered reply, a reply which elicited a sharp response from my headmistress. The fact is that in 1949, even the few outstanding women who achieved success were underrated by most men, their achievements acknowledged as some kind of fluke. Feminists were certainly not making headlines in the late 1940s.

No school I attended had offered the prospect of career possibilities to my generation of students; not even Miss Neville-Rolfe, in spite of the fact that she herself was a long way ahead of her generation. In 1948 a career for intelligent women who had benefited from a good education was still not a serious option. Young women were directed to support roles, typically as secretaries or nurses, in spite of the fact that David Lloyd George's government passed the Sex Disqualification (Removal) Act in December 1919.

Accordingly, I went off to a short secretarial course at Pitman's and rather nervously embarked on a career as a secretary at Withers. The leading firm of solicitors had six partners, of whom five of the six were Old Etonians and I was the No. 2 secretary to the hardest working of those partners, Arthur Collins, who had spent the war as the Adjutant of the Blues. Thus I benefited from Mr Collins's honed views on discipline and the very experienced wisdom of the Senior Secretary, Margaret Fairhurst, who had excelled in the War in the ATS but who was barred from officer rank because she had not taken Higher Certificate (in spite of the 1919 Act). Miss Fairhurst was a well-known character to both clients and staff in the distinctive hierarchy of Withers.

The late 1940s was a time of recovery and resuscitation for society as a whole across England, but this was particularly so in London.

Money was short, clothes were on coupons and rationing was still part of our lives, but there was a conscious effort among our elders to restore the familiarity of old ways; I remember being amazed and impressed by the determination of my parent's friends and my own friends' parents to bring us all back to what they perceived as normality. There were cocktail parties, debutante dances and hunt balls, albeit with limitations on difficult-to-obtain alcohol. We danced to the wonderful music of Cole Porter and the shock of rock and roll, newly imported by wartime American GIs! The problems associated with these endeavours served only to emphasise the happiness of their success and in spite of circumstances, these were increasingly happy years, certainly for my generation.

It was at one of these cocktail parties that I met Michael Inchbald, elegant, good-looking and more than a little challenging.

After spending the war years in India, Michael had returned to England to study at the Architectural Association. He disliked the requirement to include engineering in his curriculum, and did not qualify, preferring to identify himself as an architectural interior designer, a role in which he excelled. Although he was far better professionally educated (he was 10 years older than me) our mutual interests in antique styles and furniture as well as Interior Design, drew us together and during the course of our engagement, we travelled widely in England and France, buying beautiful and unlikely objects and furniture, finally starting an antique business in London's Walton Street and making use at the same time of the considerable spaces offered by the Milner Street house in Chelsea belonging to Michael's charming uncle, horologist Courtenay Ilbert.

During this time my fascination with history led me into the story of the skills and achievements of the interior design profession, in particular as it had developed in America where women's professional development was less inhibited than was the case in England – and of course the characteristics of the American woman were a great deal less constrained than those of her English cousins. That American women should embrace and develop the emergent profession of Interior Decoration seemed no more than natural progress and the first of these was Elsie de Wolfe.

Ella Anderson de Wolfe was born in 1859, nearly 60 years before Lloyd George's ground breaking Bill; initially she launched herself as an actress and commanded attention more for her sense of style than for acting ability. Intensely aware of her surroundings, her visual discrimination led

CHAPTER 1

Left: Michael Inchbald in his scarlet Drawing Room, 1950s.

The Gate of the Year

There are catalytic moments in life and looking back over 93 years there are some I remember with a crystal clarity. Whether or not they led on to anything, they are milestones in my life and without exception they were also turning points, moments in which my perceptions shifted or expanded, transforming my existence into an uncertain kaleidoscope of possibility. Some were funny, some dramatic and some banal, though banality is a factor unknown to childhood.

And childhood is where it starts for all of us.

I have always been a countrywoman, admiring London but not wishing to live there, yearning for green trees, green lanes and the pleasure of birdsong, never mind the freedom of living with dogs, horses and cattle. It was not going to happen!

I was born on the 16th December 1931 to a reluctant mother in Wilbraham Place, a block away from Sloane Square in London. For the past seventy years, I have lived in this part of London for practically the whole time. I stayed in the nursing home for some three months, known to the nurses as Bunty, until my grandmother, who resisted adoption vehemently, took me back to Portsmouth and put me into care with a foster mother.

My grandmother's name was Beatrice Morris. She was a pretty girl, studying art at the Slade with a view to becoming a glass engraver. She clearly worked slowly, since an exam drawing of considerable expertise (it was a detailed Corinthian capital) was considered to be so good that although it was unfinished the examiner could not bring himself to put his pencil through it as the rules decreed. Instead, it was framed and hung in her house until she died. I always loved it and made her laugh with a mixture of delight and deprecation when I constantly asked if I could have it when she no longer needed it. Unhappily it has disappeared.

But before there was any further development in my grandmother's artistic career, she fell in love with a tall redhead and in marrying him, ran away from her home in London. Her family were fairly well-to-do brewers but she appears to have been cut off in the name of respectability and I am not aware that she ever saw them again. She never referred to them and I have no idea of my grandfather's background. The young couple were established in Portsmouth by the turn of the century, my grandfather working as a dockyard worker and my mother born on November 11th 1913, the seventh child of a family living on the edges of poverty. My grandfather was killed in the First World War, no more than a statistic among the millions of young men who never returned to their families and their work. Serving as a gunner on HMS *Goliath* (RMA 3448) in the Dardanelles, he went down with her on the 13th May, 1915. My mother was no more than eighteen months old.

My mother and her closest sister described the poverty to which they were reduced. The children dispersed as soon as they could do so. The eldest son, Cecil, went to America and after the war ended in 1918, Frances, a very sparky blonde, went on stage as a dancer and changed her name to Phyllis. Confusingly, my mother's name was also Phyllis but she didn't seem to mind and accordingly changed her name to Sonia. The second eldest son, Dudley, enlisted in the Merchant Navy and retired as a Captain, a considerable achievement for a boy who had little help in his childhood.

By the late 1920s my mother was working as a model; in those days they were known as mannequins and she was clearly quite successful. Most of the Pentney children were tall and good looking, my mother handsome like her brother Dudley, with auburn hair which was bright red in childhood. In this, and in her volatile temperament she clearly took after her father, whilst her sister Frances was smaller, blonde and more fragile like my grandmother.

Of the remaining children Doris died of tuberculosis when she was in her teens, the eldest Gladys never left home until her last years, causing my grandmother considerable chagrin, and neither did the youngest, Maurice, who had suffered from meningitis when he was small.

My very early years are a blank – I have a vague recollection of the foster home, of occasional visits for tea to my grandmother who kept a child's chair for my use and always referred to me as the baby rather than using my name, but there was little or no contact with my mother as far as I know. My grandmother arranged for my christening and a friend of my mother's, Sir George Johnston, stood godfather, so she must have been there as well. My father meanwhile, had married a woman called Dora who ran some kind of dress business. He himself had been a very successful young stockbroker, and spent a lot of his money buying a pub in the West Country which he then sold to concentrate on Dora's business. His father came from a Scottish family who had gone out to Madeira in the 18th century and founded a successful winery known as Donaldsons. Their large house is still to be found in the centre of Funchal, now converted into a school. The business was sold at the turn of the 19th century and Grandfather Donaldson came back to London, entered the city and became a jobber on the Stock Exchange.

Chapter 1

My Donaldson grandfather lived near Luton with his wife Norah and was driven daily to the City by his driver. My grandmother volunteered as a nurse in the war, and it may be then that she met her husband. Unhappily he was killed in a car accident on his way to the City one day and in the early 1930s she sold the house and built a bungalow for herself in a part of the grounds. She also married the chauffeur who had been part of the accident, to the fury of my father.

My mother was a very glamorous young woman, with the kind of structured good looks which were currently being made fashionable by Joan Crawford. She looked wonderful in hats and consequently modelled them often. At some party or other she met a young man on leave from his work in the Colonial service in Africa and in the manner of a Maugham short story she married him.

John Bromley was the son of Canon Bromley of Bath, the eldest of three children.

He was a particularly kind man, and when he was told of my existence he agreed to accept me as his daughter. Since I was about two or three at the time of the marriage, this was all I knew, and thus when my mother changed her name I became Jill Bromley and for years knew nothing different.

My mother was taken along to meet her in-laws and there is a rather touching portrait photo of her, posing as the new daughter-in-law in a classic wool dress with a pretty Victorian brooch pinned to the bodice, a present from John's mother. It was all a far cry from the taboo subject of an illegitimate child that John had so generously taken on as his own.

John was a quiet, bookish man with two passions in his life, animals and Africa. I cannot resist the thought that he had painted a picture to my mother of Africa as being the most desirable place on earth and he was certainly so engaging when he talked and told his stories, that I fear my mother, urban, sparky, party-going glamour puss, was duly enthralled at the prospect of being involved in an adventure that would remove her far from her background, of which she was increasingly ashamed, and from the stain of her child's birth. I don't think the reality of up-country Africa ever took shape in her mind at this time and indeed how would it?

So life changed dramatically for both of us.

Marriage must also have been a relief, offering stability and protection from her uncertain and difficult background. As far as I was concerned, I was so young that when I was introduced to 'Daddy', the change in circumstance was seamless; and as with so many animal lovers, John was wonderful with small children. He took me riding on the beach, he put me to bed with cuddles and I was consciously very happy with him. My mother also seemed content, looking glamorous when she went out, wonderful in the evening if they went to parties, and eventually a nursemaid of sorts arrived who relieved her of the daily chores attendant upon the care of an infant.

However, all was not quite well; John disliked working in England, and he yearned for Africa. He was also aware that he could do better in the Colonial Service than in the depressed 1930s in England so they decided to go to East Africa to make a new life. This did not include me. He knew that he would be going up-country, and what the circumstances were likely to be. But he thought my mother would cope. They also shared the same view about taking a child of three or four into such a challenging life. Accordingly it was decided that they should find somewhere in England where I could be looked after, presumably until I was old enough to go out to Kenya.

The Lodge in Yapton, Sussex was a quite pretty little house, built probably in the second quarter of the 19th century. It was double-fronted, with a room each side of the front door, a central staircase and a dining room and kitchen quarters beyond. Curiously for such a small house, it had a second staircase for staff at the back, which led to a top corridor and four or five bedrooms. It was explained to me that I was going to school here and that Miss Davis was now going to look after me and teach me to read and write.

We drove through front gates into a forecourt in the centre of which was a circular flower bed filled with violet pansies. I was so entranced by the brilliance of the colour that I paid little attention to what was being said over my head. Finally, someone nudged me – Miss Davis was talking to me and she asked me a question, 'What is your favourite colour?' 'Purple' I replied without lifting my gaze from her pansies. 'How very grown up' she remarked and with that my parents said their farewells and I was swept into the house that would be my home until the spring of 1940.

My bedroom decorated in blue and yellow faced onto the front garden. For some reason I later hated this colour combination though I have no recollection of objecting to it at that time. The slatted blinds were wooden and made a clackety noise in the draught and wind, a sound I came to find rather reassuring. There was a small bed, and a chest of drawers – beside my bed there was an upright chair, and little more could have fitted into the space. The room was at the end of the corridor and when I was put to bed, the door was left ajar so that I could be heard if there was any trouble. There never was, I had long ago learnt to be compliant and to adjust to change. In fact there was to be no change for the next four years, and I slipped easily into Miss Davis's routine.

Miss Davis employed a governess/nursemaid to take general care of any children in the house, a cook to whom I was devoted, Mrs Hunt, and a gardener. I doubt if Miss Davis was a generous employer. The governesses came and went, Mrs Hunt did not appear to like them and the gardeners were at best a rather surly lot, though it must be said that children romping through their work must have been taxing to say the least.

Initially I remember several children in the schoolroom, but none of them lived in the house, so perhaps Miss Davis ran some kind of nursery school. She was certainly a good teacher and I learnt to read and write quite early. I was soon joined by another child, a little boy called Owen Leigh. Owen had the most ravishing mother to whom he was utterly devoted and she to him. She was an actress, her name was Lisa, and I imagine she was unable to care for him whilst she was working. She often came to see him, beautifully dressed, full of warmth and smiles.

The other front room opposite the school room was a private sitting room for Miss Davis and I don't think I entered it more than two or three times during my life at Yapton. When I did, I registered that it had the most hideous carpet, multi-coloured flowers on a thick beige ground, the same carpet that ran up the main staircase from the hall to the bedroom corridor. Children were not allowed on this staircase, but instead used the old staff staircase which led from Mrs Hunt's kitchen quarters to our bedrooms. I had no problem with this – Mrs Hunt was very motherly, and generally put us to bed anyway. She was a good-looking woman, her dark hair swept back into a bun, her generous figure always clothed in white overalls and her smile ever ready to greet us when we invaded her kitchen.

After breakfast we went straight to the schoolroom, where we studied all morning until lunch time. The dining room was at the back of the house, and almost fully taken up by the dining room table and chairs, with a large radio on the sideboard under the window. After lunch we went for a walk with the governess; we always wore hats and coats, and in my case gaiters and gloves. The back door led out into the garden and from there we went on to the village and one of a variety of walks, across the common past the Leg of Mutton Inn, down to the shop, along to the railway line to watch the trains go by, and sometimes to the small aerodrome in case there should be an aeroplane landing or taking off.

The Lodge had two gateways, one to the front of the house and one to what must once have been a stable yard. Miss Davis did not drive, so the garage complex had been turned into a very tidy store, where we stacked the apples in the autumn, stripped the rhubarb for jam in the summer and helped to stack firewood for the dining room fireplace. Miss Davis was a keen gardener, and we sometimes helped her planting out her beloved primulas and pansies, or in the spring we filled old egg shells, carefully saved from breakfast, with compost and a single sweet pea in each shell. These were left in the greenhouse until they were strong shoots; after crushing the base of the shell to allow the roots freedom, they were planted out into the garden for picking during the summer. It worked brilliantly!

There were few ructions at Yapton Lodge. Once, crossing the common, I was bitten by an enraged stallion, which was quite painful and threw the governess into hysterics. We ran for our lives until we reached the village shop, where the kind shopkeeper, seeing me distressed, gave me a small penknife to cheer me up. Occasionally the little tortoises went missing but they always turned up in time to be put to bed in the greenhouse where they spent the winter; and once when I was half asleep I woke to stare into two huge yellow eyes and to hear the sound of a monstrous thrumming. I must have called out because Miss Davis came running but not before the cat had crawled affectionately into my bed for a cuddle, To my disappointment he was swiftly extricated and after that my door remained closed.

Tea was between 4.30 and 5pm. Certainly we were seated at tea well before the news on the radio. The room was small but there was always a fire burning in the winter which endangered the chairs close to the hearth. Accordingly when the fire was lit, Miss Davies fixed cane shields to the back of the chairs to protect them and presumably her charges from the heat.

As soon as tea was served the cat moved into the dining room with the exactitude of an alarm clock and Miss Davies put down a saucer of milk in the corner of the fireplace. I remember so well the sound of the cat lapping the milk and quite soon we were bidden to silence, waiting for the clarion calls of Big Ben: " This is the 6 o-clock news and this is Alvar Liddell reading it – or Stuart Hibberd." One evening the presenter announced importantly – "This is the 6 o-clock news and this is me reading it" We didn't laugh, it would have been sacrilege, but I have never forgotten the wonder of this grown-up mistake, or how sorry I felt for him.

My parents made one of their rare visits to England during the year of the King's funeral in 1935 and then again in the summer of 1939. I stayed with them in a rented cottage somewhere, and I recall the atmosphere of silence that prevailed one Sunday morning. It was unusual for my mother to be so quiet and she remained so until we were all in a little open-top car which John must have hired for the holiday, bowling along on some excursion which seemed to have lost its promise.

I have a vivid memory of my mother sitting in the passenger seat, elegant in blue and white with a little panama hat trimmed in blue tilted sideways over her brow.. I see her now as she turned to my father and said:

"Are we really at war then John?"

John replied quietly "We have been at war with Germany since 11 o'clock this morning."

War was a disturbing word, but incomprehensible in any degree of reality to a child of six. To my mother it represented all the poverty, loss and degradation she had experienced when she too was a child and it seemed she was stunned to be confronted with such fear and deprivation again. They moved quietly through the next few days of their holiday.

John was recalled to the King's African Rifles, and my mother packed for him, shopped with him and constantly discussed where he might be sent. He was instructed to report to a troopship sailing for an unknown port in Africa and she went to see him off. On her return her distress was evident, though I think it was caused by confusion rather than sorrow. She wept when she discovered that she had forgotten to pack his flannel, and thus in such dire circumstances, the banal details of living take on ludicrous importance.

Whether I would have stayed at Miss Davis's had war not broken out, or for how long, I will never know.

As it was, I was returned to my small room with the clacking wooden blinds and the carved wooden African rifleman presiding over the fireplace. But of course nothing was as usual and the whole country was in a turmoil of plans, indecision and change.

Sitting with Miss Davis anticipating the news, the cat present as ever with her saucer of milk, I listened to the King addressing the Empire. His speech was slow, a determined attempt to control the stutter from which he was known to suffer, and more moving for the knowledge of his difficulty. At the end of his determined encouragement to his subjects he memorably quoted Minnie Haskins' lines:

'I said to the man who stood at the Gate of the Year, "Give me a light that I may tread safely into the unknown." And he replied, "Go out into the darkness, and put your hand into the hand of God. That shall be to you better than light, and safer than a known way."

CHAPTER 2

Education and Evacuation

In due course my mother took me to visit a school to which she proposed to send me.

She had looked at schools that she thought might be suitable but she was considerably encumbered by lack of funds. She finally tried Roehampton, the mother-house in England of the Society of the Sacred Heart. The Society was founded by Madeleine Sophie Barratt at the instigation of her brother, a priest, at the turn of the 18th and 19th centuries in France. The Barratts were a peasant family and Father Barratt was deeply concerned that the Revolution had left France, in particular the lower and middle classes, bereft of any religious teaching. The Society came to England during the 19th century when the anti-Catholic laws were being relaxed, and established the house at Roehampton. This was followed by an establishment at Brighton, and another later at Tunbridge Wells. By the time my mother was trying to get me into Roehampton, the school had become extremely fashionable; years later a past pupil assured me that when she was there seven of the pupils were princesses, a proud boast that must have caused Mother Sophie Barratt to spin in her grave. In the event, my mother was directed to the house at Brighton and I was duly enrolled.

The Sacred Heart Convent was in Hove and the Convent grounds occupied one long block of the Upper Drive. A high wall confined a

Convent of the Sacred Heart, Hove.

property of something over twenty acres, with the former private villa acting now as an entrance lodge. Beyond this was the chapel, and the wide corridor led through the purpose-built school building to large glass doors leading to the gardens and games areas beyond.

Arriving at the front door, my mother rang the bell and we waited. Eventually a small aperture opened and we were viewed; "Yes?" The voice was not discourteous but nor was it inviting.

"I am Mrs Bromley and I have brought my daughter to meet the Headmistress."

We were invited to enter and were ushered into a large room on the right of the front door. It was probably the largest room I had ever seen, and the windows at the end, opening on to the garden, were flanked by long curtains of bright orange velvet. Years later, when I returned for a reunion, the orange curtains were still there, a silent witness to the immutability of convent life.

The chapel was impressive to a seven-year-old.

I recall little of the occasion beyond the curtains, and was quite relieved to be returned to the familiarity of Miss Davis and Yapton. I was to spend Christmas there and go to my new school in January.

Twice during my time at Miss Davis's I had been taken out by a small, round woman who had an unnerving habit of gazing inquisitively at me – she was very kind, bought me toys and returned me to Yapton but I really had no idea who she was or why I went out with her. One morning, Miss Davis was sorting her post as usual when she announced – "This one is for you Jacqueline". I recall that she did not seem pleased that I should be contacted thus and she watched me whilst I endeavoured to open the envelope. It was the first letter I had ever received apart from those John sent me from Africa on airmail forms, and I was clumsy with the envelope. Finally, I got it open and something fell out and skittered across the floor. By this time everyone was anxious to know what was in the letter, but it fell at Miss Davis's feet and she picked it up – a fine three-stone diamond ring. She looked even more disapproving but handed it to me to see and told me to read the letter.

It was very brief and came from the woman who had taken me out. She was very ill, she told me, and I would not see her again, but she wanted me to have this ring in memory of her. That was all.

Miss Davis took the ring for safe keeping and sadly failed to preserve the letter. Later it transpired that the small lady was my paternal grandmother, who was dying of cancer. My mother took the ring, pawned it to pay for her passage to Africa in John's wake and retrieved it after the war. Unhappily she wore it herself and it was stolen in a burglary in 1946. It was the only thing I ever possessed that belonged to my father's family.

My mother set off for Africa and Christmas was celebrated in Yapton. John's charming brother, Christopher Bromley, arrived on Christmas Day, loaded with presents – painting books, dolls, games and two books he thought I should read, *The Tower of London* by Harrison Ainsworth which I still have, and one other which went missing, equally sophisticated. He and his friend were the greatest fun and we had a wonderful day. He died young so that I never got to know him well, but he certainly left his mark on my memory with his sweetness and generosity.

I cannot recall when Owen left, and I have no memory of saying goodbye to him. We were not close but he was a constant companion and I often wonder what happened to him.

On January 16th 1940 I was delivered to the Convent in Hove, with a new school uniform and an attitude that reflected my background which had been mostly stable but a little unpredictable. There were no tears because in truth there was no home for which to be homesick. Miss Davis was a distant figure but the time I spent with her had been ordered and largely agreeable and I suppose I thought that was the way life would be in the Convent.

On balance I was right, but there was much greater personal commitment from the nuns to the children, in spite of the nature of convent life. A small nun, Mother Lillie, was in charge of the junior school and took her responsibilities very seriously, whether it was a matter of cleaning your teeth or making sure you had a veil for early Mass. I slipped easily into Convent routine. I had been well taught to read and write by Miss Davis so these lessons were undemanding. I was delighted by a novel subject, drawing and painting, and was intrigued during my first lesson when we were all given a snowdrop to draw. Until then I had only used colouring books.

The only child I remember from those early days was Davida Campbell. Her mother was said to have run away, and she was looked after by her father who she adored. He had delivered her to the Convent, leaving her with a large silver box of chocolates to comfort her, and long after they were finished she clung to the box like a talisman. He was called up and went to war, and was among the many soldiers captured at Dunkirk. Soon Davida was informed that he was imprisoned in Germany. It was the first great shock we had of this new international conflict.

She was a fiery little person, her temper not helped by fear for her father, and frustration; it has to be remembered that she was a Protestant child in a Catholic convent, and no matter what your family beliefs, you still lived to the Catholic pattern of the House. There were one or two run-ins with the nuns, but she settled eventually and soon the rest of the class joined us at the beginning of the spring term, so that she had other things to engage her beyond her own unhappiness.

Chapter 2

I returned to Miss Davis for the Easter holidays but it was all very different. Owen was not there, the governess had gone and I was really left to my own devices, a situation so unusual in that well-ordered house that I was at first baffled as to what I should do. The schoolroom had a gramophone in it, so I played popular songs and danced by myself, or read the daunting *Tower of London* which I found difficult going. I went for walks by myself, once discovering and rescuing a ferret which had caught its lead in a hedgerow.

I found it all rather odd; one morning Miss Davis called me as I passed her room and asked me to help her put on her stockings. This also was odd – she was an essentially distant person and had certainly never asked for my help before. For the first time I becme aware of her age. Mrs Hunt came less often and the gardener had gone, no doubt to the war.

When the packing was done for my return to school, I was surprised that Miss Davis included a particularly fine Victorian doll which had been given to me and which she had always insisted on keeping safe, together with an organdie bridesmaid dress that I had worn when I was three. Neither seemed particularly relevant to convent life.

I recall Miss Davis coming to see me off and for the first time I felt uncertain about what was going on in my life and in the world with which I was familiar. I returned to the Convent in Hove where I found the usual routines were invested with an underlying freneticism and even the nuns seemed to reflect the general sense of apprehension, as well they might. The South Coast was peppered with schools of every kind and many were already trying desperately to find a house large enough for their needs which was out of the range of the anticipated bombing. The Sacred Heart had some 70 children in their charge, two of whom, Davida and I, were an added responsibility. The main house in London, Roehampton, had quickly established itself in a large country house, and the house in Tunbridge Wells had found a big mansion in Shropshire, Albrighton Hall. Mother Forbes, our headmistress, was still desperately looking for a suitable property.

Events overtook her, and she clearly made up her mind to move at any cost, the cost being the doubling up of Hove and Tunbridge Wells at Albrighton, a move which would take her closer to the safety of the West and give her the opportunity to look for herself rather than relying on agents.

Accordingly one early morning, the junior school was called abruptly, not by the comforting Mother Warilow, but by two or three agitated seniors who hurried through the dormitory urging us to get up quickly, that we had to pack and were leaving that very day. For once the pressure got the better of me and I sat on my bed weeping bitterly. One of the seniors tried to comfort me and surprised me by putting her arms

Albrighton Hall, Shropshire.

round me. It was not a gesture I was accustomed to, and to explain my distress I could only say that I had had nightmares.

The nuns were incredible, the school was wrapped and on the road that day and the main body of the children went home until accommodation was ready for them. Davida and I had nowhere to go and neither of us had relations who could step in. I am not sure what happened to Davida, but I assumed I would go to Miss Davis. No, I was told, Miss Davis was unwell. I pressed the point; I could still go to the only semblance of home that I knew. No, I was told again, she had left Yapton and gone to the Midlands. I never saw her again, and I have no idea what happened to her. Perhaps she had to go into a nursing home, perhaps she died at Yapton Lodge. It worried me for a long time and even today I have a sense of unfinished business, of never saying goodbye, an unhappy consciousness that in the end she too might have been puzzled and lonely..

So I found myself travelling for what seemed like a whole day, with another child; we were driven to a farm house, arriving around 6pm. Teatime! The farmer's wife offered scrambled eggs and to our astonishment made them out of one egg only, a goose egg. It was delicious.

I ended up on this farm in the early summer, during the new potato season. The morning after I arrived I was given a bucket of new potatoes, sat down in the orchard and asked to scrape them. I had seen Mrs Hunt do it, but I wasn't very competent and the bucket looked enormous to me; so I was transferred to some other domestic duty. My memory is vague, but I recall being sent to stay in Shrewsbury with the family of one of the seniors, Sally Grant. Her father was a doctor, it was a family of some five or six children and they lived in a Victorian terrace house, tall and narrow with a steep flight of steps up to the front door. I was teased mercilessly by the younger children, an experience I could not understand and hated. We were warned that we might hear the air raid siren at night, and if we did we had to go down immediately to the dining room. Here we huddled together under the solid Victorian dining table, a move I thought alarming since it seemed clear to me that if the bomb did come we would certainly be crushed!

I was glad to leave the Grants, and went on to a French family who also had children at the convent.

There were about eight children in this household, the progeny of Count and Countess d'Arcy; later I learned that Mother Lillie referred to them as "the countless d'Arcys". It was a fairly free-for-all household, with none of the structure of Yapton Lodge or the Convent so I found myself at a loss to settle in, though I doubt if anyone noticed.

Meanwhile the Brighton nuns had established themselves at Albrighton Hall and soon the children were collected back to school to join Tunbridge Wells and their community. The house was absolutely packed; big bedrooms were turned into crowded dormitories and when the children were in bed, the nuns wheeled out truckle beds and slept in the wide corridors. I never heard a word of complaint from anyone. It must have been incredibly difficult to organise nearly 200 people into a private house however big. It is now an hotel, but in 1940 there were only the usual domestic numbers of bathrooms and lavatories. I don't recall any disruption in the convent routine, except that we only bathed once or twice a week if we were lucky and inevitably the Junior School would not have been aware of any problems. I was still only eight in the summer of 1940. Nevertheless the nuns were concerned to relieve the pressure and Mother Forbes went on the road with a companion and a sandwich lunch, searching Shropshire for a suitable mansion for the community and the girls. Eventually she found one, Lutwyche Hall, near Much Wenlock, recently used by a boys school who I believe had been asked to leave because of their treatment of the house. Convents tended to be popular tenants.

CHAPTER 3

Lutwyche Hall

Accordingly, we packed again and climbed into buses for the journey to Lutwyche, arriving in time for tea. I felt unwell but put it down to an inclination to car sickness; when the time came I climbed into bed, only to be hauled out again to clean my teeth! In the morning I was still recalcitrant, and Mother Lillie was concerned. I was taken to the Infirmary and put to bed for observation. Mother Lillie arrived to dispel any idea of skipping lessons. Since I could not attend class, she brought the lesson to me, a kindness I considered to be exceedingly unfair. I was to learn *The Charge of the Light Brigade* and recite it to her that afternoon. And so I did, to her surprise, thus discovering inadvertently a skill for memorising which stood me in good stead thoughout my school life and later. Meanwhile I had been diagnosed by a horrified Infirmarian as having measles and it was not popular. On top of a traumatic few months, two major moves and the reassembly of the school in its new premises, one child had measles and the school was about to embark on an epidemic. And measles was not taken lightly in the 1940s.

Mother Pirquet, a tall and rather daunting Austrian nun, wrapped me in a blanket with my face covered, and carried me into the Enclosure, the part of the house used exclusively by the nuns. Entrance to this area was strictly forbidden to any of the children so the fact that I was taken in

Lutwyche Hall: the entrance front as remodelled in the mid-19th century by F.P. Cockerell.

Chapter 3

Lutwyche Hall: the entrance hall in 1974. Magnificent 18th-century plasterwork.

to this holiest of holies was a fair indication of the panic caused by the infection.

"What happens if we do go in" someone once had the temerity to inquire, to which Mother Lillie replied sharply "Children who go in there may never come out." She always was a bit of a maverick!

Happily I was not aware of this whilst I was travelling through in my blanket, a device not only employed to stop the spread of germs but to prevent me seeing the Enclosure during my progress. By this time I was feeling very ill and was not too interested in anything at all.

Lutwyche was a fine 18th-century mansion of brick and stone, beautifully sited on Wenlock Edge, overlooking a pretty valley through which ran a clear natural stream full of watercress. A wooded hill rose beyond the valley, this was Mogg, a place of beauty that informed our childhood with both magic and potential adventure. The wide terrace in the front of the house was shaded by a cedar of Lebanon, and a flight of steps led down to an extended lawn which had been lavishly planted in the days when the Lutwyche family flourished. All that was left were two crab apple trees, positioned as if they were part of a vista, and a generous group of crimson peonies which erupted dramatically each summer, defying the efforts of the grass to destroy them.

The interior of the Hall was embellished with magnificent plasterwork, no doubt commissioned from the Italian *stuccadores* of the 18th century who did so much in English country houses on their way to contracts in newly-affluent Dublin. A fine, wide oak staircase, typical of Shropshire, led up to a series of spacious bedrooms but only three bathrooms. We barely used these stairs, reaching the upper floors from a more modest staircase on the other side of the main house. A service stairway in the extension of the house led into the Enclosure where the nuns lived and slept.

For me, the first three weeks of the term were spent in darkness in a room which I discovered was Mother Forbes's own bedroom. I was visited by Mother Lillie who was my class mistress, but I was not allowed to read, or open the curtains. As I got better this became seriously frustrating and I have no doubt that I was not only a liability but a tiresome one. Inevitably the disease spread round the school but I have no idea how the nuns managed the then sine qua non that all children with measles should be kept in darkened rooms in case of danger to their sight. The day came when I was allowed to peer out of the window to surroundings which were completely strange to me. The outlook revealed a wide carriage drive which disappeared up over the hill, flanked by the old brick walls of the orchard on one side and the farmyard on the other. Eventually, I was allowed to walk in the orchard which sounded promising but proved to be planted almost completely with damson trees, another Shropshire feature. Even ripe they were incredibly sour and given the lack of sugar in the war I don't think the nuns found great use for them.

One of the new girls, Mary Alletson, a pretty girl with thick plaits, discovered my window and standing on the lawn below, brought me news of my friends; I looked forward to her visits, but it was with relief that I was finally allowed back into school life.

The Lutwyche years were idyllic in spite of the clouds of war that threatened life in England. Indeed it was only later in life that I understood properly the threat that the adult population faced with such fortitude. There were no newspapers in the Convent, and as far as I knew, no radio. Neither was missed.

We rose at 7.30 in time for Mass at 8am. In the week this was always Low Mass, and was followed immediately by breakfast in the panelled dining room, now known as the Refectory. Classes started at 9, with a break at 11 and resumed until lunch at 1. Juniors rested for half an hour after lunch, and we then played games until tea at 4.30. It was cricket in the summer on the wide lawns and sometimes in the field when the cows were grazing elsewhere, and netball in the winter on the terrace. There was no tennis court.

Seniors were allowed some leeway to cycle in the surrounding country, and at least one child brought a horse in the early days, but this practice was discontinued for practical reasons, quite quickly. I enjoyed cricket and loathed netball, but there was one great compensating factor. I quickly discovered that the drive ran alongside the stables and beyond that lay the magic of the farmyard.

Chapter 3

Davida and I spent as much time as we could there, learning to milk, not very well, learning to ride, helping with lifting mangolds, cleaning tack, above all watching with fascination the goings-on in this separate and wondrously independent world.

We went out to bring the cows home for milking, to the fields to play while the Dale girls ploughed or harvested and above all to ride the horses home from the fields.

The land immediately around the House, the Home Farm, was leased to Mr Dale and during the war years it was worked by Mr Dale himself, Norman his youngest child in his mid teens, and the five Dale sisters, Louise, Helen, Olive, Marjory and Hilda. The farm was largely dairy, with some arable and the work was consistent and hard but the Dale girls seem to have worked the land from an early age; they were strong, glowing with good health and turned their skills to any eventuality. Nothing daunted them, whether it was a fractious shire horse, a broken tractor or a pig to be killed. They rose with the dawn and didn't rest until the cows were brought in and the milk had been processed through the cooler and poured into large metal churns for collection the next morning. I am not aware that the girls were classed as Landgirls and they certainly never wore the uniform, but the Dale family was totally self-sufficient in terms of its food production.

There were two shires, Gilbert and Jewel, with hooves like dinner plates, and a bright well-mannered cob, Kit, who was popular with all of us. If there were squabbles in the farmyard, it was about who should ride Kit, since she was both comfortable and manageable. We rode the shires bareback, clinging on to their collars as they lumbered towards the stables. Only once was there trouble when Gilbert smelt Spring in the air and ran away with Davida on board. It was unnerving to watch this enormous horse cantering round the field with her, since she had no proper reins and could not hope to control him. She clung bravely onto the collar, however, and after much shouting and encouragement from the Dale girls, Gilbert was persuaded to resume his journey homewards with a shaken Davida still mounted.

Mr Dale occasionally followed hounds on Kit, who quickly learned to open gates for him. As a result of this trick poor Davida had another drama. Kit, anxious to get home one evening after a hard day's ploughing, opened the gate to the farmyard, and moved forward too quickly for Davida to throw the gate wide. It closed and her leg was crushed between Kit and the post. The leg was broken and Davida confined to a plaster cast for some weeks. She was not particularly academic and any lessons lost would have been viewed as a side benefit but it was a little while before she could ride again.

Lutwyche was a beautiful house and living in such sophisticated architectural surroundings was an education. We were also encouraged to visit surrounding properties and churches in an extension of our history studies and these exercises were helped and encouraged by the nuns. The nature of the nuns' vocation meant that not all of them were qualified to teach or were good at it. However, there was plenty of work to be done outside the schoolrooms. Mother Oakeshott, a trained nurse, was the infirmarian; Mother Clutton had spent time in Rome studying Fine Art and held study sessions each Saturday for those who wished to attend; Mother Howell, who had qualified at the Royal School of Music, played the organ at Brighton and the piano at Lutwyche, and supervised singing and music studies. I spent a lot of time with Mother Clutton studying Fine Arts and literature – interestingly these were classed as Free Study and were voluntary. I was a regular attender, and I owe Mother Clutton a great deal, in both my time as an antique dealer and in the preparation of programmes for the school that I later founded. I believe very strongly that the development of the arts is a fascinating story. In order to appreciate the developments and fashions of today, it is imperative that we understand and appreciate the changes of past centuries.

CHAPTER 4

Holidays

The disappearance of Miss Davis posed a problem for Mother Forbes. Neither Davida nor I had any close relations with whom we could spend our holidays. Davida's father had an arrangement with a Lady Cathcart who appeared to have been appointed her guardian, so Davida went there, though I don't think she enjoyed it much.

In 1940 London was enduring intense bombing which continued into 1942 with devastating effects, not only on the capital city but on the residents, thousands of whom were killed or wounded. At some point after the first onslaught I visited London and was horrified by the sight of buildings laid bare to the elements, with all the evidence of happy lives displayed in the ruins. Nursery wallpaper on the top floor, the remains of smart curtains on the reception floor, a fine marble fireplace clinging tenaciously to the wall of a drawing room, were all silent witness to life before the war. They are images as clear now as they were when I stood staring at them nearly a century ago.

Mother Forbes had a friend, Henrietta Bower, who had been able to move her large family North to her own family home, Sizergh Castle, and there I went for several holidays. I travelled first with Mother Warilow who was bound for Levens Hall, close to Sizergh. The Sacred Heart was an enclosed order, so the journey from Shropshire to

Sizergh Castle, Cumbria.

Levens Hall, Cumbria.

Westmoreland was conducted in total silence. And in case of emergency I had a luggage label tied to the buttonhole of my blazer with my name and address printed on it. Levens Hall, which had been rented by the nuns for the duration as a rest home for the various communities, boasts one of the most famous topiary gardens in England, designed by French garden designer Guillaume Beaumont, previously responsible for the gardens of Hampton Court Palace under James II. I did initially find the garden daunting. But viewed from a first-floor window, at a point when the large yew features had been rimmed surprisingly with the brilliant blue of forget-me-nots, M. Beaumont's masterpiece sprang into life and I was made aware that I was sharing a major break through in the development of design in the garden. It was my first introduction to the discipline which, much later in life, I would include in my curriculum at Inchbald as the Room Outside.

The word '*duration*' was a daily part of our vocabulary, indicating that everything was temporary, an assurance even that soon all would return to normal. In the confusion, I found the apparent stability of great houses, allied to their long histories, to be reassuringly convincing! However, I am not sure that I ever quite understood the reality of 'normal' and perhaps that gave an edge to the various entrepreneurial decisions that characterised my adult life.

My destination in the North was Sizergh Castle. After the experience of Albrighton Hall, with grandiose turn-of-the-century interiors and wonderful gardens, and then beautiful Lutwyche, the concept of a castle was not particularly impressive but I had certainly begun to appreciate the history and heritage of English estates. However, initially Sizergh was simply another place to go to without complaint, and I must have hoped that the Bowers were a less challenging family than the Grants or the d'Arcys.

Henrietta Bower was a Strickland, a daughter of Sizergh; she married a naval officer, Robert Bower, who subsequently became the MP for Cleveland, the city that took such terrible bombardment in the war years. They had a rambling house in Putney, but her stepmother, Lady Strickland, had invited Mrs Bower to move her large family away from the danger of the London bombs to the safety of the Border castle where she had been born and brought up. Here they all lived for the duration of the war, with their father, Commander Bower, commuting each Friday from London where he was still serving in Parliament.

Mother Warilow was bound for Levens Hall where there were no students, only nuns either elderly or needing rest and holidays; I believe that the Postulants were there as well. So on arrival at Kendal station we went our different ways.

The driveway entrance to Sizergh was not particularly impressive. It was essentially a working castle that began life as a defensive pele tower which had then developed over the centuries with the fortunes of the Stricklands. But the doorway into the Great Hall was big enough to accommodate a loaded hay wain, and the Hall itself was designed to store provisions and people against a siege. The reivers were a constant threat in the 11th and 12th centuries and Sizergh lay close to the Borders. The family were known to be loyal to the English monarchy and this fact would be recognised over the years. Marriages with other distinguished families, some as far afield as Yorkshire, brought the benefits of dowries and by the 18th century the castle had been extended with an elegant castellated addition replacing two gabled sections of the building.

The geography of the estate, far removed from the centre of the English Reformation and its subsequent disquieting politics, meant that like many other Northern families the Stricklands held on to their Catholic beliefs without any apparent impact on their family prosperity. During the years of the Commonwealth the incumbent Strickland opted to go into exile with Prince Charles, later Charles II, and was duly rewarded with favour when the monarchy was restored. In the dining room there were impressive portraits of the Stuart Royal family presented by the King to acknowledge the family's loyalty during the harsh years between 1649 and 1660, the equivalent of today's signed photographs of royalty.

The Bower family, like all the Catholic families at that time, was large, ranging from the eldest daughter Ann, down to the babies, Veronica and Mary, still in the nursery. Ann, an attractive blonde, was working in the war effort, but the rest of the family were all still at school. The only boy, Paul, was attractive and funny but I suspect slightly overwhelmed by a large family of sisters. The next down, Margaret, was pretty and slightly fey, popular with the younger children; then came Marianna, feisty and rather bossy, not particularly concerned with those younger than her. Many years later it came as no surprise to me that she had been appointed a Lord Lieutenant and I have no doubt that she carried out her duties immaculately.

Next in the hierarchy was Elizabeth, too young to be on close terms with Marianna and Margaret, too old to find companionship with the babies, Vos and Mary. We were approximately the same age and so were bracketed together and played, rode the ponies, sometimes went to Kendal together and in general were seen as a pair. It was an incredibly relaxed existence; the family kept a goat for its milk, and it was incumbent on one of us to milk it. This chore fell to Margaret and Marianna, the latter frequently complaining about it. I could just about milk Blackie, the Dales' very compliant little cow, but I was pretty certain that a goat would be beyond me and Elizabeth and I were never so instructed. Our chore was to feed the rabbits and clean out the hutches. I have never worked out why they were given the left-over porridge mixed with tea leaves, but they were always delighted with this offering and seemed to thrive on it. They were kept in the entrance to the Castle, a homely comment on the realities of the Sizergh history and the castle's survival; every now and then one of them disappeared in the direction of the kitchen.

Two or three ponies were kept on the fell behind the castle, one of whom had worked out how to manipulate the dangers of the cattle grid, and was therefore frequently found in the kitchen. Like all ponies they had wills of steel, but nevertheless we rode them, generally in cotton dresses and at considerable personal risk.

There was a private chapel, with an elderly priest assigned to the castle, so we went regularly to Mass as we did in the Convent. These times were, for me, very happy and perhaps the closest I came in my childhood to family life, carefree but disciplined.

The fact that Commander Bower was an MP brought us closer to the realities of the war, not least because he had the politician's habit of fulminating at mealtimes about his colleagues' performances during the previous week. No doubt his views inspired an interest in politics which has not left me. Even so war remained remote, although threatening in a way that I could not identify. The terrible bombs were far away in the South. Westmoreland remained untouched and any bombing that occurred in Shropshire was unheard of at Lutwyche.

CHAPTER 5

A new development

From the junior school we moved together into the senior school and on up the hierarchy until we were facing the more serious exams that would lead to School Certificate, which I was due to take at fifteen. But by then we were back at Brighton, my mother had not only returned from Africa but had divorced John Bromley and was planning to remarry.

She was due to collect me off the train at Victoria at the end of the holidays. Since she hadn't seen me for about three years, she came to the station with her sister Phyl. I heard her ask which one I was, remarking when she was told, that I was quite pretty! It was a bit chilling but I did not recognise her as the vibrant young woman I had last seen at Miss Davis's.

She was over-tanned and looked strained and thin; this was explained by the fact that her ship had been torpedoed off Freetown, and she had spent three days in an open boat. There had been only two women on the Dutch ship and in the chaos that followed the torpedo they were separated. My mother had been dressed in a skimpy sunsuit and thus had to endure blazing sun and cold nights until they were rescued. It must have been a terrifying experience, compounded by the fact that apart from one Dutch officer, the rest of the crew were Lascars, some of whom believed that women on board ship brought bad luck. The Dutchman explained to her that they must stay together and they took turns to sleep lest they were knifed by increasingly desperate sailors.

On her arrival in London my mother had joined the American Red Cross and worked for some time in their Piccadilly Club, Rainbow Corner. She found this exhausting. Rainbow Corner was Other Ranks, the GIs were keen on girls and they were very well paid. They drank a great deal and made passes indiscriminately, most of which may well have been harmless in themselves and it should be remembered that they were far from home; however, there was a considerable difference at that time between the English and the American culture and my mother found the job very taxing. She was alone, trying to get a divorce, encumbered with a child of eleven and the attendant worry, and wondering what lay in the future for her.

She was delighted when eventually she managed a transfer to the Officers' Club in Bond Street, where her sister Phyl and one or two of her friends were already working. Eventually Phyl, my mother and another very glamorous girl called Audrey, shared a flat in Victoria. Audrey worked in code breaking in the Ministry of Defence and I was very impressed by this fact, as well as by her scarlet court shoes! In a country now suffering from shortages of everything, scarlet court shoes were an event!

Soon my mother was drafted to Southampton, where, in company with several American girls, she drove an enormous lorry which housed a mini kitchen; or perhaps not so mini. It was specifically designed to enable the production of fresh doughnuts and the most delicious American coffee. The girls themselves drove these behemoths onto the fields beyond the embarkation points. The Naafi had their own system serving tea, and long lines of soldiers trailed up to the distribution points; the queues seemed endless, queues of young men of two countries destined for the invasion of France.

The American Red Cross rose at dawn and were in position by about 5am, swiftly followed by the NAAFI. I went with my mother once or twice and helped with handing out the doughnuts and coffee. The American soldiers were always charming and so grateful and, given the horrors they were facing, incredibly cheerful.

Cooking doughnuts generated the most delicious smell which drifted across the English line, a smell which no-one in England had experienced for as long as they could remember, and every now and then a Tommy crept into the American queue. The girls were instructed to serve them only after all the GIs had what they wanted, but the American supplies were more than generous, and if Tommy waited long enough he was normally served. If there was milk and coffee left over my mother was shocked to see it tipped into the sea. This may well have been the beginning of health and safety, since the Americans were a long way ahead of the UK on this score, but she was too well aware of the impoverished and rationed families in Southampton who would have been so grateful for these supplies.

She was in Southampton when she received a letter from Donald Whitaker, announcing that he was coming to Southampton by train, and asking her to meet him. She had seen a fortune teller, one of many she consulted, in the vain hope of knowing what the future held for her, and she was told that she would meet her future husband on a South Coast railway station. Since she and the fortune teller were both in Southampton at the time of this announcement it is all too easy to draw simple conclusions. Donald arrived in Southampton, she met him as instructed and in due course they married.

Donald was anxious that my mother should meet his parents. He was unable to arrange this during his leave and so his parents invited my mother to their house in Oxfordshire, Pudlicote; and I was included in the invitation. My mother, now committed to becoming Mrs Whitaker, was inordinately concerned to make a good impression and desperately worried that something would go wrong. We were due for the weekend, and I was with her in London while she prepared for this challenge, for that is what it was to her.

She went off to have her hair done and I was reduced to silence on her return. She had had an auburn rinse, but since she was once a redhead, the colour had reacted strongly and I finally had to admit that it really didn't look too good. Back she went to the salon to have a further rinse intended to subdue the bright colour; this was effective if she stood away from the electric light, when her hair reflected the blue rinse that was intended to correct the problem. Since rooms in the 1940s and 1950s always had ceiling lights, we agreed that I would have to manoeuvre her away from any that she unwittingly drifted under. So we packed and set out for a destination which was to be the turning point in my mother's life and which for me at that particular moment was simply another possible chapter.

During my time in Shropshire we had enjoyed tremendous encouragement from the nuns to take an interest in the Arts and Architecture. The Sacred Heart was a French order, and they adhered to the conventions of a classical education insofar as they could apply these to a girl's school. We visited local buildings of various styles and there were many. Shropshire was and is one of the unspoilt parts of England – life, apart from the early border wars, has progressed with minimum interference through the centuries and thus local buildings remained largely preserved. The main source of destruction was that wreaked on the Church during the Reformation, but the Commonwealth did not have the same impact that it had on more central parts of the country. There were wonderful places to visit and we received enthusiastic instruction. In particular Mother Clutton's Saturday Free Study sessions concentrated on Greek and Roman art and the development of the classical period in England. I was a regular attender and benefited hugely from this early introduction to a field in which I would finally make my life.

In addition, Lutwyche was a most beautiful example of its period, Sizergh with its pele tower and 18th-century additions, had proved fascinating and I had anyhow always been aware of and interested in my environment. I was told Pudlicote was a large English country house and I assumed it would also be attractive. I was also told to be quiet, courteous, say please and thank you and wait to see if the Whitakers expected me to go to bed early or stay up for supper! Since I had got used to going to strange houses and adapting to the lives of my hosts, none of this fazed me so we approached this new experience, my mother and I, with quite different expectations. I think it may be true that she

Pudlicote. Oxfordshire. 18th-century home of the Whitaker family.

drew some support and comfort from my relaxed attitude, but that didn't entirely dispel her nerves.

We arrived late on a winter's night and took a taxi from the station.

I recall perfectly driving through the gates, and to my surprise the house came into view almost immediately. My first impression was disappointment. The elevation, far from being classic, was dull, there were no steps and the front door was more like the side door to a garden. The wide proportions of the door were clearly 18th century, the overdoor was glazed and the space beyond was in darkness.

However, when the lights suddenly went on the whole scene changed; the large hall was painted red, so the illuminated space glowed with a warmth that spilled out into the winter's night. This impression was emphasized when the door swung open and a small man waved us in to the scarlet staircase hall, with the words 'Welcome to Pudlicote!' I think we both immediately felt reassured not only by his greeting but by the sparkling Whitaker smile.

Donald's father, Bernard Whitaker, was brought up in Shropshire, went to Shrewsbury School and then to Oxford. During his time at University he fell in love with the Cotswolds and resolved to make his home there. His grandfather had moved down to Shropshire from the original Whitaker lands in Lancashire, and had bought three large houses, one for each of his children. These were Winsley, Ludford and Hampton, and Bernard had been given Hampton. It must be one of the most charming houses in the county, but Bernard sold it to fund the purchase of Pudlicote and it was Bernard who painted the large entrance hall scarlet. It proved to be a house of great charm, a perfect family house.

Chapter 5

The Whitakers were always so kind and every now and then I was sent to stay with them. They went to great trouble to make my visits happy, even borrowing a pony and coaching my riding skills. At first they still had staff, a cook who reminded me of Mrs Hunt, a couple of maids and a gardener, Hicks, who was married to one of the maids.

Soon the cook left and the staff was reduced to Hicks and his wife, the big kitchen was closed and moved to a smaller room close to the dining room and life took on a pattern more familiar to my generation than that of the elderly Whitakers. Mrs Whitaker had never learnt to cook but nevertheless turned her attention to mastering simple recipes and was always so pleased when I was able to help her. One week I made her a tweed skirt and she was seriously impressed! Luckily we had treadle machines at the convent, so I was able to manage the one she had been given as a bride, many years before it was dusted off for me. The age of electricity was still a long way ahead of us!

Pudlicote provided happy interludes; I met Donald's nephew Rodney there who informed his grandmother that I 'was not bad for a girl' and after that I often stayed with his parents, Eddie and Priscilla and their younger son Martin. Priscilla had lost a baby daughter to cot death and her kindness to me to some degree reflected her grief at this loss. Both she and her mother-in-law were to tell me that they wished they had had a daughter, Mabel Whitaker going so far as to say that it could be lonely living in a house full of men! Certainly the Whitaker households were geared to boys interests, and these were mainly field sports. However, both Mabel and Priscilla excelled at horsemanship so both families hunted together. A charming sketch of Mabel, riding side saddle, flying over a hedge in front of her sons was captioned 'Mabel leads the way' and was shown to me with great pride by her husband.

CHAPTER 6

The end of the Duration

Meanwhile the so-called end of the war brought a sense of euphoria to all of us, though in fact it turned out to be something of a false dawn. At Lutwyche the Rushton church bells rang out for Victory in Europe Day, ringing for the first time since the war started, and the farming community rejoiced with the convent. The nuns immediately started on their plans to return to Brighton and these were implemented as swiftly as their departure had been four years before.

We were older and the news was available to us, so that we kept pace with the invasion of Europe, with Patten and Montgomery's race across the Continent and the fall of Berlin, but no-one was prepared for the horrors of the Holocaust.

On their return to Brighton the nuns faced new standards of living and the strict convent rules were slightly relaxed. Senior children were now allowed out at the weekends and were able to go to the cinema. Cinemas then all showed newsreels and late one Saturday seniors came back to the convent with appalling stories of the films that were taken when Belsen was discovered, stories that really didn't seem possible or credible. Thus, rather than the triumph of victory, my generation was introduced to genocide, a gross demonstration of how close humanity is to the worst of excesses.

Further, the war in the Far-East was ongoing and there seemed to be no end to the misery of those whose relations were still imprisoned or fighting. My aunt, Phyl Clyne, had got away from Singapore on one of the very last ships to leave and had arrived back safely in England. She had already been working for the Red Cross in Hong Kong and continued to do so when she arrived back in London. Her husband, Ted Clyne, had been captured and spent the war in a Japanese prisoner of war camp where he worked on the railway, and for some time she had no idea if he had survived. Eventually a small printed card arrived through the Red Cross to say that he was alive and in prison, and no more than that. She had no knowledge of his state of health or indeed where he was, but each year a similar card arrived so at least she knew he was alive.

Meanwhile, life at the convent resumed seamlessly. The main corridor frequently smelled of freshly-baked bread, the lay sisters sprinkled damp tea leaves on the oak stairs to 'lay the dust' before sweeping, we went to

Chapter 6

Mass daily in a veil, black or white depending on the Feast day, and the orange velvet curtains still hung immutably in the old drawing room of the original villa!

We had of course always been taught to sew, but sewing lessons became much more sophisticated and took place in a dedicated sewing room. With hindsight I am astounded to recall being given a roll of fine silk (where did they get silk from, it must have been pre-war stock) and shown how to cut out a pair of cami-knickers. Cutting silk is tricky anyhow, but I managed and I was then instructed in the fine stitching of French seams and scalloped hems with a view to making sexy underwear! This at a time when we ourselves were wearing cotton knickers, known as linings, underneath thick green bloomers! And one of my friends, Liane, was castigated for shedding her bloomers during hot weather and wearing only the liners. This was considered to be the height of immodesty, and I am not clear how the nuns reconciled their views with the proliferation of cami-knickers and French knickers that streamed merrily out of the sewing room.

In due course I took the results of my work home for my mother, who was delighted and surprised. She lost no time in obtaining a large quantity of parachute silk and asked me to make her a petticoat. Accordingly on my next trip home I brought her a tiered petticoat to go under her fashionable New Look frock.

My mother married Donald Whitaker at the end of the war whilst she was still working for the American Red Cross in Southampton, and spending time in London in the flat she shared with beautician Mrs Collins in Sloane Street. Mrs Collins was the long-time lover of the actress Vivian Leigh's father, who visited her regularly. However, their passion was clearly spent since they used their time together reading the Bible, (the Old Testament and the Prophecies), and analysing them in terms of the future. She explained to me quite positively that war would break out in the Middle East in the early years of the 21st century, and would accelerate into the Third World War.

London at that time was still a landscape of destruction. Bombed buildings had been made safe but that was all. Piles of shattered building material still lay on the sites of commercial and domestic buildings and everywhere amongst the rubble were the bright pink spires of the rose bay willow herb, said to flourish where there has been fire. Although I had never witnessed the fires, it was a consistent reminder of the terrors of the London bombing and whenever I see willow herb now the images of bomb damage return.

I saw a little more of my mother during this period. I generally spent about a week with her each holiday, and was sent to various friends for the rest of the time. I stayed with Diana Bowring at her grandmother's elegant turn-of-the-century house in Ascot where amazingly the garden was on the very edge of the race course. Alas we were never there in the season! I went to Wales with Mary Alletson whose mother constantly regretted that marriage had cost her a starry career in opera. Mr Alletson was kind and quiet but, I suspected, not very happy. It was a lesson in living patterns. My mother was posted to Aldermaston, then taken over by the Eighth American Air Force, and arranged for me to stay with a family whose father was a committed amateur astronomer; I found his hobby fascinating and he patiently introduced me to his celestial world with special emphasis on Saturn who obligingly appeared on several clear nights. I would so like to have learnt more.

Aldermaston was the ultimate Victorian pile, built in the last quarter of the 19th century after fire destroyed the original manor house. The gardens were laid out in the same period and included a very large ornamental lake inhabited by an exotic collection of water birds. The splendour of the property encapsulated all the magnificence of the British Empire at its peak and I left it with a passion for birds! It was the last great house in which I spent time during this game of hopscotch which encapsulates my childhood. Apart from any other considerations it was a privileged review of art and architecture as well as the English countryside. I learnt so much from such infinite variety and, had it not been for the war, I would have spent four years in a Convent in Brighton, where I would have had to make do with the Brighton Pavilion! On our return to Brighton it was indeed one of my first stops!

Although her life was beginning to resolve itself, my mother was unhappy and this made her endlessly discontented. In today's terms, would we call this depression? She was a very competent and intelligent woman who was much happier when she had work to do and could enjoy the company of colleagues. She was also blessed with good looks and a model's flair for dress, a flair which extended to the interiors of her houses which were always successful.

Her association with Americans, which she hugely enjoyed, also gave her odd ideas about how a child should be dressed. On one excruciating occasion she insisted that I pile my plaits on top of my head with two bows either side. Given that I have a large head, and that my plaits were exceptionally thick, I looked and felt ridiculous. At that time she thought it funny, but on the whole the responsibility of a child, and an illegitimate one at that, was a difficult burden but one with which she did her best to cope. I had no idea of the facts of my situation, nor did I know that she had not told the truth to her new husband.

After her marriage, my mother took a little house in the suburbs and waited for Donald to return home from his posting in Egypt and for his demob. I remember her going to meet him, leaving me in the house to 'arrange some flowers to welcome him home'. I didn't resent Donald but

Chapter 6

I was sad that John had disappeared and really thought that welcome home flowers were my mother's responsibility. However, it was the season of golden rod and dahlias so there was no real challenge!

Still serving in the Warwickshire Yeomanry, Donald was posted to Catterick where he was allocated a quarter called The Hagg, and where I now spent my holidays. Troops were still streaming across the Channel into Europe and it fell to Donald to make speeches on their departure, a job he loathed and for which he felt he was not fitted. His war had been totally uneventful and here he was encouraging others into the bloodiest of battles.

This era lasted a few months, Donald was demobbed and now faced a quandary. Trained as a private land agent, he had to address the fact that there were increasingly fewer landed gentry with the means to delegate their estate responsibilities. In the 1930s he had worked for the Bastards in Devonshire, whose estates were so extensive that they employed two agents, and there he had led a life of privilege way beyond his means. A house was provided for him, his days were leisurely and certainly unencumbered by all the regulations which have developed since that time, and he also had free access to the field sports on the estate at all of which he excelled.

As the days after the war drew to an end he was searching for a livelihood with many thousands of others like him, in a period of grave depression.

Eventually he was offered a directorship in a famous (and the oldest) firm of land agents, Drivers Jonas, unhappily for him based in London. In addition he was given a few months to study for, and take, the qualifying exams in order to become a Chartered Surveyor. To his great credit he worked hard at his studies and succeeded but it was a worrying time for both of them. He in particular was concerned that it had been a long time since he had studied anything, although he had been to the Staff College, rather to the surprise of his Nairobi friends. In fact, he claimed never to have failed an exam and I do believe that was true. Any written work he did was carried out with the greatest clarity, beautifully written and annotated; and having marked much work myself in later years, he must have come as a joyful relief to a jaded examiner struggling with poor grammar and terrible manuscript.

CHAPTER 7

New family patterns

After we left Yorkshire, Donald rented a large cottage at Iver, Buckinghamshire, belonging to a Mrs Fowler, a rich and eccentric woman who lived in the pretty Georgian main house with some 12 or 14 dogs of various sizes and pedigrees.

Donald was able to study for his surveyor's exams, my mother bought herself a dog, a spaniel she called Spur to whom she became devoted, and I spent my holidays there. The property adjoined the late Duke of Kent's home, Coppins, and the entrances to the two houses were close; the Duke was killed in a plane crash, but his black chow haunted the Coppins gates, and I always assumed he was still waiting for the return of his royal master. The chow put on a fair display of royalty but very occasionally he could be tempted to walk down the road with me when I went shopping for my mother, but as soon as the Coppins gate was out of sight he would return and take up his usual position. He was very handsome, but there was definitely an air of the puppy belonging to Prince Frederick of Wales, who prompted Alexander Pope's couplet;

"I am His Highness' dog at Kew'

Pray tell me Sir, whose dog are you?"

When Donald's results came through his success was a tremendous relief to him. He was accordingly installed as the Country Partner in Drivers Jonas and faced the prospect of finding somewhere to live in London.

Drivers Jonas was founded in the 18th century, the first firm of land agents working on a commercial basis. The partners did not live on the estates they handled, largely because most of the estates were in London. They counted the Abel Smith estate in Mayfair and the Ilchester estate in Kensington among their London clients; and Dyrham Park with its sister estate at Porlock had been handled by them for decades. The Partners were anxious to develop their country interests and given the climate of decline in the world of the aristocracy and landed gentry it was clearly a propitious moment to expand in that direction. Donald was to lead the country side of the firm forward, and there is no doubt that he was a promising candidate to do so; educated at Eton, particularly good at games and field sports, his friends were drawn from the very section of society that Drivers Jonas were hoping to capture.

Chapter 7

All seemed to augur well when his ten-year contract with the firm was confirmed.

However, finding a house in post-war London was not easy. There was a great deal of bomb damaged property that required restoration. Houses still intact had often been abandoned during the war years and therefore required extensive rehabilitation and there were draconian limitations to the amount of money that could be spent on any given building. Repairs to the fabric were accepted but practically nothing was allowed to be spent on the aesthetics. Luckily Donald was able to go to the files of his own firm, where he hoped to find a suitable property at the limited price he could afford.

Eventually he was offered a cottage in Shepherd Street, off the Market. My mother loved mews houses, I have never understood why, and she was delighted. She was less pleased when she discovered why it was available.

25 Shepherd Street was on one of the firm's estates, and had recently become available because the tenant shared it with another woman in the same profession of prostitution. It was therefore deemed to be a bawdy house and, as such, illegal, so that Drivers Jonas were able to repossess it and offered Donald a lease; for this privilege he had to pay the resident tenant a sum of money referred to as payment for fittings. I remember that the several hundred pounds he had to find brought him a pair of old light fittings. My mother's view was more to the point. "Unfortunately, we inadvertently bought the goodwill", she remarked, and so it would prove.

Shepherd's Market was the centre of prostitution in Mayfair, and trade flourished. In the heart of this very grand area of London the Market was a village with a grocer, butcher, tailors and cleaners; indeed everything you could want was to hand within a stone's throw, and in addition to these everyday requirements were the ladies of the night plying their skills with relentless enthusiasm.

They each had their own pitch, whether on a corner, near a shop, or a little further down the street, and they guarded these pitches with iron determination. A most beautiful blonde, known as the Queen of the Market, stood opposite the grocer, her hair and clothes immaculate; I couldn't understand why she had become a tart, her looks were so outstanding, but I was still at my convent when we moved in! Another wondrous redhead, not unlike Rita Hayworth, arrived each morning for work in a white Rolls Royce, but I never saw her soliciting. Most of the girls (which is how they were identified in the Market) were good looking but those two were outstanding and they irritated me because I thought they had so much to offer that they could surely have done better than take to the streets. Possibly the white Rolls Royce provided a clue.

My mother never allowed me to go out without a hat – going bareheaded would have indicated that I was on the game! A hat made it clear I was not part of the action! Silk head scarves, then fashionable, were not allowed either – they were frequently used by the girls, who otherwise went hatless. There were clear parameters of behaviour and everyone was expected to observe them. Once I went to collect a coat from the cleaners and started to remove the coat I was wearing to leave it in the shop. The assistant was horrified; "Don't do that dear, it really upsets the girls and they might come in and start a fight!" By the same token it was important not to linger beside any of the 'pitches' even if the girl was otherwise engaged. Since I was by now 14 or 15, it was not unusual to be eyed up or addressed by some man who no doubt had a schoolgirl fetish, and it was vital to walk straight on as if nothing had happened. Anything might annoy the girls, and being young didn't help.

My mother had converted No. 25 very well but had insisted on putting in a bow window which made the little elevation look like a Victorian shop front. In order to do this she had enlisted the help of builders working nearby, W. Wright and Son, a firm who would prove to be a part of my life for the next sixty years. She was delighted with what they had done but by the time they were finished I was rising 16 and she was concerned that the atmosphere of the Market was hardly right. In addition to this consideration her prognosis that No. 25 carried its own 'goodwill' proved to be correct. Donald was away quite a lot since he was looking after a wide spread of country properties and my mother was concerned by the leftover clients who rang the bell sometimes late into the night. So she slept with a bucket of water beside her bed when he was away and she went house-hunting.

It must have appeared to be a useless proposition; either houses were expensive, or they required more money to be spent on them than my parents could offer. Donald, with a new and demanding job, was well aware that he was luckier than many demobbed officers, but was bewildered by the challenges facing him. He had gone straight from his home at Pudlicote in Warwckshire to private land agency, where he was provided with everything to which he had been accustomed in his own family. In addition he worked with and for like-minded public school boys; if he lacked home comforts, this was compensated by the fact that he was an engaging and good-looking young man skilled in social pursuits and was constantly in demand for dances, tennis parties, house parties, shooting and hunting, at all of which he excelled.

By contrast he was now living in London, which he disliked, and was constantly on the road between clients, often spending the night away. A number of his clients were the newly-rich farmers, who had worked so incredibly hard during the war and were reaping the benefits. In addition to their own land they were beginning to acquire the lands of the gentry, which were coming on the market to offset death duties or in sad recognition of the lack of heirs. In the late 1940s and 1950s the tide of difficulties faced by the landowners of England became an avalanche; the break up of estates of any size, and the destruction of wondrous houses for lack of funds was to prove seismic in the social changes already making themselves felt, in the aftermath of a war which was the second in a generation.

Two of Donald's main clients were the Gotobeds of Norfolk, a well-known yeoman farming dynasty for whom he had great respect, and another equally large family in Lincolnshire with whom he stayed quite frequently. This was the main kind of work that he was doing, advising on agricultural methods and land acquisition, rather than administering a large estate; the one historic estate that he did manage belonged to Justin Blathwaite who was a school friend. At the same time he was familiarising himself with a countryside which had, during his absence, changed considerably. Returning soldiers often did not wish to go back to the hard life of the farm, however paternalistic their employers may have been. So estate cottages were coming on the market for very little; one school friend of mine later told me that she and her husband sold up a number of their village cottages for £1000 each, and this in the heart of the Cotswolds. "….to little men with suitcases full of cash" she added bleakly.

Thus the tied cottage became a thing of the past and working farms were looking to the possibilities offered by the new familiarisation with America and all things American. This meant that machinery was the way forward, and of course machinery heralded the requirement for fewer hedgerows, and much larger fields, a policy that took no heed of the destructive impact on wild life. Nevertheless, Donald had a job and he got on with it as best he could, and was happy in the process to revive old friendships and, with the help of my mother who he adored, to start again with a different life to the one which he had once envisaged.

And my mother familiarised herself with London's estate agents.

In fact Drivers Jonas were most helpful and we looked at a number of houses, one particularly nice one on the Ilchester estate, but in the final analysis they were simply beyond Donald's means. My mother was increasingly concerned about the suitability of living in the Market and spent her days trawling rather hopelessly around the agents, faced always with the question 'and what can you afford, Mrs Whitaker', the reply to which was sadly predictable. This repetitive interchange was once again taking place in the office of an agent near Gloucester Road, and included the fact that 'my husband has just come out of the Army', a statement made more in despair than with any hope of sympathy. But it resonated with an elderly lady who was in the office purchasing a flat.

Mrs Tennyson d'Eyncourt walked across to the desk where my mother was sitting, sat down beside her and told her "I am so sorry for all you young people trying to cope at this time – I have a house in Hereford Square you can have. I prefer now to live in an apartment and I have no need of the house. No, I don't want any money for it, I shall be glad to hand over the lease to you!" My mother's grateful astonishment may not have been matched by Donald that evening; no one could have credited the story and Donald would have been the first person to question the condition of the building. However, it was true and it was a genuine gift. I think Mrs TD had lived in the country during the war, but the house was in good condition and the lease had ten years to run; thus 29 Hereford Square became our new and very attractive home.

CHAPTER 8

Les Dames de Saint Maur, the House of Citzenship and Amberley

I had, meanwhile, left the Convent but not before tragedy struck our class. Davida had notice of her father's imminent release from prison in Germany and she was walking on clouds. The bad news was truly terrible – Lt Campbell's plane had crashed near Paris and everyone in it was killed. They were all prisoners of war. It is thought that most of them crowded to one side of the aircraft, from which they could get their first sight of the iconic city and that this movement tipped the plane off balance. I saw Davida for a moment, unable to speak, her arms slack at her sides and the tears pouring unchecked down her face; and then she was gone and I wondered about her future. She now had no-one to look after her and only the shadowy Lady Cathcart for support.

Friends of my mother's had decided to send their only daughter, Patricia, to the convent of Les Dames de St Maur and accordingly I too was enrolled there. My formal education ended therefore as soon as I took School certificate and I embarked on studies of shorthand typing, accountancy, cookery and French. The School was housed in a grand villa on the edge of the Oatlands Park estate, and we were two English girls with eighteen French girls there to learn English. A cluster of similar villas had been part of a commercial development built in the early 1800s by a very rich man called Ball Hughes, known to his friends as Golden Balls, who was not only well known for his extravagance but also as a generous member of the art world.

Les Dames de Saint Maur was a teaching order, the foundation of which was supported by the morganatic wife of Louis XIV of France, the Marquise de Maintenon. By contrast the Sacred Heart order had been founded by a member of a peasant family, Madeleine Sophie Barratt, but both Orders had similar educational aims in the years of their foundation linked to the preservation of the existing Catholic religion.

At the end of a year I was a fairly competent shorthand typist and could play off-the-cuff bridge in French. I hated it, and in fairness to the nuns, I would not have chosen to be trained as a secretary. In fairness to my mother she was anxious to train me in subjects that would support my future.

By the time I left school I was still only 16 and my mother was constrained to find some form of Higher Education. For reasons unknown to me she opted for an institution called the House of

Oatlands Park Estate. Originally a royal palace but owned in the early 19th century by the incredibly wealthy Edward Ball Hughes.

Citizenship and her decision coincided with the acquisition of 29 Hereford Square.

Two women ran this faintly eccentric establishment. One of them, Miss Dorothy Neville-Rolfe, was the pro-active thrust behind the venture and the other we rather suspected to be the financial support. Miss Neville-Rolfe, whose semi-political lectures generally turned out to be based on a passionate belief in female potential, was something of a pioneer in the post-war fight for feminist power. Since that time we have seen numbers of powerful people who are not only women but who are not averse to expressing their own feminist beliefs in terms of aggressive defence. This attitude has not always advanced their views, however sensible. There is no doubt that in 1798 when William Godwin wrote his Vindication of the Rights of Women, his views were astoundingly perceptive and it took far too long for his opinions to be given credence. Unhappily, at least in this respect, Victoria and Albert gave out the wrong message. Or was it just Victoria?

The new school was two blocks away from No. 29 and I was to be a day-boarder; a fellow student, Anne Emmet, whose mother was a distinguished politician and therefore unable to look after her in London, came to live with us.

While Anne and I pursued our studies at the House of Citizenship, my mother started somewhat unrealistically to talk about my 'coming out'.

Anne came from a happy family, but perhaps suffered from the same kind of loneliness that I now recognise prompted me into a character of passive independence. Her mother had taken on great responsibilities in Sussex during the war and thus her presence in Anne's life was episodic in daily terms. Anne's father died soon after she was born, the youngest of four children; Anne was brought up in the nursery and school room until the time she went to Roehampton. Thus we had similar backgrounds, and a similar outlook. This led to mutual understanding and our early year together at the House of Citizenship cemented a lasting friendship; it must be said that the starting point was certainly the fact that we were both Sacred Heart girls. She was quite opinionated, not least because she was very proud of being a direct descendant of Irish rebel Robert Emmet's brother, Thomas, who wisely left Robert in Ireland and went to New York where he made a serious success of his life as a lawyer!

A dear schoolfriend, Anne Emmett, later Anne Money-Coutts.

I had spent seven years in the Convent, with minimal links with my mother, so that the nuns and Lutwyche constituted my family. Religion was a philosophical refuge which helped in the difficult relationship I had with my mother, and whilst Anne was more relaxed it nevertheless proved to be a strong bond in the early years of our friendship. We discovered that we were the only convent educated Catholics at the new School and we rather arrogantly took the view that we were on the whole better-educated than the Protestant students who had been to a variety of the best English Schools. Confirmation of this came with the fact that we were the only students who did not have to go to compulsory spelling lessons, and we were also the only ones who had any background knowledge of the fine arts.

Anne went home to Amberley Castle at the weekends, which left me with my parents. My mother was very controlling so I found myself going regularly to the Hurlingham Club where a number of her fellow Kenyans gathered for tea, reminiscing on their wondrous life in Africa and bemoaning the fact that English weather was dreary, English life was boring, English finances were dreadful and there were no cheap servants. My social perspectives started moving to the left, which would have horrified Anne's uber-conservative mother.

Mrs Emmet at this time was serving as a magistrate, and as a Conservative backbencher. She was hard-working and one of the most committed people I have ever met. This did not leave a lot of time for Anne; in addition, Anne's older sister Lavinia was out in the world. She had already had a coming-out dance at Amberley, which was attended by the young Princess Elizabeth. Christopher, the elder brother and heir to Amberley, was newly-married and running the estate, and her younger brother David was at University; which left Anne fairly alone. Soon she started asking me home for the weekends and I was pleased with the idea, if slightly nervous of meeting Mrs Emmet whose daunting achievements and rather remote character had taken shape in my mind as the result of Anne's stories.

Amberley Castle is a spectacular building, once the summer palace of the Bishops of Chichester, attacked during the Cromwellian wars and thereafter serving as a farm house. The magnificent entrance

Amberley Castle, Sussex.

was approached by a long downhill drive which devolved into a very large courtyard, now serving as a substantial garden. The remaining buildings were to the left of this entrance but the courtyard/garden was dramatically enclosed by the old battlemented walls, giving an impression of romantic privacy. We arrived that first time at night, and the dwelling area appeared to be in darkness; I noticed that Anne was quiet as we entered a large hall, a quietness that made me wonder about her relationship with her mother. The hall was dominated, not only by an impressive staircase, but more importantly by a magnificent pair of bronze stallions sculpted in Paris in the 1920s, an immediate indication of Mrs Emmet's appreciation and taste.

In a minute she appeared, a woman who had been pretty but who was aged as my mother was not, and who clearly gave little or no attention to her appearance. Her grey hair was curled tightly round her face, her clothes were simple and totally unimaginative, and her expression was unemotional. I was greeted quietly and courteously but I was deeply impressed by the silent strength that seemed to emanate from her presence and was immediately aware of a personality which both baffled and intrigued me. As Evelyn Rodd she had married into the Emmet family and the young couple were given a London house, furnished down to the tea towels. Preferring to live in the country, they swapped the house for Amberley, moved the contents into the run-down building and embarked on a programme of restoration which brought the old Bishop's palace back to life and its former distinction. I found it fascinating, and a distinct contrast to the fighting castle of the Borders that was Sizergh.

Evelyn Emmet's cool welcome masked a very warm heart, and I came to look forward to the Amberley weekends. Anne's maternal aunt Golly had married the painter Simon Elwes, and their two older boys were frequently there. The eldest, Peter, was about to join the Army and Dominic was still at Downside with the youngest, Timothy. They were all charming, amusing and extremely intelligent and it was the first time since the days at Sizergh that I relaxed and truly enjoyed the company of a happy family.

CHAPTER 9

Debutantes and work

In 1951 I was twenty, part of the fading London scene of formal dinner parties and dances, irritated to realize that any talent I might have had for drawing and painting fell a long way short of career potential and further irritated by parental determination that I should take up shorthand typing and settle into secretarial work. I was generally considered to be a bit arty, not a compliment in England at that time. Meantime my mother was determined that I should, in the parlance of a previous age, "come out". The interpretation of this expression was then quite different to the spin put on it in the current world of gays and transgenders.

Coming out, in the post-war years, was surely a vain attempt on the part of the pre-war generation to capture past splendours and in the sense that we had a very good time, it certainly succeeded. I was so impressed by the determination and generosity of all those parents who devised wonderful dances, cocktail parties, picnics for the 4th June and Ascot, in what was an attempt on the part of the parental generation to forget the war and turn back the clock. However, the young anywhere will create their own pleasures and romances, and the years of war had changed more than the debutante season.

Anne was to have a glamorous coming out ball at Amberley, a truly romantic setting and in due course this happened when she was seventeen. For reasons best known to her mother, she was not presented at court whilst my mother was determined that, in the absence of a dance, she would organise this for me. Accordingly she went to the Lord Chamberlain's office and put my name down. When she was asked for my father's credentials, she told me that she had explained my illegitimacy and pointed out that I should not be excluded on these grounds. I find this story inexplicable and rather unlikely. Nevertheless the fact is that my name was accepted, the date for the Presentation was fixed, and a new silk dress was ordered.

The day came, and Donald and my mother were both suffering from the effects of a long evening in the 400 night club. My mother declared that she could not attend the Palace but Donald, with a clearer understanding of protocol and its effects, hovered over her until finally she conceded that perhaps she could get up and dress, and we all followed suit.

When we arrived at the Palace we were ushered into the Ballroom which was lined with tiers of seats to accommodate hundreds of people. My mother and I climbed up to the highest level, in order to see better, but Donald said that his hangover precluded the climb and chose instead to sit at the lowest level. In due course my mother received a scrap of paper, kindly handed up through the tiers, with a scribbled message to the effect that Donald was not only asleep but snoring! She returned the note with a request to wake him up and keep him awake!

In due course the King came in, accompanied by Queen Elizabeth and the two Princesses. I was surprised at how small they all were, and the King was very slight. He appeared to be wearing make-up and I was told that this was to conceal fatigue and to highlight his presence for those like ourselves who were some distance away. They moved together round the room, preceded by an elderly Admiral with what looked like a small ivory staff. This he deployed to pat the stomachs of those who moved forward in their eagerness better to see the monarch. Occasionally the royal party paused to exchange words with someone known to them, or to whom they were introduced, and that was the only action. There we all were standing on our metal tiers, dressed to kill, and there was the Royal Family being gawped at – I suppose it was ever thus at Court.

In due course the Royal Family left, we descended from our top tier, scooped up Donald, and went off home to resume normality.

Many people fail to give the Royal Family credit for the work they do, which not only absorbs their days to an extraordinary degree but is frequently boring and where Presentations were concerned must at that time have seemed ludicrous. When they were discontinued I was not surprised.

Meanwhile the process of coming out continued, largely due to my mother's determination that I should succeed socially and marry well, a policy which I found deeply embarrassing. There was a considerable degree of bargaining on the social scene, largely involving the view that debutantes whose parents could not afford to give large parties and dances were not invited to anything. Reciprocity was vital. In the event I went to a number of dances and cocktail parties and enjoyed most of them hugely. Annie and I often went together, and we organised parties for charity balls as well. My mother very kindly gave one or two small parties for us at No 29, where Donald acted as butler and deeply impressed my friends with his good looks and practised charm. One girl was heard to enquire whether the handsome young man was Jacqueline's boyfriend. It made his week!

London dances were frequently held in Londonderry House, once the scene of brilliant political receptions, or 27 Knightsbridge, which had a large and elegant ballroom. Popular hotels were the Hyde Park, where a friend from school, Maureen O'Brien, had a wonderful coming-out dance, decreeing that the girls should all dress in white, pink or green. The elderly Lady St John of Bletsoe lived in a huge house in Lennox Gardens and let out the ballroom for parties, but I do not recall going there. There were very few large houses with ballrooms left functioning after the war and quite a lot of the parties were given in country houses. Kind hostesses laid on buses to bring their London guests down and back; dinner parties were always organised before dances, either in London or for country dates, so that the possibility of meeting new friends was endless. We wore long evening dresses and white gloves and the boys appeared sometimes in white tie, frequently their father's, but as time wore on it was generally a dinner jacket.

After the dance, we went on to nightclubs – that is to say many people did but I was forbidden this wicked luxury. Indeed, I was supposed always to be back at home by midnight, which led to some interesting Cinderella moments, but on the whole I am amazed at what I managed! This success was largely due to the fact that No. 2 Walton Street, the house that had succeeded 29 Hereford Square, had a large stone staircase, which of course, did not creak and thus allowed me to creep silently to bed in the small hours. An Italian friend had a different challenge. She frequently wore taffeta – well, we were nudging the New Look and dresses were tight-waisted with very full skirts; taffeta is very alluring but it rustles! So during the day she secreted her dress in the downstairs loo, waited for her parents to go to bed and as soon as she had changed the rest of the evening was a lot of fun!

Another of my challenges was the loud clang made by the taxi driver's metal flag which disturbed the silence of the early hours. I always instructed the driver "It is No. 2 on the corner but please drive round the corner into Walton Place." There came an evening when, as I leaned forward to offer my instructions, the driver turned to me and said "I remember, Miss – drive round into Walton Place!" I was quite shocked; it was the catalytic moment when I decided that enough was enough and I would have to start taking charge of my life.

One day to my horror, my mother announced that she was going to the 400 in the evening – I had been there the night before, and whilst I was hardly a celebrity, it was a small nightclub and the very sweet staff were inclined to greet one warmly by name! So I gritted my teeth and waited for morning.

My mother was all sweetness and light ; she had gone into the Ladies' Room of the Club and was greeted by the rather motherly lady who had presided there for years. "Your daughter was in last night Madam!" "Impossible', my mother responded sharply, "she is not allowed in nightclubs." "Oh, I assure you Madam" and she described my dress, one

Jacqueline Inchbald with antiques.

that I had taken over from my mother. "I know her well, she is so pretty, she looks so like you!"

Nothing was said about my intransigence, then or later!

My first job was at the General Trading Company in Old Park Lane near Londonderry House. Originally a large stable complex, horses were housed on the first floor, which they accessed via a long ramp, and carriages were accommodated on the ground floor. These spaces had been converted in the 1920s to the requirements of a large shop, the ramp now supporting a wide staircase. The Company had been started as a gift shop, and was very popular, particularly with country people, who found it convenient for elegant household goods, china, crystal, painted accessories and even antiques. It was famous for its Wedding Lists and was also well known for a selection of bath oils and soap. It was not generally known that the bath oils were manufactured on the floor above the shop by any of the employees who might be temporarily surplus to requirements. Basically it was a mixture of oil and pungent essences which we stirred in a large vat (I particularly recall the sweet pea essence as being slightly overwhelming) and then bottled. It remains one of the more eccentric skills that I have acquired in a long and varied career.

I learnt a lot about porcelain and glass, not least from an elderly Russian aristocrat who brought in fine 19th-century dinner services gleaned from the endless sales of country houses that were constantly being closed for reasons of economy. Whole services of wondrous Spode, Minton and Derby were purchased for anything between £50 to £80 and if old Mr Part who owned the shop was not in the buying mode, the Russian would mutter bitterly that the English had very little appreciation of the finer things in life. "All they want is Greek Key or Indian Tree" (both of them bog-standard but popular china patterns) he fumed to me once and I have to say I did see his point of view. But then of course there were no longer the domestic staff to care for past beauties. Large dining rooms were being put to other uses, and people were even being tempted to eat in their kitchens, would you believe?

I later went to work as a secretary at Withers; this was an eminent firm of solicitors, with six partners and a supporting team of specialists, the Managing Clerks. I did a brush-up course of shorthand typing at Pitman's but I was still fearful that my shorthand would not be up to the requirements of a lawyers' office.

In the event I worked as under secretary to Arthur Collins, who was the only partner with two secretaries, and probably the most hard-working partner as well. He regularly went home to Yorkshire for the weekend with a briefcase full of papers. His main secretary was Margaret Fairhurst, known in the Office and by the clients as Miss Fairhurst, a

Chapter 9

model of courtesy and efficiency. She had served during the war as a Wren and had she passed School Certificate would certainly have been an officer, even in that demanding and rather snobbish Service. Her management skills were outstanding and I learnt more from her during our two or three years together than at any other time – or so it seems to me from the perspective of the years. She might have deserved the label 'formidable' but she was kind, fair and always very helpful though she took a cool view about my filing abilities.

Arthur Collins was well known during the war as the Adjutant of the Blues, but it was only later in life that I understood the implication behind that appointment. He was a very cool character, and since I was the subordinate secretary I had no problem with this. To him I was always Miss Bromley, aged eighteen – they were different times! On one occasion I asked Margaret if I could leave around 2.30pm one Friday because I was to go to a dance in Dorset, and she said I must ask Mr Collins personally, which was a bit daunting. However between Mr Collins and my mother, I preferred to chance my luck with my employer and duly formed up nervously with my request.

There was a long pause whilst he gazed at me thoughtfully and I prayed that I would not be fired on a basis of frivolity; eventually the silence was broken. "There is no need for you to leave at 2.30," he remarked " You can take the 4.20 from Waterloo and it will get you there in plenty of time". I was grateful, but doubly impressed by his grasp of the South Western time tables!

So off I went to stay with the Welds, where at dinner I sat next to a young man who told me he was a magician. This statement was something of a conversation stopper; was this an adequate way to make a living, did he have a rabbit in his vest pocket? I never saw him again but the evening remained remarkable for the fact that on the way home from the dance Jo Weld, who was driving us in a crowded Rolls, pointed out a hot rick, smoking dangerously and doomed to burst into flames at any moment. He proceeded to give us a comprehensive lecture on how not to build a hot rick; I had not heard of a hot rick before and have never encountered one since but I still know quite a lot about them! Sometimes the useful acquisition of information comes to light in curious circumstances.

My mother was a dedicated control freak, certainly as far as I was concerned, and she was determined that I should leave Withers and work nearer home. Accordingly I was coerced into a job that was vacant at KLM, the Dutch airline that had its headquarters in Sloane Street, next door to Harvey Nichols. I was to be secretary to the Treasurer and I was to go home to 2 Walton Street where we were by then living, for lunch every day.

It was the very last thing I wanted to do – I had already gone through the motions of interest, first in acting and then in production, followed by an ambition to become a lawyer. The idea of working in an Accounts department in KLM, however elevated the executive, appeared to me to be a crushing form of Limbo: but as far as my mother was concerned, discussions were never an option. The Treasurer, Mr Zegers, had only just arrived in the UK from Holland when I started work for him and could barely speak the language. The first task he gave me involved working out something to do with the world-wide timetables; apart from baffling me, I never did grasp the reasoning behind it and suspect that he really did not know what to do with me. I think I was there to improve his English and perhaps I did. He was extremely nice and we became friends. Working for a Dutchman was very different to working for an Adjutant in the Household Division! In the course of my almost non-existent duties, he asked me to send flowers to a girl in Holland. Red roses travelled regularly to Amsterdam together with carefully sealed notes. Eventually he confided that the girl was his mistress and he was clearly hopelessly stricken! Soon it was announced that because he was preparing to settle in England, his wife would be paying an introductory visit and he warned me that she could speak no English at all – he also begged me not to mention roses.

I was young and fairly pretty and Mrs Zegers disliked me on sight. I could not think what I had ever done to displease her but the explanation was soon forthcoming. Mrs Zegers had found out about the girlfriend and assumed that I was the culprit. There was nothing I could do about it.

Having learned a great deal from Margaret Fairhurst about running an office, I now learned as much from KLM how employees should be treated. I arrived in the office a week before Christmas and was presented with a dozen eggs and a Dutch cheese for a Christmas present. In 1952 these were both like gold dust to rationed England. I tried to return them, pointing out that I had done nothing so far to merit them, but I was told that I was now an employee of KLM and that was the way they treated their staff.

In the relatively short time I spent with KLM I was deeply impressed with their staff policies and learnt a great deal that has been of help to me ever since in my own business administration. Life at home had become increasingly difficult and I finally decided to leave. I explained this to Mr Zegers who immediately told me that he would find me a job in the Manchester branch; I thought it so kind of him, but I was appalled at the idea of going off to a strange city and a new job, never mind the problems of somewhere to live.

CHAPTER 10

Michael Inchbald and a new perspective

So I ran away from home and went to stay with a cousin of Anne's.

Part of the reason was that at some time in the year I had met Michael Inchbald at a friend's party and discovered that he was the designer responsible for a dazzling exhibition at Peter Jones. Part of the dazzle could be attributed to the American influence, brought to the UK not just by the freewheeling American servicemen and women who so transformed English social life, but also by *American House and Garden*, a Condé Nast magazine that encouraged both diversity and exploration. The rules that appeared to govern the disposition of space, the treatment of furniture and the acceptable pattern of lifestyle in this country appeared to have no relevance to the work of the American Interior Designers featured by Condé Nast.

Michael Inchbald at his desk in the Conservatory at the end of the Drawing Room.

The meeting with Michael Inchbald, brilliant, good-looking and funny, if unpredictable by nature, was to be life changing.

Michael had followed me into a friend's cocktail party; we went up together in the lift, drifting into the crowd without speaking. Eventually I saw him making his way towards me and before I could say anything he asked with an innocent detachment "Tell me, why do you wear a Poor Bleeding Russia?" He referred, of course, to the silk scarf I wore to protect my hair from the rain, the very type of scarf that the late Queen wore all her life when she wasn't wearing a hat or a tiara. It was a provocative introduction, a fast ball which startled me as he had intended; Michael could be very droll and often, I would learn, his work would reflect his sense of humour. We chatted and parted, until one day I saw him peering through my Sloane Street office window at KLM and waving merrily. Soon we started seeing each other and his career as a designer fascinated me. I had never met a dedicated and trained designer before and his commitment to his work, together with his undoubted talent and its possibilities was impressive.

Before the war he had spent a little time at the Architectural Association on the understanding with his father that he would qualify as an architect. When war broke out in September 1939 he tried to join the Artist's Rifles; it was a popular regiment and more experienced artists had got there first! He then tried for work in camouflage which would have involved joining the Royal Engineers, but it was explained to him that whatever regiment he joined he would not be in a position to choose how or where he would serve. Instead he joined his father's original regiment, the Berkshire Yeomanry, and was posted to India. His brother Tony was commissioned into the Grenadier Guards and later killed at Camino in Italy.

When Michael returned at the end of the war, he rejoined the Architectural Association for a time but his experience there was not a success and he went back to his parents' house, Hailebourne, commuting to London when he had any work. During this time he was employed by Peter Jones to mount an exhibition to highlight the Antique Furniture Department and the Interior Decoration Department. Queen Mary, an accomplished aficionado of the world of antiques, requested a visit and the subsequent success of Michael's spectacular manipulation of style, colour and texture was confirmed when Peter Jones mounted a second exhibition.

Soon Michael went to live with his maternal uncle Courtenay Ilbert at No. 10 Milner Street, a house which was literally bursting with Clocks; clocks of all sizes, styles, periods and nationalities. There were also three large cabinets containing many hundreds of watches in the same categories, and the value of this collection was difficult to calculate. Very few people knew that Courtenay was one of the most knowledgeable authorities on the measurement of time in the world and his collection included the names of the world's greatest makers. On first acquaintance Courtenay appeared slightly withdrawn, not unlike Evelyn Emmet, but that was simply the courtesy of an earlier age. In spite of amazing achievement, both were unassuming and Courtenay's laconic responses to conversation could be a little daunting. Michael, I discovered, was well known for his preference in girl friends, so when his mother asked her brother, Courtenay, what he thought of Michaels's new girlfriend, Courtenay remarked that they were all the same … "long legs and blonde hair".

No, said Rosemary, she's got dark hair! "Oh," he remarked, "makes a change, doesn't it?"

Courtenay Ilbert, by profession an engineer, continued to live in the very large house that his mother had purchased when she was widowed; his spare time was devoted to the care and development of the collection of horology that he had started whilst he was still at Eton. Apparently, aged twelve and in his first half, he had purchased a tray of watch parts in a local sale; it appears that the now defunct jeweller had been working on watches and of course the auctioneers had lumped everything together so that Courtenay's purchase was no more than a total muddle. Family myth has it that by the end of a week, he was the proud owner of three working watches.

In 1952 the clock collection occupied the whole of the thirty-foot drawing room, together with several cabinets of shallow drawers which housed the extensive collection of watches. Every maker of any significance was represented in the Ilbert Collection and every inclusion was noted for brilliant mechanical achievement and/or outstanding design innovation. All the great makers were represented: Tompion, Quare, Breguet among so many. He was a very retiring man of great modesty; in the first days of my association with Michael I was often to see him raise his fingers to his lips as we passed the clock room, an indication that we must not disturb his uncle, so I took a while to get to know him. When I was twenty I left home and Michael found a room for me in the Convent in Cadogan Street, very close to No. 10.

Each weekend he went to his family home in Buckinghamshire and one day he arranged with his uncle that I could use his apartment at the weekend when he was away. It was much nicer than the confines of the Convent and it was the beginning of a great friendship with Courtenay. Because I still had nothing to do I started to sort out cupboards in the basement of No. 10 that were full of glasses, porcelain and artefacts once part of Courtenay's mother's extensive entertaining. Long neglected, disused and very dusty, I took great pleasure in sorting and cleaning them, storing them carefully in better order than I found them. Courtenay was aware of this, surprised but pleased that someone was trying to bring back some of the order of his mother's life.

Courtenay Ilbert with his collection of watches.

Every Friday evening Coole arrived to help with the upkeep of the Collection and when they had finished their work, Courtenay took him out to supper in Beauchamp Place. Coole was a valued employee of Courtenay's great friend, horology dealer Malcolm Gardiner and his visits were fixtures in Courtenay's life, as was lunch at the Spanish Club with Malcolm every Saturday.

The walk from Milner Street to Beauchamp Place was as far as Co could manage; aged around twenty he had been a keen skier with Arnold Lunn and twice broke the metatarsals of his feet as a result of the poor ski bindings. These injuries made it impossible for him to march and thus he was not able to do any military service in the 14/18 War – he once showed me his class photographs: "I am the only one left" he said quietly. One Friday evening, Co knocked on the door of Michael's flat and asked me if I would like to join them for supper. I was enchanted, so off we all went on the short trek to the restaurant in Beauchamp Place and this became a Friday ritual. Coole was highly intelligent and very funny and the conversation ranged far beyond horology.

On Saturday Ffoulkes arrived in the morning, also to work on the Collection with Co. Ffoulkes, known to Co and everyone else as Fookie, was also a horological expert. He and Coole came to the house to concern themselves with the brilliant masterpieces in the Collection, to avail themselves of the interchange with Courtenay, who by this time was considered to be one of the greatest horological experts in the world, and indeed to help with the maintenance of the collection. Courtenay was also renowned in this relatively small, and very select circle, as an unassuming man of great modesty who welcomed anyone with a serious interest into his house and his collection. And every Saturday, without fail, he lunched with his close friend, Malcolm Gardiner, commonly referred to as Plum. This odd nickname arose from an occasion when a French expert peered at Malcolm's work on a watch and declared in horror "A plumber has been at this watch!".

This was greeted with unfair delight by Malcolm's many friends and thereafter he was known as "the Plum".

So the household at 10 Milner street settled into a pattern – I lived nearby, and worked for a Mayfair antique dealer – Michael did more dealing than designing but the advent of Hugh Wontner changed that balance and I found myself more closely involved with Michael's work, not least because he was colour blind, and this I found fascinating. We began to spend our weekends visiting wonderful houses and looking for beautiful objects.

It was a happy time, shattered by a dramatic family disagreement which prompted Michael to ask his uncle if I could have the top floor of the house, now unused, as a flat. I had a small legacy from my grandmother and Michael used this to redecorate and furnish, and so I moved into Milner Street with three girlfriends, took over the running of the household and joined Michael in his dealing and interior design business.

And in due course Michael's work on what had been the staff quarters was featured with great success in *House and Garden*.

Michael

By the time I met Michael, I had spent time in a variety of houses dating from the 500-year-old Sizergh Castle through the 18th-century Lutywyche Hall to a small villa built around 1900 in Yapton. I had taken note of all of them and been intrigued, not only by their construction and cosmetic appeal, but also by the history and lifestyle of the many people who had called them home. In spite of my academic ignorance therefore, Michael and I clearly had many interests in common and I began to help him with secretarial work, shared visits to places of interest to us both, visits which included antique dealers and auction houses. We married in 1955 and lived as a family of three with Courtenay, all of us more than interested in artforms and historic achievements. It was a very happy time, during which Michael and I developed an antique business in Walton Street. Michael had always bought in the sort of furniture and artefacts that he knew could be useful in his design work; this potential stock had been stored in the little coach house at the back of the courtyard at No. 10. It was now moved into the Walton Street shop, the new Mrs Inchbald was installed to run the place and Michael initially did most of the buying which he hugely enjoyed. I also bought, but mostly smaller things and the occasional picture. Michael was always concerned about my penchant for the Victorian period and sometimes complained that I was filling the shop with Victorian junk! I took the view that there was a great deal of spectacular artwork in the 19th century, and it was only towards the end of the reign that wealth and social complaisance gave birth to the vulgarity of the final years. Interestingly, picture dealer Jeremy Maas once commented, as we stood together at one of Christie's Victorian sales, "You want to be careful Jacqueline, there is a lot of ullage in this period!"

David Hicks

At this time a young David Hicks was living with his mother just beyond Sloane Square and had of course completely redecorated her very pretty classic terrace house; in due course he invited us to dinner.

David's style was quite different from Michael's; whilst Michael was a committed classicist, David's early work was consciously simple, relying on colour and pattern for a result that was best described as cool elegance. His drawing room offered a background of shell-grey walls and carpet, plain white curtains outlining the tall early 19th-century windows, and white upholstery accented by a sparkling selection of Thai silk cushions. I thought it enchanting.

It was a wonderful summer evening when we left to walk home to Milner Street and Michael was quite depressed. Conscious that David, in his early twenties was much younger, he had started to brood about the lost years of training that he had spent in India, in his view doing very little of anything. In spite of the dazzling success of the Peter Jones exhibitions he felt that David was coming forward with youth on his side and that the work that he, Michael, had just seen, encapsulated a new spirit, a freer outlook which would perhaps resonate with the adventurous vision of a post-war generation. The sharp use of colour in David's work also emphasized Michael's own disadvantage, the colour blindness that had prevented the development of his talents in wartime camouflage techniques.

But there was very good news to come.

Courtenay received a telephone call from a total stranger; could a Mr Wontner, who had an interest in watches, visit Mr Ilbert? An interest in watches was catnip to Courtenay so a time was arranged and we waited to see what, if anything, could justify this interest. In due course a good-looking man of around middle-fifties appeared, Hugh Wontner,

Sir Hugh Wontner, Lord Mayor of London, 1973

who turned out to be Chairman of the Savoy Hotel. His grandfather, who was a prison Governor, had a challenging hobby – he was a secret watchmaker! Hugh explained to Courtenay that his grandfather had made three watches in all, which for an amateur otherwise fully employed was not without merit, and that he had signed them all "RENTNOW", effectively Wontner spelt backwards, to ensure his privacy. Hugh wanted to acquire one, if possible, and having heard of Courtenay's massive collection of watches, just thought that he might find one of his grandfather's at No. 10!

Unhappily Courtenay was unable to help and nor could he find any official reference to Grandpa Wontner. The real beneficiary of this encounter was Michael! As soon as Hugh saw Michael's incredibly smart flat the Savoy acquired a new designer and he was immediately commissioned to redesign the Hotel's famous ballroom. It was the beginning of a long and happy association. Not only was Hugh very charming, he had done quite a lot of acting and was interestingly well read; he also had an engagingly thespian sense of humour. Working with him was the greatest fun, presenting not only a welcome challenge but a sense of future security. The skills of interior decoration were not well regarded by the architectural profession at that time and certainly did not have any professional status, so that those who specialised in the decoration of houses faced financial as well as working uncertainty.

In 1956 Courtenay was taken very ill and moved into a nursing home in North London, miles from home. In the days following this horror, on one of my visits, he told me that the nurse greeting him in the morning had recited Hickory Dickory Dock to him! Since he had no problem with his mental abilities, he was outraged and in his now broken voice wondered whether he could come home. The doctor was doubtful but common sense prevailed and he returned to Milner Street; his bed was installed in the old dining room, we acquired a wheel chair that gave him access to the clock room and he was ready for the string of old friends who trooped in to see him and wheel him into the clock room for all the old familiarities of shared interests and kindred spirits. In 1956 Courtenay died in his own bed, in his own house.

In 1958 my son Courtenay, was born, quickly followed in 1960 by my beloved daughter Amanda, and my old top-floor flat was now the nursery, with a very sweet nanny installed as well. Thus I was freed to continue to support Michael's work. But before these happy events, we were faced with the problem of the Collection and its disposal. Courtenay's own views were not crystal clear. "It is my life's work" he told me "and of course I would like it to stay together – on the other hand" he added " I have had such wonderful fun putting the collection together that I feel badly about denying other collectors the same pleasure." And so we were left puzzled as to the outcome; in the end it hung on money.

Chapter 10

The value of this collection was, in some respects incomprehensible. It was the work of a whole lifetime, starting as it did with that tray of watch parts purchased at the auction of a dead watchmaker by a bright and inquisitive 12-year-old who, within days, restored three watches. I met that schoolboy when he was in his sixties and he was as fascinated then by the prospect of possibility as he had been in his teens. It was his enduring sense of mechanical adventure which made him such an engaging and charming companion. But apart from the collective value, the collection included some of the finest known examples of timekeeping; Earnshaw's 509 award-winning chronometer which travelled on the Beagle with Darwin was there, together with the spectacular skeleton clock supposed to have been commissioned by Louis XVI from Breguet and subsequently claimed by the Napoleons, who installed a diamond cypher on the marble base. When Michael, always fascinated by anything palatial, exclaimed over this, Courtenay, deeply unimpressed by anything at all other than skill, remarked quietly, "It is still a very good clock".

Jacqueline with Courtenay and Amanda.

All the great names of British time keeping were represented in this astonishing array. The watch collection, where it all started, was now seriously large. At sometime in the history of Russia, a great many of the Czarist artefacts were put on the international market and Courtenay predictably purchased quite a large number of watches. When they arrived however, it was discovered that the gold and jewelled cases had all been purloined in transit and all Courtenay was left with was the movements: he was absolutely delighted. He had exactly what he wanted without the costs of all the jewellery!

In all the circumstances it seemed inevitable that the only method of disposal had to be the auction room and Christies were approached to prepare a catalogue and allow Courtenay's treasures to be enjoyed as he had enjoyed them. However, many people considered that it would be a national loss if the Ilbert Collection were to be dispersed, and that it should instead be lodged in the British Museum, a permanent memorial to Courtenay and an invaluable source of inspiration and knowledge to the horologists who would follow in his footsteps.

Since I had secretarial experience and some grasp of administration, it fell to me as a competent family member to co-ordinate with the British Museum during the negotiations for the sale and movement of the collection.

One day, thinking about the move, I recalled Courtenay's story of how he considered that he had no alternative but to take the entire collection down to the basement in a desperate attempt to save everything from the depredations of the Luftwaffe. This involved removing all the weights and movements. Together with the cases, each longcase might have involved three trips down the basement staircase – given the number of clocks involved that was a fairly herculean effort and Courtenay had perforce to do it by himself. Luckily the threat never materialised. When I first visited the Clockroom, the clocks had been restored to their appointed places, and were wound and working; being in that room was an extraordinary sensation, rather like walking into a giant heart.

CHAPTER 11

The School

1960 was surely a turning point for all of us, offering as it did the end of the miserable post-war austerity and the beginning of an era which allowed freedom of thought, aspiration and achievement, the beginning of the sixties! It was in 1960 I decided to start a Design School.

I remember the end of the war in 1945 as being excruciatingly slow. Berlin fell in 1945. The horrific discoveries of German atrocities in Europe added to the misery that the Nazi administration had wrought not only in the United Kingdom, but to the millions of people who lost their lives, whether passively or aggressively, in the conflict. In the midst of all the celebrations, the sound of the church bells we had not heard for so long, and the wondrous reunion of servicemen with their families, but we knew that the war was not over. There was still Japan.

And Japan took another year.

Nevertheless, there must have been a quiet optimism in the government that allowed its ministers to consider what would happen to the country 'after the war has ended'. It was that optimism that generated the foundation of the Design Council in 1944, and led to plans that would promote British design, British industry and British technology to an exhausted world. It was a brave plan and could be said to have had an unqualified success in its primary aim. I doubt if anyone realized the true extent to which the Council would influence the British themselves in their knowledge and appreciation of design and designers.

Prince Albert of Saxe Gotha, consort of Queen Victoria, encouraged public interest in design when he launched the Great Exhibition of 1851. This magnificent display of British industrial achievement, housed in the Crystal Palace which in itself provoked gasps of astonishment from visitors, was the first and probably the most successful and provocative of events that inspired others throughout the 19th century. Looking back on this success in terms of imperial status and manufacturing achievement, the Labour Government of the late 1940s took the view that it might be worth revisiting the establishment of English industrial supremacy by celebrating the centenary of Prince Albert's essay into marketing and public relations, a project so successful that it still resonates in the 20th century.

Herbert Morrison, Labour Member of Parliament for Hackney South

James Gardner

and a former Minister for Transport, was an enthusiastic supporter of the enterprise, which commanded a budget of no less than £12 million. The Labour party was well known for their encouragement of art and architecture as well as for determination that the vast portfolio of historical achievement in the UK should not only be preserved but shared. Now the government decided that England must demonstrate to the world that the war was over, and that the consequences of that war were in no way going to inhibit the English ability to recover, renew and once again excel. Accordingly, after four years of preparation, the Festival of Britain was opened in 1951, bringing to the British people the concept and importance of design and a new understanding of designers. Since the exhibits were displayed nationwide, the project became an exercise in education across every level of society, bringing not only pleasure to the public but opportunity to aspiring artists.

There was no greater supporter than the King himself, who was personally anxious to show to the world that in spite of the tribulations of war, Britain was still very much in business.

The Festival had been pre-dated by a smaller and much less ambitious exhibition mounted by the Council of Industrial Design in the Victoria and Albert Museum, with a similar aim to educate the consumer in the role of those behind the products which support daily life. Misha Black was a leading figure in the philosophy of the project, which featured a wide variety of presentations and products, from Black's witty essay "The Birth of an Egg Cup" to the prototype railway carriage designed by his studio. Designers' identities and achievements, lost in the chaos of the war years, came to public attention in this event. Robin Day and Ernest Race were just two of the furniture designers whose careers would prosper over the next decades and whose names would become familiar in retail circles. A significant figure in both events was James Gardner, awarded an OBE for his supervision of the Britain Can Make It exhibition and his work on the Festival, where he designed part of the South Bank Exhibition and Battersea Park pleasure gardens. He had an extraordinary career, starting as an apprentice jewellery designer at Cartier, later engaged on camouflage design during World War II (he assured me that he was very good at fake tanks!) and finally ending his days as one of the most influential designers of museums on an international canvas. He was the epitome of a modern Industrial Designer, able to turn his talent to any conundrum. It was James Gardner who involved Michael Inchbald in the V&A exhibition, and this was one of Michael's first commissions when he returned from military service in India.

I went to neither of the Exhibitions that proved to be such a milestone in the design world, nor did I like the furniture and graphics that I saw on the posters and in the media. Much of the furniture, with its

Chapter 11

splayed legs and disappointing veneers, had more than a hint of the type of Economy furniture produced in the war under the influence of proletariat Scandinavia. Both quality and individuality were sacrificed in the name of practicality and financial viability, a sacrifice that was inevitable in a country that had remained under siege for four years.

So when in about 1950 I was told that there was a magnificent display of interior design at Peter Jones I was determined to go and have a look, not least because I had become interested in window dressing and thought I might learn something.

Robin Day

Peter Jones was a firm already well known for the Interior Design department, though I was not aware of that at the time. Several designers started their careers in this department, not least John Fowler, who worked there as a painter of furniture in the 1930s before he joined the firm started by the redoubtable Lady Colefax. The department was responsible for the decoration of many of the great country houses, and the client list was impressive. There was also an antiques department, and both sections were managed by a particularly impressive lady who had been in control for many years.

When I finally got to the Exhibition I was not disappointed. Here was the familiarity of elegant antique furniture of the highest quality, arranged into 'rooms' indicating to the buyer how to assemble and manipulate style, texture and colour. In addition, there were innovations and witty asides. A bedroom was furnished entirely with the pearl-inlaid black lacquer furniture so popular with Victorians of the 1860s, the soft furnishings in brilliant pink echoing the nacre lights in the pearl and challenging the glossy black surfaces of the lacquer. A set of dining room chairs of *c.* 1800, sabre-legged, quietly elegant, was covered in a yellow McLeod tartan and looked immediately quite different from expectation, combining the shock of fashion with the familiarity of classicism. Magnificent armchairs by Thomas Hope were upholstered in leopard skin and I was enthralled. I had no idea how I could possibly break into this world. Even the window dressing idea had fallen foul of the financial and parental diktats that had precluded any art training. So back I went to my typewriter at Withers banging out legal documents, from thence to KLM and finally, just short of 21 years old, I left home and authority, found myself a job in an antique shop and, with Michael's help, a room in the Convent in Cadogan Street.

At some time during the year I had met Michael Inchbald at a friend's party and discovered that he was the designer responsible for the dazzling display at Peter Jones.

Part of this dazzle could be attributed to the American influence, brought to the UK not just by the freewheeling American servicemen and women who so transformed English social life, but also by

57

American *House and Garden*, a magazine that encouraged both diversity and exploration.

It was not until some time later that I met the designer of this spectacle. When I did, his career in design and his dedication to his profession fascinated me; I had never met a trained designer before and his commitment to his undoubted talent and its possibilities was impressive. Indeed when Paul Reilly, Director of the Design Council, came to see the magnificent rooms that Michael created in No. 10 Milner Street after his uncle's death, he remarked that he had never met a designer so fascinated with his own ingenuity! Marriage to Michael marked the beginning of a lifetime's involvement with design, and more particularly with the integrity and status of the designer, but I had a great deal to learn.

Sir Paul Reilly, Director of The Design Council and great supporter of Michael Inchbald.

Eventually the new world, with a social structure based on success rather than bloodlines, was a major influence on 20th-century lifestyle. Domestic mobility was an important factor in promoting the idea of decoration or refurbishment. In America a change of job often meant a change of state or city and so a newly-mobile society was all to the benefit of the emergent profession of interior decoration.

In 1931 interest and professionalism in Interior Design had progressed to the point where the American Institute of Decorators was formed as the presiding body, in order to preserve disciplines and standards in what was a new profession. Interior Decorating was now taken very seriously but the American rate of growth was not matched in England where architects considered themselves to be the exclusive guardians of anything to do with buildings .

War is an all-embracing disaster, impacting on every aspect of life. Artistic education is no exception. Young designers, whether working or teaching, were inevitably called up at the beginning of the war and by 1944 students in England found themselves being instructed by a tranche of the much older generation. In addition, many designers did not return from active service and others changed direction in the wake of such a serious life upheaval. This was another reason why the UK interior design world fell dramatically behind New York, and whilst The Festival was much needed, it informed about the fact of design, introducing rather than influencing.

It was however, a beginning. Simultaneously Condé Nast launched the English version of *House and Garden* under the editorship of Anthony Hunt. The first issues were not particularly successful, partly because the images were drawn from America and partly because a great many featured products were not available in the UK. The dedicated reader had almost certainly seen it all before in the American version, also available in the UK. One of the reasons for this paucity of content lay in

Chapter 11

the fact that there was little of contemporary interest to photograph in austerity Britain.

However, womens' magazines, prompted by the American concept of lifestyle, had found a new story in interior design and started to feature designers and their opinions on the home pages. The word was getting out, and the glamour of the Peter Jones Exhibition generated much publicity, most particularly when Queen Mary requested a private visit.

By 1960 I had been running Michael's studio for him for several years together with an antique business which we had started, which dealt largely with French and American dealers. English *House and Garden* magazine was now fully established as the designer's bible and all the womens' magazines, weekly and monthly, were regularly featuring interiors and Interior Designers. In my role in the studio I was very aware that although I had learnt a great deal of office management at Withers, secretarial work for a leading firm of solicitors was not really adequate experience and I decided that I should find a centre of design learning.

Condé Nast

There was nothing.

The options were only a full-blown architectural training or the courses run by polytechnics which offered shopfitting and window dressing studies as the nearest suggestion to interiors. David Mlinaric, who worked in the Inchbald studio, having studied, at the Bartlett, but that too was architecturally based. The alternative was Parsons in New York but by now we had two small children and my absence would have been unthinkable.

So I thought the unthinkable!

I decided to open my own School and with this in mind I rang Paul Reilly, then head of the Design Centre. I expected my plan to be considered risible, but Paul was not only enthusiastic but very supportive. There and then he gave me a list of possible lecturers who might help and so I devised a programme, largely based on what I did not know! This ignorant approach had the benefit of highlighting what students did actually need to know. Eventually progress with the syllabus would highlight a great deal more besides!

With all the current burgeoning interest in interior decoration and design, it had become clear that in the interests of designers' clients, formal training was required to protect their interests, and the idea of the Inchbald School was soon given the extensive publicity that initially put the venture on its feet. Decorating editors loved it, the good idea was a runaway success and it was then my responsibility to consolidate the educational gravitas and justify the original decision. Good ideas don't stand on their own merits; they require the energy to implement

Front of No. 10 Milner Street, with architectural details highlighted by Michael Inchbald.

below: The first-floor drawing room at No. 10 Milner Street (Stanley House), created from two large bedrooms.

Chapter 11

left: Michael Inchbald's original design for his bedroom c.1950, blackberry walls and pale grey paint.

below left: View from the Blue Bedroom through sliding doors to the Drawing Room.
below right: view from Hall into Morning Room.

61

Jacqueline Inchbald c. 1968.

the concept and the determination to continue in spite of the worries of a young business. Private schools have to be managed on the same principles as any other business in order to ensure that the product, the educational programme, retains both authenticity and authority.

I feel guilty that I was too ignorant in 1951 to appreciate the Festival of Britain: it created a sea change in the way that the English people regard design and that in itself was an educational victory.

1960 was the moment to extend the professionalism of interior design in the UK, and a centre of educational excellence to train interior designers was badly needed. So in 1960 the Inchbald School of Design, with seven students in its first term, was established to provide just that service.

The first group of students, September 1960.

CHAPTER 12

The Development of Interior Design

The development of Interior Design and Decoration as an identifiable career has taken much longer than is generally thought. It was certainly flourishing in the 19th century, but as a trade. It was not until the 20th century that it finally crystallised into a profession at once fascinating and challenging.

It might well be argued that the dazzle of decoration was born in the theatre, with the desire to entertain, to divert but importantly also to impress. If this is an acceptable proposition it may logically lead back to the early 17th century and to the architect who brought back to England the spectacle of the European Renaissance, namely Inigo Jones (1573–1652). It is difficult to deny that Jones' studies in Italy, and his work for the English crown would influence architectural and design perspectives for over two centuries. His introduction to the possibilities of studies in Greece and Rome engendered the interest of the privileged class, paving the way for the refined form of architectural education which would henceforth be known as the Grand Tour. In the days when private tutors were the norm in the big houses, and public schools could be less than enjoyable, the idea of rounding off one's tuition with a tour across Europe to glamorous new countries, full of light and sun and discovery, must have been truly appealing, no matter how uncomfortable the coaches nor how flea-ridden the coaching inns.

These educated and mostly privileged adventurers set forth to enjoy themselves as well as garner new knowledge, and the result of their studies had an invaluable impact on cultural life in England. There is no doubt that Jones' pioneering studies in Italy established the classical tradition which flourished with such enduring success throughout the 18th century. From the tapestries and panelling of an earlier age, Jones transformed established interior design with the cool elegance inspired by Vitruvius, taking the transformation further by emphasising the light and colour, the comfort and fashion of Italian achievement. Travel and study, the common denominators of design knowledge, were the tools that forged his over-riding talents and brought him to the attention of the English court. A felicitous relationship with a powerful patron, no less than Queen Anne herself (1574–1619, consort of James I), reinforced his success, enabling a spectacular revision of the taste and fashions of the Tudor monarchs.

In an age when military and field sports were the entertainment of

Inigo Jones
1573-1652

the day, the evenings of the Court were filled with music, dancing and theatre. Masques were a form of theatre, early cabarets devised to fill tired evenings, engage the audiences of the court and by such diversion cement the dependency and loyalty of the aristocracy to the new Scottish King, James I, who was already known for his interest in architecture. Briefed by the Danish Queen, Inigo Jones collaborated with poet Ben Johnson to provide presentations of ever-increasing glamour and ingenuity including movable sets and breath-taking costumes which in turn influenced early Stuart fashion. Anne of Denmark does not attract great regard in history but she must have been an engaging client, with a great sense of fun and drama, perhaps still lacking credit for her interest in the world of artists.

Given this talented triumvirate, the Palace masques became a noted feature of Court life; Inigo Jones progressed in royal favour to further architectural patronage, finally leaving his mark not only on London but on the character and form of the English house.

One of his smaller but most significant buildings in terms of interior design was the Queen's House at Greenwich, commissioned by the Queen for her personal use. The two collaborators must now have formed the friendship which so often springs up between designer and client, a friendship based on shared interest and experience, and mutual understanding; it is interesting to speculate on the nature of their discussions regarding Anne's new enterprise.

This house was surely a personal requirement for the comfort and privacy which prove so elusive in palaces, incorporating a closer relationship between the building and everyday life, demanding a quite different brief to those engendered by the Court and its rigorous demands. The Queen's House was to be something of a blueprint for many other buildings, reflecting the very human desire for the intimacy of family and friends as opposed to the pomposity of a palace environment. James Stuart, VI of Scotland and I of England, took the crown left to him by Elizabeth in 1603 determined to establish his dominion over what had long been an aggressive enemy and an aristocracy of doubtful loyalty. Accordingly, he undertook a programme of image enhancement which today would be described as public relations. He had a passion for splendour and for the arts and he set about establishing his Court as a centre of culture. As part of his plan he commissioned Inigo Jones to redesign the sprawling palace of Whitehall. Although the development remained unfinished, one of the finest buildings of the reign, the Banqueting House, was completed by the king's son, Charles I, with an apotheosis of James by no less an artist than Rubens; it stands today an exceptional example of Stuart patronage. Apart from his desire to continue his father's scheme for the royal palace, Charles was himself a serious collector of fine paintings.

He employed an accomplished agent, Endymion Porter, to assist in his purchases, counted Van Dyck and Rembrandt amongst his circle of friends and commissioned Bernini to create a fine bust of himself aided by the famous triple portrait painted for the purpose by Van Dyck.

Under the Stuarts, architecture, design and the fine arts all flourished and it was felicitous that the first two Stuarts, James and Charles, were contemporaneous with some of the most brilliant artists of the century. James's grandmother was French Princess Mary of Guise and his mother, Mary Queen of Scots, was brought up in France. French influence was thus a strong factor in his education. In addition he was sharply aware of the necessity of impressing and dominating his English subjects with a show of majesty allied to determined management.

The Queen's House, however, emphasised both culture and domesticity rather than swagger and was surely an influence on the later Chiswick House and Marble Hill, both commissioned with a requirement for private use, but lacking nothing in terms of elegance. Can the character of the English country house be traced back to the interesting partnership between a Danish queen and an adventurous English architect? Unhappily the beginning of the Civil War in 1642 brought any form of culture in England to an abrupt halt and indeed generated an era of destruction that was not matched until the advent of the German bombing missions in 1941. The royal treasures and jewels were broken up and sold for cash, Charles' magnificent collection of paintings was sold and scattered across Europe whilst numerous fine houses throughout the country were damaged or destroyed.

Craftsmen and professionals were drawn into the armed forces on both sides, a situation that is the inevitable result of any war but particularly so in the event of civil disruption. As a result the interruption of skills impacted across the whole area of education and shared experience, to the detriment of artistic and design progress. Further there can have been little or no patronage through the Commonwealth years until the day in 1660 when Charles ll returned from exile to claim the crown. The new King brought with him the restoration of Court life, and personally generated an era of patronage and artistic challenge. Like his father and grandfather before him, he was both artistic and inventive, wasting no time in reestablishing the splendours of majesty deemed so important to the reputation of monarchy. New Crown jewels were commissioned to replace those dispersed by the Commonwealth, and the king set about trying to retrieve at least some of the Stuart Collection of fine art which had been sold off by Cromwell. England gave him a riotous welcome home but Charles remained aware that monarchy required the seductive powers of both glitter and entertainment and these were delivered by his exceptional personality and his capacity to entertain, not just his Court but his people.

The Influence of France

Charles II had spent nine years in Bruges, where he established the Court in exile, whilst his mother returned to her native France. He was, however, a frequent visitor, not only to his mother but to the Court of his cousin, the French king in Paris.

It was during these years that the superlative Château of Vaux-le-Vicomte was being created close to Paris to the order of Nicholas Fouquet, Superintendent of France, as his personal residence. The design team responsible for this, the most beautiful private house and garden in France at the time, perhaps even in Europe, were architect Le Vau, garden designer Le Nôtre and the painter Le Brun. Together this incredible trio designed an estate of elegance and beauty that appeared to have no financial parameters. Fouquet had risen to power during the young king's minority, enjoying an independent authority which clearly encouraged complaisance. When the enterprise was complete, Louis was invited to celebrate the magnificence of his senior courtier and nothing was spared for his entertainment. Unhappily the king could hardly fail to note that one of his servants, the servant with access to Government funds, had far outdone the monarch himself in terms of grandeur, and inevitably such apparently limitless expenditure was called into question. Fouquet's brilliant achievement proved to be his downfall.

The success of his designers in producing a domain of such outstanding beauty and brilliance was surely part of their brief, intended to enhance the reputation of a spectacularly ambitious figure. Louis XlV was in his early twenties when he was entertained so royally at Vaux, and he was deeply shocked by the parade of wealth and power that he encountered there, and which undoubtedly appeared to him to be a challenge, not only to his royal status but to his personal authority. No-one had yet experienced the full impact of Louis's determination to brook no rival from either Government or aristocracy, so his immediate reaction sent a shock wave through the Court. Fouquet was tried and imprisoned for life and there was no appeal. The charges were 'peculation' and, much more significantly, 'lése majesté'. The design team had exceeded the brief with immeasurable success, but with disastrous results for their client. Vaux was a public relations programme that disastrously backfired, but which provided an inspiration for the creator of Versailles and a blueprint for his isolationist policy. Louis recognised the impact of Fouquet's bravura property and learned the lesson of public relations, of outward show providing an overarching dazzle, a blinding crowd pleaser that could promote and at the same time dominate.

Determined to exceed the splendours of Vaux, Louis lost no time in deploying Fouquet's designers to create a centre of magnificence at his father's old hunting lodge in Versailles. Against this background he invented a title for himself, 'the Sun King' and deliberately created a seat of central government at which those members of the aristocracy who aspired to placement were expected to attend; thus he shackled his senior subjects to his personal and imperious will, and the splendours that his artists created ultimately became the very bedrock of the monarchy's eventual disintegration. He instructed the Vaux creators to build him the Palace which would become the "most beautiful Palace of the Western world", a Palace that in 2017, over three hundred years after it was built, could attract over 17 million visitors anxious to see the glories that the finest European designers and artists of the late 17th century could produce. No subsequent design team has ever matched or even challenged the magnificence of Versailles and nor did the multitude of courtiers who lived there ever claim that it was comfortable. Comfort was not the priority. Unsurprising then, that the king should decide like the Stuart Queen that he would build a residence providing an escape from the duties of monarchy, a small and comfortable house that offered privacy, where he might enjoy the company of his family and close friends beyond the etiquette of strict court controls. This building, the Trianon de Porcelaine, a design conceived by the now famous M. le Vau, was clad in blue and white decorative tiles, an approach that was both charming and innovative. Unhappily the tiles did not stand up well to the elements and the porcelain Trianon was dismantled in 1686 to be replaced by the larger and more impressive Grand Trianon, clad in red marble. It was formally opened by the King and his second, morganatic wife, Mme de Maintenon, becoming a refuge for royal privacy, a place where life could be led on a more normal footing than was possible in the main Palace. Later in the reign it was frequently used as a guest house for eminent visitors, but by 1703 it was the permanent family home of the Grand Dauphin, the eldest son of Louis XIV, who resided there until his death in 1711.

The development of these smaller houses, albeit still grand, was a reaction to the desire of the upper classes for comfort above display. The finances of wealthy clients enabled architects and designers not only to exercise their ingenuity to the full, but also to progress in terms of their own professional status. The talents and expertise of the teams which created Vaux le Vicomte and subsequently Versailles, had effectively crystallised the political impact of interior design and decoration, but at the same time such talents led on to the next stage of client requirement, a greater provision and control of comfort, both physical and psychological. Apart from the development of a style more sophisticated than palatial, the element of comfort was introduced as a primary consideration. The heavy, carved wooden chairs, perhaps with a seat cushion, were replaced by elegant frames with seats and backs designed and fitted by a new breed of craftsmen, the upholsterers. The handsome wooden panelling gave way to painted finishes and the tapestry hangings would slowly be replaced with damasks and velvets stretched over flat walls, a precursor to wallpaper. Small spaces, small rooms, small houses require more thought and attention to detail than larger areas, but the idea of smaller houses still recommended itself to the clients of the late 17th and early 18th centures. The fashions adopted by royalty and the aristocracy were soon copied by the successful classes and would evolve into the establishment of a social pattern which in principle would dominate social mores until the catastrophes generated by two world wars in the 20th century. By the late 17th century French designers had established an unquestionable domination in matters of architectural innovation and interior style, whilst the cash-strapped Charles II, apart from the trappings of majesty, tended to bestow his patronage on other men's wives and the emerging recreation of horse racing. Charles died in 1685 and the accession to the throne in 1689 of his niece Mary, with her husband the Dutch Stadtholder, William of Orange, was destined to reinvigorate the arts in England, bringing an injection of Dutch taste and Dutch artefacts which provoked a new perspective of decorative possibilities. The reign witnessed not only a restoration of Hampton Court and its gardens, a particular interest of Mary's, but there are numerous smaller country houses throughout England with Dutch features and more agreeable interior layouts dating from this new influence.

Treasure from Asia

The Dutch were a successful middle-class people well before the development of the middle class as we now know it in England. Combined with a practical outlook on the priorities of everyday life, this identity engendered a quite different attitude to domestic interior planning and was the perspective that the Dutch monarchy brought to England on the accession. Decoratively speaking, one of the most interesting aspects of Holland's contemporary culture was the strong connection with the relatively new Indian market. Three years before Queen Elizabeth I died in 1603, she granted a Royal Charter to the Governors and Company of Merchants of London for the purpose of trading in the East Indies. The most desirable products at the time were spices and salt, the market expanding into the valuable saltpetre, an ingredient of gunpowder, and developing further into more luxurious goods such as cotton and silk. Vasco da Gama had already discovered this market, making landfall in Kolkata in 1499, but the hazards of the sea journey round the Cape of Good Hope were such that even the adventurers of the 16th century found the challenge more than a little daunting. Familiarity and good seamanship prevailed however and the Dutch who, like the Portuguese, were a maritime race, established the Dutch East India Company, Vereenigde Oostindische Compagne, in March 1602. This official date had been preceded through the century by robust trading; further, the Dutch at the time were the only merchants allowed into Japan where, among other products, they purchased Japanese Imari porcelain, introducing these skilled accomplishments to the European market. Both England and Holland were thus established in India virtually simultaneously and it should be noted that Charles II's Queen, Catherine of Braganza, brought not only Tangier but Bombay to England as her marriage dowry, both of them very considerable contributions to England's subsequent imperial ambitions as well as to English culture. By the beginning of the 18th century the influences on design fashions were not only challenging but international. New skills were adapted by European manufacturers and the possibilities for potential designers were both stimulating and provocative. The route running through Turkey, Persia and Turkmenistan, which came to be known as the Silk Road, had generated a trading communication system across the whole area. Until the three European seafaring nations, Portugal, Holland and England, found their way round the Cape and to India, this was the major marketing network for the exotic products such as carpets, silks and porcelain that Europeans perceived as fashionable and desirable. There were also a number of trading ports on the West coast of India and in due course these increased in importance with the advent of the Company merchants. The style of design and decoration known as 'Queen Anne' can be attributed to such new opportunities.

Tea became the popular drink, generating both silver and porcelain designs and the elegant productions involved with its service. Indian cotton was fine quality and much cheaper than silk. Furthermore the Indians had refined and perfected the art of block printing and their fabrics were coloured with dyes that were fast to light, qualities that recommended them to the general public. Chintz, fairly rare in the 16th century, achieved tremendous popularity in the period after Queen Anne ascended the throne in 1702, and remains closely associated with the more relaxed and more generally available fashions of her reign. Initially used for bedcovers, curtains and wall hangings, it was also seen as desirable for clothes, partly for the brilliance of the colours but also for the skills of the Indian fabric designers who combined the familiar patterns of Mughal and Islamic art into the culture of the European public, producing classic products which played a significant part in 18th-century interior fashions. These cloths, revived in popularity by 20th-century interior designer John Fowler, are still used extensively today, a tribute to those long-ago Indian artisans.

State Support

In the late 17th century upholstery was emerging as an increasingly important skill and one of its leading proponents was Frenchman Daniel

Marot (1661–1752) who enjoyed a successful career spanning the late 17th century, through the reign of William and Mary and well into the Hanoverian period. Marot is an important figure in the development of Interior Design, not only because of his contemporary success, but because, as a skilled engraver, he chose to record his extravagant and detailed designs for the benefit of his peers and, as it turned out, for the benefit of posterity. The son of an architect/engraver, Marot was trained in the latter skill by his father and spent time studying and working at the Gobelins Factory in Paris, under the aegis of Jean Bérain, another leading designer of the period. The Factory was founded in 1440 by a Flemish dyer for the manufacture of the tapestries so popular at that period.

Tapestries and paintings were the basis of interior design but with the development of style there was increased interest in gilding and upholstery and Marot excelled in the structures of curtains and furniture covering, as well as being renowned for his fabric and leather designs. In 1662 the Factory was purchased for the Crown by Minister of Finance, Jean Baptiste Colbert, who then established an extended programme of activities, renaming the establishment as Manufacture Royale des Meubles et Tapisseries de la Couronne. This demanding title indicated that the new responsibility of the Gobelins was to be proficient, not only in the designing but in the production of anything required for the interior design and decoration of the royal palaces. It was thus inevitable that such extensive programmes would incorporate a training centre of decorative arts, a school for interior designers who required such a diversity of accomplishments to carry out their commissions, royal or otherwise.

Colbert was deeply concerned with the trading superiority of France, as well as with the aesthetics of architecture and applied art. He was himself a patron of the arts, a leading figure in the establishment of Art Academies and a pioneer of art and design education. And in the reorganised Manufacture Royale, Marot's tutor Jean Bérain (1637–1711) was a leading figure. Born in the Austrian Netherlands, Bérain worked under painter Le Brun and was established at the Louvre when he was appointed "dessinateur de la Chambre et du Cabinet du Roi". His reputation as a designer and stylist was soon firmly established and his body of work is extraordinary, ranging through applied decoration, fashion and furniture design, as well as excelling in the fantasies of theatre design for both Molière and Lully. Like Inigo Jones, he is a one-man demonstration of design virtuosity, his influence extending well into the period of the Regence and the fashions of the Rococo. And as the King's favoured designer he was in control of the output of an important royal department, the Menus de Plaisir du Roi. This organisation devised and designed any Royal event that had to do with the private or political life of the monarch, whether State visits, royal weddings or funerals. The appointment allowed Bérain to indulge both talent and fantasy and he must have revelled in such liberty. His work demonstrates the various and innovative influences which permeate this period of his life. In 1686 he no doubt oversaw the decorations for the receptions accorded to the Embassy from Siam, whose exotic cortège was received with amazement by the citizens of France. The Ambassador brought with him sumptuous presents, others more practical, all of them intended to encourage trade between the two countries. Gold, so beloved of the Siamese, tortoiseshell, the brilliant silks for which they are still famous, carpets, lacquer and porcelain were all included and all contributed to the knowledge and inspiration of the French designers and the all-encompassing talent of M. Bérain. He was a designer who experimented endlessly, establishing an outstanding domination over his contemporaries. He developed a form of decoration identified as 'grotesque', displaying at once both fantasy and wit. The introduction to Europe of Chinese art and artefacts was reflected in his innumerable proposals for surface decoration and became identified as 'Chinoiserie'; he developed the diverting fashion for 'singerie', the depiction of monkeys in the elaborate dress of the day, disporting themselves in paintings and wall murals, even on ceilings. His 'grotesques' developed into what became the Regence style, and the later and better known fashion for rocaille or Rococo. And in 1692, astonishingly to the modern mind, the King instructed him to design the exteriors of the new ships being built to replace those lost in battle. His most famous marine commission was an elaborate design for a warship, *Le Roi Soleil*, which transformed a three-decker into the appearance of a massive piece of fine cabinet work, the grandeur of which must surely have made it an immediate challenge to the enemy had she ever encountered one. Many years later the artists of WWII were creating similar delusion!

As a student of Jean Bérain, Daniel Marot would no doubt have pursued his career in his native country had it not have been for the revocation of the Edict of Nantes, a revocation that condemned French Protestants at best to discrimination, at worst to exile. Marot chose the latter option, fled to Protestant Holland and was lucky to be recruited into the service of the Stadtholder, later William III of England. In this capacity he worked on a number of royal and Government buildings and carried out extensive work for the family of Orange at their hunting lodge, Het Loo, (the House in the Woods), another modest but charming retreat for a royal family. When William and Mary acceded to the English crown and moved their Court to England, Marot followed and continued to work for them, most particularly on the restoration and renewal of Hampton Court Palace. The designers of the 17th century were blessed with patrons, mainly royal, who were themselves lucky to be part of a new age of travel and discovery, an age which brought so many international opportunities which would, in due course, contribute to

INCHBALD

Lord Burlington
1664-1704

the development and success of the design profession. Interestingly, a number of these designers chose to publish their work for the benefit of others, thus creating a domination over the movement of fashion and taste. Design was turning into a recognisable and desirable occupation, albeit one which perhaps relied on opportunity. However the 17th century saw the beginnings of formalisation and the basis of formal training.

Louis XIV's policy of political centralization, his autocratic style of Government so well supported by his brilliant design team, would eventually smother the status of his own aristocracy, but in England there was a new impetus born of travel and art education and English aristocrats were at the heart of it.

The Architect Earl

England's burgeoning artistic development in the 16th century was crippled by the Civil War in spite of the strong legacy of James I. The emergence of a more European culture in London came in the wake of the 1660 monarchical restoration and a newly-European court, a movement heavily underwritten by the later accession of Dutch William and his Stuart wife. France, on the other hand, recovering from its own Civil War of the Fronde, was dominated by an imperious young Louis XIV, determined not only to establish his authority but to encourage and engage architects, painters, and designers to provide a background of splendour, a mirage that would disseminate his royal divinity both in France and abroad. In this he has something in common with James Stuart, a monarch not only fascinated by the arts but one who was anxious to deploy them as a tool of communication with which to impress and overwhelm his doubtful subjects. The Civil War of the Fronde in France resulted in autocracy and culminated in political disaster, whereas the Civil War in England created a democracy, outcomes which had much to do with the character of the peoples involved. By the end of the 17th century England had survived over half a century of civil and political turmoil. In 1694, the year in which Richard Boyle was born, Dutch William and Mary were joint monarchs in a country which had settled into peace and the pursuit of foreign interest and foreign conquests. Queen Anne, forever associated with small, red-brick manor houses, succeeded her sister and brother in law but still the Court of St James remained haunted by the claims of the very Stuart family from which both Queens had sprung. On her death in 1714 Anne's half-brother James landed in Scotland laying very reasonable claim to the ancient thrones of Scotland and England, a claim that was difficult to refute. Only when James had been driven by force out of the country did George, his cousin and Elector of Hanover, set sail from the Hague to claim the English throne through his grandmother's bloodline. In that same year, 1715, Richard Boyle's father died and the boy of eleven became the 3rd Earl Burlington, the owner of extensive land holdings in Yorkshire, Ireland and London, with all the potential that implied. This child, encumbered so young with heavy responsibility, was destined to be one of the leading figures of the design world. He developed into a man of great culture, influencing not only the development of the arts and architecture in 18th-century England, but the structuring of English taste. Initially his preferences were painting and music, and these talents were encouraged by a musical mother.

*William Kent
1685-1748*

Such preferences were broadened by the specific travel programmes identified as the Grand Tour, a form of privileged education which had become fashionable with the Restoration of the monarchy in 1660 and which remained as an integral part of a gentleman's educational experience throughout the 18th and part of the 19th century. Generated by the English Renaissance, the work and influence of Inigo Jones had promoted interest in both the classic architecture and the philosophy of Greece and Rome. Symmetry and balance, logic and moderation were all presented as a desired ideal and what better way to study these principles than to travel to the countries that had inspired them? Between 1714 and 1719, the young Burlington undertook three Grand Tours; during the last one he visited the Veneto and there developed a newly-found passion for architecture and in particular the architectural works of Palladio. In the course of his travels he met another Yorkshireman, William Kent, the modest protégé of generous county neighbours, who had spent time studying in Italy and working as a painter. The two shared their enthusiasm for the works of Palladio, and continued travelling together, finally visiting Paris on their way back to London where the peer installed Kent in his London mansion. Burlington House was and is, a vast mansion built round a square on the North side of Piccadilly. The house to which Kent was introduced was handsome but old-fashioned and Burlington was keen to restore and enhance both the building and the interiors. Initially he commissioned Colen Campbell, instructing Kent to design and oversee the interiors. Kent was primarily a painter but this commission presented an opportunity to move on to the world of interior and furniture design. In collaboration with Campbell, Kent worked on the first example of neo-Palladianism, a style which would proliferate around the English counties, frequently as a result of a newly-educated and appreciative upper class, benefiting from Mediterranean experiences.

Lord Burlington also owned a large property at Chiswick, with land running down to the River Thames. Here he himself essayed a small work of architecture, a garden house he called the Bagnio; he was sufficiently pleased with this achievement to include it in the background of a portrait painted of him around 1719, clearly an early

Chiswick House

demonstration of his new interest. His original intention regarding the Chiswick property was to modernise the old house in a working partnership with Kent, but after a destructive fire he decided to build the kind of classical villa which he had so admired on his visit to the Veneto. Relatively speaking, it was to be a small house, echoing the human scale of the Queen's House of some hundred years earlier, but nevertheless featuring rooms with impressive proportions and magnificent decorative embellishments. Here he intended to instal his increasing collections of paintings and furniture and in this small building, architecturally perfect and with magnificent interiors, he would entertain the artistic and political friends who were now an integral part of his life. Most collectors are keen to show off the fruits of their erudition and Burlington was no exception. Chiswick is no more than six miles to Hyde Park Corner, easily accessible by carriage to and from the London heartland and thus the villa eventually became a centre of intellectual and political exchange allied to the discussion and enjoyment of Lord Burlington's continuing acquisitions. The property was further enhanced by the creation of a landscape garden, incorporating fountains, follies and features of interest for those guests who chose to seek out these idyllic beauties. In contrast to the pure discipline of the villa's architecture, the style of the garden was relaxed and picturesque, setting a fashion which captured the imagination of other landowners anxious to impress their visitors with erudition and the challenge of the unexpected. For this pioneering work, a complete change from the formalities of French influence, Burlington's close friend Kent was responsible, adding a new facet to his achievements and establishing his reputation as the father of the English landscape garden. William Kent and his patron had together produced a centre of intellectual exchange against a conscious background of both elegance and splendour, a background which was in itself an attraction and the foundation of a fashion.

Chapter 12

Burlington's idyll demonstrated the attraction of the smaller house situated in the clean air outside the city, and his engaging personality and generous hospitality seem to have encouraged the further establishment of smaller houses in the area. At the time that the villa was being constructed, another house nearby was commissioned by Henrietta Howard, Countess of Suffolk. Her 1724 brief to architect Roger Morris conformed to the fashionable interest in Palladianism but was designed to specific requirements suitable to her lifestyle. She had for some years been the mistress of the Prince of Wales and Lady in Waiting to his wife, Caroline of Ansbach, a dual identity which indicated a degree of tolerance and wit on her part. Unsurprising that she should consider a retreat designed on her own terms for her pleasure and her retirement, a house with a riverside garden offering the convenience of water transport to London in this newly-fashionable area. Marble Hill is a less demanding form of Palladianism than Chiswick. Losing nothing in terms of elegance it nevertheless displays a softer, more welcoming style than the perfectionism of Lord Burlington's masterpiece. The interior plan is not without machismo, including as it did a Great Room with capriccios painted by Panini and a floor plan reflecting the very personal requirements of Lady Suffolk. It is an individual and comfortable house which can be described as a home. It provided her with an elegant and attractive background. Lady Suffolk and Lord Burlington, both of them familiar with the Court of St James, had two other neighbours who would provoke interest in their houses and gardens and further the intellectual reputation of Twickenham society.

The first to join this circle was Alexander Pope, a successful poet brought up in Twickenham, who purchased a riverside property with a curious handicap. The road in front of the house cut him off from his own garden. In order to access the garden safely and privately, Pope created an underground tunnel which he then transformed into a spectacular grotto, lined with shells and stalactites, semi-precious stones and shards of looking glass. Lit by candles, the walls presented a shifting excitement of sparkling surfaces, transforming his tunnel into a dramatic and theatrical grotto, a far cry in garden design from Kent's romantic landscape. Nevertheless fashionable visitors were amused and intrigued by the ingenious conversion of necessity into drama and Pope's grotto was the forerunner of a number of shell follies and grottos, a fashion that lasted beyond the end of the century. Later on the same local society was impressed by the building commissioned by Horace Walpole, writer, collector, art historian and politician, and the younger son of First Minister Sir Robert Walpole. Sir Robert had commissioned William Kent to build the magnificent Houghton Hall in full baroque grandeur to echo his outstanding political successes. By contrast his son Horace bought a small riverside cottage called Straw House, and proceeded over the years to build an astonishing folly, a 'little Gothic Castle' often referred to as Gothic Revival but perhaps more accurately termed Gothic Invention. Whatever the identification, Straw House now known more glamorously as Strawberry Hill, provided inspiration for the Gothic Revival movement which persisted well into the 19th century and coincided with the romanticism of 18th-and 19th-century literature. 'One must have taste to be sensible of the beauties of Greek architecture," Horace remarked with some degree of self-deprecation, "one only wants passions to feel Gothic" and so he proceeded to release his passions into the development of his fantastical project, a 'small' house that on completion boasted twenty-two rooms, filled to the brim with his library and his haphazard collections of artefacts, curiosities, paintings, coins and anything else that caught his attention. He was the ultimate individualist, inventing a new craze for chivalry and romance, backed by a talent for seeking out objects and details of interest with which to enhance his architecture and interiors. There was however, another facet to his interior skills. 'I did not mean' he wrote in his *Description of Strawberry Hill* 'to make my house so Gothic as to exclude convenience and modern refinements in luxury. The designs of the inside and outside are strictly ancient, but the decorations are modern'. He had 'a thousand plump chairs, couches and luxurious settees covered with linen of blue and white stripes adorned with festoons,' echoing a relatively new demand for comfort and simplicity, whatever the favoured style. In due course and in response to the publicity generated by his vision, he was prevailed upon to issue tickets for four visitors a day between the hours of 12 and 3, who were generally conducted round the house by his housekeeper. Society had become fascinated by Horace Walpole and he revelled in this interest, since he himself remained committed and intrigued by his own artistic achievement and connoisseurship. The interiors reflect a scholarly interest in all things Gothic but it is the design of applied decoration in the Gothic manner that is particularly impressive in its careful detail and accomplished application to the interiors of Strawberry Hill.

Walpole avers that his interest in Gothic was a rejection of the Italianate styles that had taken such a strong hold in England, in favour of a period in English history which he considered to be glorious, a time when the Christian Church exercised a mystic dominance over both layfolk and politicians. Church Architecture presented supreme grandeur and with it power and superiority; today this too would be classed as public relations, encompassing as it does the power of the senses to impress the subject. Whatever the name, it has for centuries been deployed as an agent of religion, its very success bestowing a plenitude of talents and funds. Ritual and magnificence reinforced the message of the Church as the supreme authority and thus encouraged the greatest talents of the Middle Ages into the service of Christ. The more powerful the Church became, so the more wonderful buildings, paintings and sculptures were raised in support of the gospel, and the intellectual subjugation of the crowd. The sheer scale of the cathedrals leaves the modern world astonished by the feats achieved by architects and artisans armed with ladders and wooden scaffolding. The shock of the Nôtre Dame fire, the anxiety that it could never be restored, is a significant reaction to the disaster and to the importance that France and the world still attaches to this edifice some 900 years after building was started.

*Robert Adam
1728-1792*

In decorative terms Walpole drew on medieval magnificence with a light hand. The tomb of Prince Arthur in Worcester cathedral provided inspiration for wallpaper; the structures of two other royal tombs created the chimney piece in his library; staircases and plasterwork all confirm an amazing level of erudition without descent to the banal. However, the most telling detail of progress lies in that phrase 'a thousand plump chairs'. These charming, if eccentric smaller houses were built essentially for privacy and relaxation but designers were increasingly aware of the demands of physical comfort needed to extend the enjoyment of a new leisure. Swagger was still important but it wasn't always the primary consideration. Originality and intrigue were the new challenges. Walpole's masterly adaptations of his chosen, if eccentric, classic style were taken up to some extent through the 18th century although the brilliance and balance of classical Greece and Rome were revived and the fashion furthered by Robert Adam, an architect soon to be famous for his adaptation of the style to the requirements of the 18th century

Urban Adaptation

The three Adam brothers were the sons of a Scottish architect, who trained in their father's studio. Robert, the most famous, went on a Grand Tour between 1754 and 1758, a period shortly after the discovery of the villa of Herculaneum in 1738 and the city of Pompeii in 1748. The spectacular revelations regarding architecture and art which resulted from these excavations reinforced interest in classicism and through Robert Adam gave rise to what is now known as the Adam Style, synonymous with the English style of the 18th century. He was an architect who designed every detail of his interiors using his preferred motifs to produce a unification of interior design more generally associated with mid- and late- 18th century- France than England. Furniture, light fittings, door furniture all received his direct attention; even carpets were woven to match exactly the intricate plaster work and decorative paintings on the ceilings, so that the overall look was one of total co-ordination. It was a novel concept and its success was measured by the volume of work which he achieved during a relatively short life, and by the influence that work has exerted on the history of public and private buildings in England. The buildings he created in this much lighter classic style established him as a dominant figure during a century of political progress and architectural elegance, confirming his body of work as typically English, in spite of the fact that it was wholly inspired by antiquity. His furniture was unusual because he often painted it, and gilded the highlights, features that the French initiated. Painted furniture did not really recur significantly until Syrie Maugham used the same decorative form, sometimes to the outrage of more conventional critics. One of Adam's major urban projects was the purchase of the remains of the Bishop of Durham's London palace, on land which then fronted on the riverside between Somerset House and Whitehall. On this site he and his brothers built a terrace of twenty-four classically designed houses, with vaulted terraces and wharves providing connection with the river. Although it was not a financial success, the Adelphi, as it was called, housed the association of art manufacturers, now known as the Royal Society of the Arts, which remains there to this day. Perhaps it was on this account that the development attracted a number of artists, authors and actors as tenants.

This concept of terrace housing, with which we are now so familiar, was developed in London after the Great Fire of 1666. A Huguenot builder, Nicholas Barbon, turned developer in the face of necessity, and started rebuilding the city in rows of similar dwellings. This basic design innovation effectively saved both time and money, since the houses shared party walls, and the materials were common to the whole enterprise.

In fact the terrace was a design form of urban development which had already been anticipated in Paris with the Place Royale, now the Place des Vosges. This major enterprise was commissioned by Henri IV and was intended specifically as urban housing for the aristocracy of the city. Henri went so far as to include a house for the Queen, though she hardly used it. The terraces formed a square, with a road running through the middle and extensive gardens, approached by magnificent gateways which emphasised the private grandeur of privilege. So although the terrace house is associated with English cities, the concept originated with a French designer and a French royal client. The Place Royale predated the work of John Wood in Bath by over a century, but when Wood, architect, builder and speculator, started on his ambitious idea of a revivified and beautiful city he started a trend, both elegant and practical, which swept through English cities for the next two centuries. First devised for fashionable Bath, the principle of terraced housing was adopted by developers and city councils for the entire range of urban dwelling. The consistency of the architecture indicated a consistency of interior planning, with domestic offices at basement level serving dining and morning room at ground level, and drawing rooms on the first floor offering better light and a distance from the street that alleviated both the noise and the smells of horse-drawn traffic. Lower-class houses rarely had basements and perhaps only one upper floor.

The continuing development of such urban formats of terraces, squares and avenues, built largely for the professional classes, decreed patterns of lifestyle that would dominate society until the dawn of the 20th century and the cataclysm of the First World War. However, the social mores of this aspirational class required more than elegant elevations; attention was drawn to the requirements of a much larger market of people who were educated, efficient and able to afford the sophisticated niceties of design and decoration previously the preserve of the privileged classes. Cabinetmakers were becoming increasingly more organised and one or two made serious names for themselves and their products. Success in cabinetmaking had a great deal to do with patronage but the new trend to disseminate knowledge through printing was increasingly important and in due course the English cabinetmakers started to publish their work with considerable success.

The Designer/Cabinetmaker

Thomas Chippendale's book, *Gentleman's and Cabinetmaker's Directory*, published in 1754, went into three editions and included every detail of interior furnishing down to Chinese 'sophas' and even clock cases. So Thomas the cabinetmaker was perhaps more accurately described as an interior designer, coping, as he did, with every detail of the space, handling his commitment to interior work in much the same way as architect Robert Adam. The title of his book is interesting; he is attracting not only the attention of his peers but of his clients, identifying them as Gentlemen and no doubt hoping to attract their business. Public relations, still unidentified as a career, is nevertheless brought into play in the marketing ploys of these great artisan/ artists.

Chippendale's contemporary, George Hepplewhite (1727–88), established a more delicate house style, in line with the light-hearted classicism of Robert Adam. When the designer died his resourceful widow, recognising the marketing benefits, collected his designs together and published them as *The Cabinet makers and Upholsterers Guide*. In due course Thomas Sheraton (1751–1806) followed this success with his own *Cabinetmakers and Upholsterers Drawing Book* in 1791. This work was actually subscribed by no less than 600 cabinetmakers and joiners, a very clear indication that there was not only a market for the information, but a very real demand for it, particularly from those skilled craftsmen who either lacked design ability or worked too far from the metropolis to keep up with fashion.

Chippendale, Hepplewhite and Sheraton are all noted as the greatest of the English cabinetmakers, but their books embrace much more than furniture design. The contents include the skills of the upholsterer and the question of fashion and taste. The use of the phrase 'Household Furniture' rather than interior decoration, indicates an emphasis on everyday requirements which include both comfort and practicality. Later, in 1805, Sheraton went further and produced an encyclopaedia, *The Cabinetmaker, Upholsterer and General Artists Encyclopaedia*. The notion of formalised design education was crystallising in the public mind and the phrase 'interior design' was coming into use. Financially comfortable people in the middle classes were increasingly interested in the fashions of the day and the improvements that could be made to their life style and their status in the community. Elegant interiors were one way of demonstrating social success; ownership of a carriage and horses gave birth to the phrase 'carriage folk' used throughout the 19th century to indicate social arrival, a period when a private carriage had the same importance as a new 21st-century sports-car. The 18th century produced a potent mix of privileged amateurs and professional talent which generated a fascination with the concept of interior design amongst a much wider public than ever before. The general characteristics of this newly-ambitious class included better education, greater financial security and a much wider knowledge of other cultures, either through formal education, travel or a rapidly expanding media. Painters and engravers still played an important role in the dissemination of both knowledge and awareness and by the middle of the 19th-century magazines were informing on every kind of fashion and skill. In 1839 the Art Union Magazine featured contemporary artists, sculptors and engravers with information that was both interesting and relevant to readers concerned with building or improving their houses, as well as those sufficiently informed to wish to start collections. Such aspirations arose from a desire to impress others and to enhance interiors with something beyond the obvious and the practical. The established order of the aristocracy was filtering down to the professional classes and social aspiration would take design to new levels. Given the industrial and technical developments of the succeeding two centuries the pre-eminence of this elite section of society would be challenged by the power of money and its spectacular possibilities.

New Money

The beginning of the 18th century saw a further immense source of wealth flowing from the sugar plantations of the West Indies.

By the end of the 17th century the East India Company, newly established by force of arms and astute business dealings, had created fortunes that had as great an impact on society as did the much later discovery of oil. When Clive returned from India his capital appeared to be so immeasurable that he was called before Parliament to answer for his political actions and his financial integrity. Describing the treasure house of gold and jewels that had been made available to him, he remarked angrily that he 'stood astonished at my own moderation'.

Whether or not that was true, he brought back with him the incomparable Arcot diamonds which he presented to Queen Charlotte, commissioned Capability Brown to build a mansion on the Claremont estate, and landscape the surrounding gardens, and built a further smaller mansion in Shropshire. His colleague in India, Warren Hastings, was also arraigned before Parliament to answer for his conduct, an action also prompted by the wealth he brought home. Hastings purchased Daylesford, a mansion in Gloucestershire, and instructed architect Samuel Pepys Cockerell to redesign and decorate it with reference to his successful career in the Company. Furniture was created using ivory and silver brought from India, together with embroidered materials for curtains and upholstery. When his stepson died in the mid-19th century the house was sold and the contents auctioned, the catalogue providing interesting details of the interior artefacts. In 1946 the house had deteriorated under the tenancy of the US army, and was purchased by Lord Rothermere. He instructed both architect Philip Jebb and decorator John Fowler to restore the building and the interiors, and Fowler used the old detailed sale catalogues in his efforts to restore it as faithfully as possible.

Claremont, 18th-century Paladian mansion in Surrey by Vanburgh.

In 1805 Cockerell was also commissioned by his younger brother Charles to build him a mansion in the Neo-Mughal style, the copper onion dome and red sandstone elevations something of a surprise in the verdant Cotswold countryside. This sensational house, Sezincote, financed by Sir Charles Cockerell's Indian service with the Company, stands today in its unlikely setting, an icon of British supremacy on the sub-continent. In spite of his confident handling of the Mughal style the architect never went to India, drawing on the extensive publications of coloured aquatints produced by Thomas Daniell and his nephew William. India was all the rage and the Daniells' *Oriental Scenery*, published between 1795 and 1808, proved to be an unqualified success with a fascinated public. The media had become a major source of information and education. The Company's successes continued but the flow of wealth from overseas was now increased by sugar revenues. The magnitude of these inevitably affected politics and policies through the sheer power of finance, creating ex-patriot millionaires who still perceived themselves as British and therefore concerned with the affairs of Britain. The international income of Britain, allied to the undaunted entrepreneurial powers of those who travelled abroad in search of wealth and adventure, were the foundations of the 19th century acceleration to empire.

Sezincote House, Gloucestershire.

One of the largest and richest estates in Jamaica was owned by Peter Beckford, who had risen to be Governor of the island. Beckford sent his son William to England to be educated at Westminster and Balliol and thereafter to take a position in the City at the head of the West Indian merchants, known colloquially as the Sugar Kings. It suited the ambitions and inclinations of the Governor's son to enter City politics. He was appointed an Alderman of the City of London and Lord Mayor, eventually representing the City in Parliament. This daunting figure, known always as Alderman Beckford, died when his son, also William Beckford, was ten years old, already showing signs of artistry and self importance rather than any inclination to follow in the merchant footsteps of his successful family. William's name would become inextricably linked with extravagance, architectural and decorative drama, and unhappily, social scandal.

On the death of his father in 1770 the child is said to have inherited the equivalent of £90 million, which allowed him liberty to do as he chose throughout a self-indulgent life. The extent of the Beckford income from the Jamaican estates was notorious and it is worth noting that income tax was not introduced by Pitt the Younger until 1798. It is reported that when this tax was imposed, sugar baron Porter of Paradise in Barbados received a letter from the Treasury explaining that he had paid more than his due – the tax was liable on income, not on capital! Porter's income was so great that the figure he submitted was assumed to be his capital position. For the young William Beckford then, nothing was impossible.

The house where he was born and raised, Fonthill House, built in the Palladian fashion, embraced and popularised by Lord Burlington, was so luxurious that it was nicknamed Fonthill Splendens, giving the child an early sense of status. As the only legitimate son he was spoilt, tutored at home rather than enduring the rigours of Eton or Westminster, and eventually embarked on an extensive programme of Grand Tours through Europe. He was a diligent pupil and totally entranced by architecture, design and decoration. The original Fonthill is described by a contemporary as 'superbly brilliant and dazzling'. Porphyry busts, walls hung with silk and velvet, picture gallery, tapestry room, state bedchamber, were all redolent not just of new money but the self-aggrandisement that had been so lavishly displayed at Vaux le Vicomte. It was clearly important to the Alderman that the Beckford fortunes should be visibly confirmed by expenditure as well as the manner of his family lifestyle. So the young Beckford, well-educated, intelligent and in no way short of funds ,was in a position to indulge any or all of his creative fantasies. There were many, but perhaps the most outstanding undertaking was the creation of Fonthill Abbey, a startling building devised by Beckford and architect James Wyatt on a spectacular scale in the High Gothic style. It was certainly the reason that William

Beckford's name is still remembered in the design world, partly for the concept, partly for the extraordinary extravagance of the architecture and the interiors, and not least for the disaster attendant upon careless construction that resulted in the partial collapse of the building soon after it was completed.

Beckford's Abbey did not in any way conform to the idea that grandeur might be modified. What started as a romantic garden pavilion in the form of a Gothic ruin developed into a monumental demonstration of elegant vulgarity and snobbery. Benjamin West, the American President of the Royal Academy, was enraptured, stating that he was lost in admiration at "so vast a combination of all that is refined in Painting, Sculpture and Architecture," but designer Thomas Hope remarked that "the new building at Fonthill subjected every one of its details to disadvantageous comparisons with the Cathedral at Salisbury". Hope's sharp comment was all too pertinent. Whilst self-indulgent Beckford was probably the client from hell, James Wyatt has a great deal to answer for in the casual implementation of William's dream. Wyatt, now the darling of architectural patronage, was working on many other projects which included Wilton for Lord Pembroke, Doddington Park for the Codringtons (also sugar barons) and Windsor for the monarch, any one of which might be said to have been major enterprises. Further, the architect was known to be brilliant but unpredictable in terms of his contacts with his clients and his builders and Beckford himself spent a great deal of time travelling abroad during the course of construction. This client/designer relationship was thus unhappy from the start of the project, and it says a great deal for Wyatt's reputation that Beckford continued to employ him though there was a clear threat of dismissal. When Beckford was not in Europe, he spent his time at Fonthill urging the workforce to hurry, and forcing them to work through the night by the light of bonfires. Both client and architect allowed shortcuts, and Wyatt deployed a new form of concrete, compo cement, that was insufficiently tested and finally proved to be unstable. In addition to this chaotic approach, the foundations of a tower, initially built of wood, were not strengthened when the tower was rebuilt with the much heavier compo cement, leading to its eventual collapse. The client's reaction to this was unusual: "We shall rise again" he wrote to Garter King of Arms, "provided the sublime Wyatt will graciously deign to bestow a little more commonplace Attention on what I supposed his favourite structure". As far as his client was concerned, Wyatt was clearly still in business.

Beckford's absences during building were largely due to a sojourn in Paris where, in the period after the execution of Louis XVI in 1792, the aristocracy of France was imploding and the artefacts of that supremacy were coming on the market in a flood of fear and low prices. William's purchases included the bureau of King Stanislaus Leczinski of Poland, which found its way into his Grand Drawing Room, Gibbons' library, and what was left of Sir William Hamilton's Greek vase collection. Meanwhile, the fact that the income from his sugar estates was faltering did not deter him from the spending habits of a lifetime. However, in a gesture of economy he decided to demolish his father's Fonthill Splendens claiming that he could deploy the fabric to the new Abbey. So the splendours of Palladianism gave way spectacularly to the Gothic echoes of Walpole's Strawberry Hill.

The Abbey took years to complete, bedevilled by dreadful project management and poor quality materials. When it came to the interiors, silks,and velvets, gilding and carving were all lavishly bestowed on an imperial scale. Reception rooms were hung with an impressive collection of old masters and embellished with gilded and jewelled objects of every description, and this in spite of Beckford's diminishing Jamaican revenues. Comfort posed a problem; the reception rooms were not only enormous, they were also immensely high so that the building was difficult to heat. It is said that sixty fireplaces were kept alight through every season but the warmest, and they were filled with scented coal, surely the forerunner of the scented candles so popular today. Unhappily it is difficult to imagine William cuddling into Walpole's 'plump sofas' in a room whose ceiling rose to 128 feet above him. Eventually he found himself living alone in this "poetic and almost uninhabitable place" of which he had dreamed for so long. Finally he sold the estate to an arms merchant and went off to live out his years in Bath, where he built another tower. The Abbey was a figment of his imagination brought to reality by an over-abundance of money. It was a stage set, demonstrating financial success and the social aspirations that prompted him to include in his stained glass windows the armorials of those knights who signed Magna Carta, and then to claim descent from all of them! It could also be described as a master-class in public relations. In spite of Beckford's undoubted erudition and discriminating taste, his childlike pretensions provoked more astonishment than admiration, and when the playwright left for Bath, the theatre fell dark. Nevertheless it could be said that his social aspirations were satisfied when his only daughter became the Duchess of Hamilton.

Born in the mid-18th century, William Beckford died in 1844, seven years after the accession of Queen Victoria, some six years before the Great Exhibition ushered in the confirmation of England as probably the greatest industrial nation of Europe at the time.

Banker Hope and the Middle class

New money, generated by fabulous sugar fortunes, and the wealth brought to England by the pioneers of the East India company, would now be augmented by the industry of the manufacturing entrepreneurs who in their turn required a tangible affirmation of success and superiority. And there was an increasing number of skilled artisans and designers, anxious to oblige, who would start laying down the foundations of a profession that was still virtually nameless. By the end of the 18th century the communication of news and information disseminated to the general public was gathering pace. In the 17th century news had taken the form of pamphlets but in 1702 Edward Lloyd, the founder of Lloyds Insurance agents, established *Lloyds News* and in 1709 Richard Steele established the *Tatler*, later joining Joseph Addison to start the *Spectator*. *The News* was concerned with business and shipping news, but both *Tatler* and *Spectator* also featured current affairs at a more social level. *The Gentlemans Magazine* was inaugurated in 1731 and 'covered any subject which might interest the educated public'. The range included business and finance, literature and politics but did not feature design or decoration. Clearly the 'general public' did not include women! The cabinetmakers who went into print were enthused by the public interest in the distribution of fashionable news and their assumption was clearly correct and successful. Their publications were professional in their illustrations and the detailing of their designs, and were of general interest in the recording of current style. None of them, however, set out to display and explain the methodology of creating furniture and fashion for a given space until the advent of Thomas Hope.

Illustration from Thomas Hope's Household Furniture and Interior Decoration.

It was Hope who, in the title of his book about interior design, refers to *Household Furniture and Interior Decoration*. This phrase moves the subject matter into a much wider domain than the design and creation of furniture and decorative finishes by offering the reader information which is directly relevant to everyday living requirements. It takes the point further by including the 'how' and 'why' under a newly-minted identity.

The Hopes were a Scottish family who established themselves in Amsterdam, trading there throughout the 18th century as insurance brokers, merchants and most importantly bankers. They operated at political level, employed by the Rotterdam authorities to oversee the transport of the immigrant English Quaker community from Holland to Pennsylvania, a contract which continued through the century; they also dealt in the less lucrative slave trade. In addition, the Seven Years War (1756–63) offered great opportunity for business speculation, an opportunity which Hope and Company were quick to exploit.

The family took on a partner, Pierre Cesar Labouchère and by the time he married the daughter of English banker Sir Francis Baring in 1796, the Hope family had moved to England and the two banks were forming close ties.

The motivation for this move was the threat of Napoleon's occupation of Holland, a threat which would last until the Emperor's defeat in 1815; and the temporary result for the Hope family was the abandonment of their Dutch property. However the strong influence of the bank in Holland and the felicitous link between Hope & Co. and Baring & Co. led to the lucrative part they played in the Louisiana Purchase in 1803, a matter of some 828 square miles of America sold by Napoleon to Thomas Jefferson for $15 million. The reason for the sale was the requirement for money to facilitate the invasion of England. In the event both the imperial vision and the imperial finances were failing and Napoleon was defeated at Waterloo. Given the impressive service charges relevant to the Louisiana Purchase, the Hope interests in Holland and England were munificently restored.

The 18th century had thus been a period of spectacular growth at the bank so that when Thomas started on his lengthy Grand Tour of the Mediterranean seaboard he travelled not only in great luxury, but as the member of a family that had long patronised and invested in art and artists with every indication of educated appreciation. His initial aim was to study and record all that he had seen and experienced in the so different cultures of the Mediterranean, and he illustrated his travels extensively with his own considerable drawing skills. In 1795 he returned to London where he addressed the problem of redesigning a Robert Adam house in Duchess Street, at the same time embarking on a comprehensive programme of interior decoration and furniture design for all of which he was personally responsible. Hope was not educated as either an architect or an interior designer; nor did he have the practical studio/workshop experience that would have qualified him for either of these professions. It is, however, very difficult to identify him as an amateur. Where Burlington, working closely for many years with Kent, could justify his sobriquet as the Architect Earl, it is less easy to class others in the same way. Lady Suffolk was clearly a client, albeit one of taste, and Walpole, writer, collector, antiquarian, worked closely with architect John Chute and writer/designer Richard Bentley, going so far as to refer to this triumvirate as the 'Committee'. It was a droll, if successful partnership, identifying Walpole as both educated client and inspirational designer. Hope however, erudite, exceptionally talented and blessed with apparently limitless wealth, relied on his own artistic skills to convey his proposed designs and decoration.

By the time Thomas was born, the family were considered to be very much part of Amsterdam high society, but to Thomas's consternation he did not receive the respect or status to which he was accustomed when he moved to London. This social challenge had not been faced by his distinguished predecessors in the design world and it seems that the creation of the Duchess Street house was an attempt to showcase his undoubted talent and knowledge, his boundless resources in part making up for a lack of aristocratic blood. Society was slow to respond but eventually he arranged for visitors to come and view his work in the same controlled way that Walpole had opened Strawberry Hill so many years earlier. There is an element of patronisation here, but also a genuine desire to educate and influence. Certainly there was a great deal to see, and Hope's system of displaying a series of collections in rooms that echoed their theme was interesting and innovative. An Indian room included paintings of India by Thomas Daniells, the Flaxman room featured a fine marble by the sculptor himself and the Vase room, displaying the Hamilton vases, was suitably embellished with furniture and decorations inspired by the classical details of ancient Greece. This thematic approach would be echoed more than a century later by William Pahlman mounting his exhibitions in the furnishing department of New York's Lord and Taylor.

Marriage to Louisa de la Poer Beresford, the pretty daughter of the Bishop of Tuam, improved Hope's social status and he purchased a small country estate, the Deepdene, where he built an Italianate villa of great charm, set in a garden laid out in the still-fashionable picturesque style. The design of the house was derivative, but it inspired much of early Victorian architecture; Osborne House, on the Isle of Wight resonates in the overall design but interestingly the interiors of the Deepdene, faithfully recorded by Hope in full colour, demonstrate a distinct emphasis on comfort as well as introducing a fashionable domesticity which looks a great deal more inviting than the ecclesiastical splendours of Beckford's folly. Like David Hicks he favoured brilliant colours and like Beckford he chose exotic materials. The Deepdene was not an agricultural estate in the manner of the landed classes, it was more a family refuge from all the publicity engendered by Duchess Street and his book. Thomas Hope, at once brilliant and flamboyant, did not quite fit into the image of the English gentleman. He was perhaps too clever and, more importantly, perceived as foreign. But with an elegant wife and the Deepdene he created his own identity, and his interiors, so beautifully recorded, have ensured his place in the hierarchy of design.

Strawberry Hill and Fonthill were both the subject of numerous drawings and engravings by a variety of artists, but Hope supervised his own records. After an initial and unenthusiastic reception by the cognoscenti of the art world, it was recognised that the Duchess Street house and its furnishings were indeed of considerable significance, as well as appealing to those more interested in the very latest fashions. Copies of the furniture started to circulate and it was for this reason that Hope published his book, *Household Furniture and Interior Decoration*, preparing the drawings himself for the engraver George Dawe, to ensure that copyists would get every detail right. The publication was a curious mixture of pride and pomposity, ensuring that his beloved designs preserved their identity and he, the designer, was not credited with inferior products. Reprinted in 1971, the book still holds a fascination for the student of interior design and decoration.

The Amateurs

Sometime around the middle of the 18th century Mrs Montagu, highly intelligent and more than comfortably rich, declared herself to be 'sick of Grecian elegance and Gothick grandeur', turning instead to the 'gaudy gout of the Chinese'. She was an early aficionado of Orientalism but given her interest in decoration and building it is unsurprising. Her subsequent forays into the subject were startling.

Writing round to her friends she invoked their help in gathering feathers for a scheme she devised for her new house in Portman Square. The project was no less than ten years in the making and she herself designed and oversaw a series of hangings, the feathers sorted and sewn in careful patterns. It would appear to have been a daunting project, particularly for a woman with no training, but the lifestyle of the day allowed for painstaking effort and women of every level were competent with a needle. The scheme provoked a great deal of comment, the most famous from the poet William Cowper: "The birds put off their every hue To dress a room for Montagu". Mrs Montagu, christened by Dr Johnson the 'Queen of the Blues', was the first of the Blue Stockings. In Portman Square she organised the Society of the Bluestockings, increased the size of her new garden by an acre and employed Wyatt and Capability Brown to romanticise her country house, Sandleford. She had no training, but her intellect, her capacity for management and her wealth would have made her a formidable competitor in the world of 21st century design and decoration.

In 1823 Lord Blessington travelled with his beautiful wife and the equally beautiful Alfred, Count d'Orsay, to Naples where he rented a virtually unfurnished palazzo on the high ground above a city which was humming with French fashions and French glamour. Empress Josephine, brought up in the heat of Martinique, established a fashion for light draperies and curtains to cool rather than shield. In this respect her influence on the contemporary style of France and the work of her architects, Percier and Fontaine, was evident not only in Paris but in Naples, where General Murat and his Bonaparte wife Caroline now ruled as monarchs newly-established by the Emperor Napoleon. The Blessingtons spent several years in the Belvedere, overlooking the bay of Naples, entertaining an almost permanent houseparty of British visitors and expatriates. There was no kitchen in the Belvedere because the Neapolitans preferred what we now call takeaways. Food was brought in to order from local kitchens, so Lady Blessington's housekeeping responsibilities were reduced to indicating how many people would sit down to lunch or dinner. This prolonged holiday was turned into a form of Grand Tour; lunch was frequently a picnic in some ancient site where the company could exclaim over the marvels of another age and the ubiquitous Count D'Orsay, always in attendance, could sit with his pencil and sketchpad recording the scenery.

Charles Matthews, a young architect later to work with Pugin, was another long-term guest and not unnaturally he too was keen to record what he saw. Both were intrigued and delighted to be introduced to topographer, Sir William Gell, known to the party as 'Rapid Gell" on account of his newly-invented optical device, a *camera lucida*, which facilitated much faster and more efficiently recorded images.

The Belvedere boasted a spacious reception room containing individual tables or desks where members of the party could write or draw as they wished when the weather precluded sightseeing. Lord Blessington himself had a more private area with a desk large enough to accommodate plans for the mansion he was building in Mountjoy Forest in Northern Ireland. He too was a frustrated client of James Wyatt whose casual attitude was impossible to harness from so far away. Accordingly he made daunting journeys home across the Alps to try and progress the building, but the combination of absence and a determination much inferior to William Beckford's, left only the foundations and basement kitchens established before his funds ran out and he gave up. However, he addressed the matter of the gardens and forest himself, augmenting the plans of his father Lord Mountjoy, who had planted 80,000 trees on the 36,000-acre estate.

On one occasion, despairing of Wyatt, he invited Matthews to Ireland to look at the site and brought him back to Naples with a view to working with him on the designs for Mountjoy. Arriving at a hostel in North Italy on their way, they were informed that there was a shortage of post horses and they had to wait nearly a week before they could travel on. Confined by weather to the inn, Blessington proposed that they paint the sitting room to cheer it up and this they did together, covering the walls with fanciful murals. The reaction of the innkeeper is not recorded but the 20th-century invention of television may be responsible for much that is lost in artistic achievement.

The progress of the Blessingtons continued through Florence and Rome, and gives an insight into the interests and accomplishments of this and many other house parties at home or abroad, interests which were in no way unusual in that period before the advent of the camera and its domination. Their grand tour turned into something resembling a modern cruise, made up of travel, sightseeing, theatre and fun. Finally they settled in Paris, where Lord Blessington designed his wife's rooms. 'Lord B,' she wrote in her diary, 'has all the merits of taste, and the upholsterer that of the rapidity and excellence of execution'.

'Upholders,' now identified as upholsterers, were thus undertaking the responsibilities of today's interior designer/ decorators without necessarily supplying the designs.

Interior craftsmen

The development of firms serving new money co-incided with the financial and industrial success that international money streams brought to England. The story of the Crace family, established by 1780 as John Crace and Company, is of particular interest, not least because they were one of the earliest recorded interior decorators. Their artistic origin lay in coachbuilding and this of course involved painted finishes, painted panels, gilding and upholstery. The detailing in carriage or coach was significant. Windows were fitted with blinds and curtains, seating made up in silks, velvets or fine leathers all suitably trimmed with passementerie, with fixtures carved from ivory and precious woods. Door handles were often made of silver, incorporating initials or coats of arms, whilst travelling coaches included space for books with wells in the floor to accommodate travelling essentials, not least a chamber pot. Further, due to the luxurious nature of the finishes, the general make-up of the vehicles required careful mainternance, all of this closely related to the decoration and preservation of luxury interiors. Whilst we were at Lutwyche a friend and I discovered a small and very elegant carriage in one of the stables, in nearly perfect condition. The interior was carried out in violet: violet pleated taffeta, fine violet leather upholstery, ivory tags on the violet blinds and silver carriage handles, all the wondrous products of skilled hands taken for granted by a more elegant age. I sometimes sat there, mesmerized by the display of quality, and wishing that I could be part of that world.

John and Frederick Crace's establishment could claim George III as a regular client and they would go on to do extensive work for the King's son, the Prince Regent. John worked constantly with architect Henry Holland and in the course of a commission for the Duke of Bedford the fourteen-year-old Frederick joined his father at Woburn to learn painting and gilding. In 1794 he returned to London to work at Carlton House in order to learn graining and marbling, finally addressing not just one trade but as many as his father felt appropriate. By 1800 both Craces were involved in the creation of the splendours of the Carlton House interiors.

Architect Henry Holland was instructed by the Prince Regent effectively to reconstruct the old house with an emphasis on French neo-classicism, a commission that began in 1783 and lasted during the years when Europe was shaken by the revolutionary events in France and the advent of the Bonaparte regime.

Chapter 12

After the execution in 1793 of both Louis XVI and his Queen, Marie Antoinette, the contents of the great palace at Versailles were put up for auction in 17,000 lots over a period of two years. Concurrently the fine houses of the nobility were looted and the libraries and works of art likewise sold off to rich foreigners like Beckford. One such collector proved to be the Prince of Wales.

The Prince was an admirer of the understated classical elegance which had evolved from the heavier styles of the 17th century and, since it developed during the reign of Louis XVI, had become identified with that monarch. In order to pursue this interest he invited marchand mercier Dominique Daguerre, interior decorator to Marie Antoinette, to London to supervise the group of French craftsmen working on Carlton House interiors in the Louis XVI style, as well as overseeing the purchase of new pieces commissioned from famous French ebenistes including Weisweiller. At the same time he demonstrated an interest in Gothick design. When Horace Walpole visited the house in 1785 he must surely have been amused to see the magnificent Gothic dining room installed on the lower floor, echoing his own inspirational work at Strawberry Hill. He recorded his opinion, declaring that the house was a model of 'taste and propriety'. The Prince was a discriminating client and since Carlton House was the official background for the Court of the Prince of Wales, later to be Regent, he was anxious to create an atmosphere of royal authority. He extended his influence to the garden, instructing William Townsend Aiton, later director of Kew Gardens, and assistant Humphry Repton, to redesign the gardens which had originally been laid out by William Kent in 1732 for Frederick, Prince of Wales.

John and Frederick Crace's trade card.

Repton's family had sent him to Holland to be educated and learn Dutch in the hope that he would become a merchant, but although he benefited from his international experience, this ambition did not mature and aged 36 he had achieved little or no success. However, encouraged by an old friend, founder of the Linnean Society, Sir James Edward Smith, he had studied botany and gardening and so it was that he found himself working with Aiton on the gardens of the Prince. This rather unlikely development intrigued him with its potential and in 1788 he sent out what he described as a circular but which would now be called a brochure, explaining to various pre-eminent members of society including the Duke of Portland, that he was embarking on a profession of landscape gardening, (a term he coined himself) and offering his services. Unlike his predecessor Capability Brown, he did not undertake contracting services, contenting himself with providing the designs in an engaging form which would continue to influence the designers of both interiors and gardens that came after him.

He painted watercolours of both Before and After schemes,

demonstrating the impact his talents would have on the landscape should his designs be adopted. These paintings were then bound as a book, always in red leather, for presentation to the client so that his proposals could be implemented by estate contractors and staff. It was a masterly development in the process of design presentation, including as it did an immediate visual appeal to the client, the establishment of a corporate house style conveyed by the identically-bound Red Books, and the publicity to be gained by the presence of his elegant works of art in the libraries and drawing rooms of some of England finest mansions. This novel system meant that the client was charged a design fee for the book, rather than the ongoing costs of the design implementation; it made less money for the designer but Repton had no grounding in the realities of garden design. He was an accomplished visualist nevertheless, as well as being a master of watercolour, and these talents were the basis of a successful career.

The palatial history of Carlton House was short. Buckingham House, presented to Queen Charlotte in 1775 and known then as the Queen's House, was available to the Prince on his mother's death in 1818 and no doubt represented something like home. Fourteen of her fifteen children had been born there and it was perhaps the memory of childhood content that prompted George to start renovating it as something of a private house. In 1826 he decided to transform it into a Palace with the intention that it would be the main residence of the monarch. This work was continued by William, his brother and successor but finance was difficult and building dragged on over some ten years, until the first Royal occupant to move into the Palace was George's niece, Queen Victoria. It seems the work was badly done, or badly designed, and it proved to be a most uncomfortable residence until the Queen's marriage to the competent and talented Prince Albert brought efficiency, order and comfort (including warmth) to the new residence.

The Development of a Design Firm

In 1787 Prince George had rented a house in the tiny Sussex village of Brighthelmstone, close to the sea and sixty miles not only from London but also from royal responsibility and unpaid bills. This retreat allowed him greater freedom to appear in public with his morganatic wife, the Catholic Mrs Fitzherbert. The marriage was officially denied but nevertheless the political cognoscenti knew of it and in the years before the Catholic Emancipation Act they feared possible repercussions. Socially she was treated by his friends with the respect and status due to the wife of the Prince but it was not an easy situation and the privacy of a small Sussex village must have appeared particularly inviting. Soon the Prince commissioned Holland to build him an elegant house, close to the sea, where he could entertain his court uninhibited either by an

Chapter 12

Brighton Pavilion

exasperated father or by a Parliament appalled by his excessive spending. This degree of freedom from supervision or unfortunate publicity inevitably slid into a period of wild parties, stories of raffish friends and more extravagance. However, there were still sixty miles of carriage ride between the Prince and authority and he determined to build onto and improve the house that he had initially called the Royal Pavilion. Even the name seems light-hearted, confirming its identity as a house for entertainment and amusement, palatial indeed but in no way designed for the stilted formalities of court rules. In 1811 the Prince became the Regent with the status and responsibilities of a ruler. Ignoring financial advice he commissioned John Nash to extend the Pavilion, adopting a curious style between India and China, so that in due course the grey seas of the English Channel provided a back drop to a building as exotic and fanciful as had ever been seen in Sussex. Onion domes were startling enough but the interiors, with a mix of exotic styles in both interiors and furniture, were something quite new and here was a serious client for the Craces, father and son.

Designers like Crace needed a full studio of talented and hardworking specialists; these were the apprentices, learning to perfect their skills under the tuition of the master. Their studies, both practical and inspirational, included every detail of furniture and furnishing, but the successful middle class required status as well as perfectionism and status was associated with the aristocracy and their achievements. Clients demanded the symbols of social superiority just as much as they wished to demonstrate success with obvious expenditure; and as always, the market created the suppliers. In a period when history appeared to

Frederick Crace and Son's trade card.

be increasingly romantic, draughtsmen learnt everything concerned with the development of style and past fashions. By the middle of the 19th century decorating firms could offer their clients brochures which illustrated the variety of styles that had been established through the 17th and 18th centuries, from the flamboyance of the Tudors to the sophisticated interiors of the Age of Enlightenment.

Most of these firms started under the auspices of a talented specialist. In 1785 the trade card of John Crace pronounced him to be a Painter and Gilder and his son Frederick confirmed this, describing his father as 'a house and decorative painter – considered very eminent in his profession'. The development of their business interests and the demands of their work on the Pavilion had involved both father and son in the supply of materials, carpets and wallpaper; the wider requirements stretching to furniture, beds and upholstery. Gradually the scope of their services and products expanded; in 1802–4 they billed the Prince £179 for "attending the Prince at Brighton and arranging the furniture, china etc ….." which exercise involved them spending over three hundred days with their client during this time. Effectively John's son Frederick and his grandson John Gregory were by now providing the services of the modern interior designer/decorator as we understand the description, but they would still have been identified in general terms as Upholders, or upholsterers. In the early years of the century they set up new premises in London's Wigmore Street, trading under the name of Frederick Crace and Son. In due course they arranged a showroom where they could give receptions for clients and fellow artists. Crace and Son were moving into the world of public relations and a glamorous invitation card announced the "Inspection of their new decorations in the Renaissance and other styles on Wednesday evening next…" The date of this Reception was June 3rd 1839, two years after the Coronation of the young Queen Victoria. They had now been in business for seventy years and their success was a prototype for the emergence of similar firms staffed with artists and artisans of the highest skill who were delivering the services of the interior designer.

The Crace family firm would trade on with increasing success throughout the reign. In 1873 they employed more than 100 staff and were dealing with a broad spectrum of leading English manufacturers. These included Gillows (furniture makers), Mintons (china and pottery), and Jacksons, the firm of plasterers who had worked for Robert Adam and still preserved the casts they had made for so many of his leading buildings when I started Inchbald in 1960! The last Crace, John Diblee Crace, finally closed the original Crace firm in 1899, in spite of the fact that they were still receiving excellent commissions and enjoying a reputation that had endured for well over a century. He set out his reasons for this surprising decision as being the 'harassing anxiety attached to the employment of men, caused partly by Trade

Chapter 12

Union action and finally by the Employers' Liability Acts.' This heartfelt statement from an employer of the 19th century no doubt resonates with working design firms of the 21st. *Plus ca change, plus ca c'est la meme chose.* He further points out that 'It was the practice of both my Father and myself, to personally direct, and supervise by frequent visits, every work – large or small.' This commitment to quality and detail is a sine qua non in the profession of designer/ decorators of any age and involves a heavy workload. With no son interested in the firm, J.D. Crace henceforth continued as a consultant but the glowing products of his talented family still exist to inspire and amaze.

A similar and equally successful firm, Howell and James, was started in 1819 by James Howell and Isaac James, silk mercers. Their premises were in Regent Street and initially they dealt in retail jewellery. By the time the widowed Lady Blessington returned to London in 1831, Howell and James were establishing themselves in large premises and providing furnishings and decorations for London society. They may well have worked on her house in Seamore Place, but when the lease ran out in 1836 and she moved to Gore House in Kensington, they certainly worked there to the designs and instructions of Count D'Orsay. Seamore Place, the hexagonal dining room clad in mirror, and the drawing room decorated in gold and white, had epitomised both the glamour and erudition for which her salon was famous. Gore House was much bigger, a country house on the outskirts of London, with a forty-foot library decorated in green with curtains of green-figured damask, dark green Brussels carpet and a garden large enough to accommodate a cow! D'Orsay went further, covering the upholstery in apple green, including the two state chairs originally made for Carlton House and acquired by Lady Blessington at the sale held in Buckingham Palace on the orders of frugal William IV.

The drawing room, less well used unless Tom Moore or Frans Lizst were invited to play the piano, was decorated in crimson and gold, and somewhere in these lavish interiors, among a number of fine paintings, hung portraits of Lady Blessington and the author, Mrs Inchbald, both of them by Sir Thomas Lawrence. Silk curtains, Aubusson or Brussels carpets, and the accompaniment of fashionable and elegant furniture amounted to considerable capital expenditure. Lady Blessington's jointure was dependant on her late husband's Irish estates, and even as she moved into Gore House landowners were already suffering from the economic effects of the potato famine, a national disaster which would finally decimate both the fortunes and the population of that country. As her finances became more precarious, d'Orsay's reputation also suffered from his gambling habit and burgeoning debts, causing alarm to one of their major debtors, Howell and James. Accordingly the firm took out insurance on her life against a debt of £3,500, an action which would guarantee that they had first claim on her estate. This protected

Thomas Lawrence, Portrait of Elizabeth Simpson Inchbald, c. *1796. Oil and black chalk on canvas, 71.1 x 63.5 cm*

INCHBALD

The Great Exhibition, 1851.

the firm but did not appear to encourage a modest lifestyle. By 1844 it was evident that both d'Orsay and Lady Blessington would have to sell up and live abroad in much reduced circumstances.

The firm, now known as Howell James and Co, put in an execution for debt, and Messrs Phillips were instructed to put the contents of the house up for a sale which took three days to complete.

The Blessington household retired to Paris but Howell James and Co, now established as a leading business firm, went on to great prosperity. By 1865 they employed over a hundred female workers, were selling the design products of the tutors and students of the South Kensington School, and taking an active part in the design activities which included the Great Exhibition and its several imitators. In 1884, this long-established purveyor of furnishings and decoration became a Limited Company and changed its name to Howell and James Limited.

The Aftermath of the Great Exhibition

There is no doubt that Prince Albert's grandiose idea of showcasing British art and British manufacture in 1851 was of untold benefit to both professions, not only promoting England as a leading nation in culture and commerce but also highlighting the effect of superlative publicity. His death was a great blow to England but his legacy was of huge importance to the art world.

In particular the success of his Exhibition provoked interest in the education of designers. Whilst the apprentice system had not only prospered but also produced spectacular talents, it was largely confined to studios with specific skills so that it lacked the breadth of opportunity and vision enjoyed by the privileged aristocrats of the Grand Tours.

The Royal Academy was initially the heart of the fine art world, an institution founded in 1768 by George III, a man too often associated with a debilitating illness and too rarely praised for his contributions to culture. The foundation was in part due to the support of Sir William Chambers in his capacity of head of the Office of Works, a position which carried considerable authority and influence. The overall intention was to provide specific education for young artists and to further promote English art and artists through the presentation of their work to the general public. The Academy school did not educate designers but, as an early centre offering professional art education, it promoted the idea of dedicated study linked to practical work as well as including the benefits of presentation and marketing. Interestingly the educational programme was based on that of the Academie de Peinture et Sculpture founded in Paris a century earlier by Louis XIV.

Graduates of the Academy School would include painter James Barry

RA, architect Sir John Soane RA and painter JMW Turner RA, among many other luminaries, so that this innovative programme could be said to have got off to a flying start, not least because the first President of the Royal Academy was the great Sir Joshua Reynolds himself.

Initially it was housed in Somerset House, once the London residence of Anne of Denmark. Unsurprisingly she had commissioned Inigo Jones to contribute to the development of the old Seymour family mansion, transforming it into something more regally appropriate. Subsequent occupants included Henrietta Maria, and Charles II's queen, Catherine of Braganza, both of whom were Catholics, which may have contributed to the belief that the palace was a hotbed of popery. It was a large building and over the years had served in a variety of uses, which included an army barracks, offices and occasional accommodation for visiting dignitaries.

In 1780 it seemed expedient to house the new Royal Academy in the faded but fine rooms of this once royal residence and from that date the Academy's annual Exhibitions were held there. In 1837, the year of the young queen's accession, a felicitous decision was taken to move the RA to Burlington House, so closely associated with the Architect Earl and the art world of the early 18th century. The vacated spaces in Somerset House were then given over to a new institution, the Government School of Design, set up to promote design and the practicalities of design, as opposed to the Fine Art tuition of the Academy or the scholarship of the British Museum. Contemporary interest in the arts and the linked benefit to industry encouraged development in all forms of public art education, including learned societies, emerging museums and of course the media. Henry Cole, civil servant, artist and designer, took a major part in the progression of this relatively new movement.

Cole was brought to the attention of Prince Albert by his interest in art and design exhibitions and was recruited on to the board of the Royal Commission for the Exhibition of 1851 under the Prince's presidency. This famous and successful exhibition "of the Works of Industry of all Nations" was one of the outstanding civil events of Victoria's reign and Cole played an important part in the organisation and management of it. Apart from the magnificence of the achievement itself, the Exhibition generated a surplus profit of £186,000 and Cole lobbyed for this sum to be put towards ventures dedicated to science and art education. His success in this endeavour resulted in the purchase of land in South Kensington where a home was built for the Museum of Ornamental Art, an institution previously located temporarily in Marlborough House. This Museum, of which Cole was a director, was transferred to the new site in 1855 and renamed The South Kensington Museum under his continued directorship.

He determined that his museum should serve as wide a public as possible, believing that education was surely the cornerstone of any society. He decided that the new forms of city gas lighting could facilitate longer opening hours for visitors to the museum, allowing a wider section of the public to benefit from his work. He described these longer visiting times as "hours most convenient to the working classes" and established himself as a pioneer in the general advancement of knowledge and culture to a much wider public.

Frank Parsons

The combination of gaslight and Henry Cole's convenient hours also impacted on the number of working hours in industry and the quality of lighting required for such demanding tasks as lace-making or even reading /learning. Born in 1808, he lived until 1882, a period of spectacular discovery. In this context it should be remembered that whilst the computer is credited to 20th century genius, the first steps in this challenging invention were taken in the early 19th century by Charles Babbage and his assistant Lady Lovelace, the daughter of Lord Byron. The commercial innovations of the 19th century, the development of manufacturing, transport and communication, must surely remain unmatched until the leap forward of technology in the late 20th century.

In due course logic suggested that the Government School of Design should be relocated to the same site as the new museum, and renamed the South Kensington School. Once there it flourished and developed in reputation until 1896, when it was renamed The Royal College of Art, an institution of university status, and granted a Royal Charter. In the 1960s it was housed in its own building and now enjoys a worldwide reputation as probably the leading centre of post graduate design education.

American Example

In New York in that same year, 1896, American impressionist William Merritt Chase founded the Chase School, to instruct on a broader base than fine art.

The name was changed in1898 to the New York School of Art and in 1904 the school employed Frank Parsons, a man who could well be called the father of the interior design profession. Parsons took the view that artists and designers should look to industry rather than relying on the patronage of rich clients. "Art is not for the few," he stated "for the talented, for the rich and nor," he added tellingly, "for the church".

Effectively he refuted the idea that art was elitist at any level and he considered that both the art world and industry would be wise to recognise a mutual benefit and act upon it. "Industry is the nation's life … and industrial art is the cornerstone of our national art." Working on

Parsons School of Design

that dictum he developed courses in Fashion Design, Interior Design (originally called Decoration) and Graphic and Advertising Design. These three programmes amounted to a new concept now identified as 'lifestyle', envisaging as they do so much of daily challenges and decisions. By 1911 Frank Parsons was the sole director of the School and had established new priorities and possibilities for those artists who make such a practical contribution to society, namely the designers.

In 1921 William Odom, a protegé of Parsons and himself a graduate of the New York School of Art, opened a studio in Paris which he called the Parsons Paris Atelier, dedicated to the study of European design and decoration. Here was a 20th-century version of the Grand Tour, this time taking both students and formal educational programmes overseas in order to study Western culture in Europe. When Frank Parsons died in 1930, William Odom became President of the School and in 1936 the school's name was changed to the Parsons School in commemoration of an inspired designer and educator who, with his former pupil Odom, transformed not only the profession of interior design but its image.

Parsons School of Design dominated the educational levels of the 20th-century interior designer until, like the South Kensington School, before it, it was absorbed into the University system of New York.

The nature of American society was quite different from the patterns of the European countries from which many Americans had emigrated. There was no issue of breeding or background in the land of the free; their aristocracy was dictated not by background or blood but by success, and money was the powerful demonstration of that achievement. These two factors automatically engendered untrammelled ambition, not least because it was evident that those at the top had accessed their status through their own talents and efforts, without benefit of privilege. The desire to improve, whether it be position or life style, was universally urgent and inevitably led to a desire for both information and education. In this atmosphere, the new American plutocracy looked to Europe not only for inspiration in the building of mansions suitable to their new affluence but for artefacts with which to furnish them, and this enterprise was energetically promoted by an art dealer, Joseph Duveen, later to be ennobled for his philanthropy.

Duveen was the son of a Dutch immigrant, an expert on Oriental porcelain, who settled in Hull and built up an extensive business in art dealing. His son, also Joseph, developed the firm into the sale of furniture and paintings, opened an establishment in London and discovered a lucrative market in the United States. New American money, building mansions based on the palaces of Europe, required the furnishings to complete their schemes, and Duveen, a sharp and erudite dealer, was only too willing to engage with the architects responsible. Famous for the sagacious comment: "Europe has a great deal of art and America has a great deal of money", he duly proceeded over the years to take full advantage of this.

Once again Europe was pillaged for its treasures from ruined aristocrats in the wake of World War I, in much the same pattern pursued by collectors of French treasures over a century before. Duveen's clients included the most powerful of the new age barons, JP Morgan, Andrew Mellon, John D Rockefeller and William Randolph Hearst among those whose appetite for culture allied to philanthropic inclinations (which they felt guaranteed immortality) would eventually be the foundation of America's greatest museum collections.

Celebrity status

By the end of the 19th century the camera had added a different dimension to news and therefore to fashion, disseminating as it did a vastly increased number of images through the pages of existing and new magazines. It did not yet however, replace the artist in the media.

In 1868 twenty-six-year-old Thomas Gibson Bowles borrowed £200 to found *Vanity Fair*, a new magazine which would feature current news, social narrative and fashion. This marked an interesting shift in popular journalism, introducing a wide spectrum of information and gossip to capture public interest. His success was measured by the fact that within twenty years he sold out for £20,000 in order to fund his further ambition to become a Member of Parliament. This he did, serving as member for Kings Lynn for some fourteen years.

Elsie de Wolfe

His various projects and his position as a publisher indicated a wide circle of interest and friends, and in due course he decided to incorporate this into the magazine. Accordingly he employed Leslie Ward, better known as Spy, to capture the personalities of the day rather as the camera now captures the 'celebrities' of the 21st century. The Spy cartoons are an early example of personal publicity; to be featured in *Vanity Fair* was a matter of some satisfaction, however diffidently expressed. It was an indication of success and popularity for the politicians, lawyers, artists and beau monde who were selected for Ward's 'comic impressions' which the artist himself stated 'should always (be) devoid of vulgarity'. Literary caricatures were well known, whilst the work of cartoonists tended to be limited to royalty, aristocrats or politicians who had captured the public interest by their actions, whether popular or not. Generally speaking, cartoonists were not flattering. The Duke of Wellington's nose was famous, as was the Prince Regent's stomach!

Spy, however, took his work to a different level. His depictions were at once accurate but elegant, so that the drawings actually pleased the subject, quite apart from the social cachet of being included in this extensive gallery of luminaries. Soon pride dictated that the images should be framed and it was not long before they were featured in groups in London clubs and private studies. It was a hint at later celebrity.

The First Lady Decorators

Theatre has always been a world of its own. The entertainments of the Stuarts featured the Queen and her eminent ladies in waiting with no hint of criticism. The public theatre did not, however, feature actresses until after the Restoration in 1660 and inevitably there was a link between some of the most popular and their off-stage affairs. Nell Gwynne referred to herself as the 'Protestant whore' which suggests that exposure on stage indicated a relaxed attitude to the strictures of society. This inference, fair or not, haunted the profession of actress until at least the early 20th century; the middle classes of the 19th and early 20th century took the view that 'going on the stage' was not a desirable occupation for ladies! It was an attitude that echoed criticism of those girls who in some way made an exhibition of themselves and thus were deemed to be vulgar. On this basis, personal publicity must also be vulgar so when a young woman called *Elsie de Wolfe* decided to become an actress there may have been raised eyebrows in her family. Her thespian skills proved to be unremarkable, but she designed her own clothes, wore them with aplomb and quickly established a reputation for individuality and personal elegance which appeared to compensate for her lack of formal stage training.

Soon de Wolfe attracted the attention and affection of theatrical producer Miss Elisabeth Marbury. Rich and talented, Marbury was well known in New York society, and lauded for bringing European artists and writers to the New York theatre, including both Oscar Wilde and George Bernard Shaw. She was a member of the highest social circle, exclusive to the four hundred people who could fit into Mrs Astor's ballroom! Snobbery had overtaken the robust pioneers of America at last! Miss Marbury's contact base was thus of inestimable use to her glamorous friend, who now turned to interior decorating as a career.

In due course the two women set up house together, the house decorated by Elsie in the French manner and financed by Marbury. The refreshing and different interiors led to a number of introductions from Marbury's circle, which included prominent architect Stanford White. White was newly commissioned to build the Colony Club, founded by and for upper class women in protest at the time spent by their menfolk in the numerous New York clubs founded, it was said, in imitation of those in London. The club needed an interior decorator, and de Wolfe was put forward. Her designs were so successful that she was repeatedly commissioned with similar briefs for clubs in a number of the large American cities, centres of industry reaching for culture. Her career was launched and Henry J Frick was a major client although it was sometime into the 20th century that de Wolfe's work in the Frick mansion was recognised as interesting.

Syrie Maugham

It is constantly claimed that de Wolfe was the first of the interior decorators as we understand the term and she encouraged this belief. It is certainly true that she was one of the most successful, then and later. Part of her success had to do with a determined perfectionism in terms of presentation, public relations and a flair for dictating life style, ensuring that whatever the circumstances she was always seen as a style leader.

In 1913 Elsie capitalised on her new popularity by writing a book called *The House in Good Taste*. This work outlines the rules and principles of her views on design and decoration and confirmed her position as an arbiter of taste. It enjoyed considerable success and provides an interesting insight into fashions in the year before war broke out in Europe. However in 1897 *The Decoration of Houses* by New York socialite Edith Wharton and architect Ogden Codman had already drawn public interest to the facts and practice of design rules and to the notion that this was an artistic skill which could be extended through education and knowledge. Elsie was a pioneer but Edith Wharton could certainly claim to have been the first of the lady decorators. The difference between them is simply the fact that one had no need to earn a living and thus did not require either clients or publicity, whilst the actress morphed into a role that provided a prototype for the successful 20th-century interior designer. Elsie's use of the phrase 'good taste' raises the issue of 'bad taste' with all the reservations generated by 19th-century society on taste of any kind. If art equates to freedom of expression, perhaps taste falls short as a criterion of art; and surely interior design is an art form?

One of the major interests in Elsie's rooms is the constant use of French furniture, in particular the later and often provincial furniture of the Louis XVI style. These were pieces that fitted into the proportions of the smaller apartments now being rapidly developed in the US. The turn-of-the-century decorator was rediscovering the combination of comfort and elegance that Marie Antoinette had sought when she commissioned her Petits Appartements in the vastness of Versailles.

Whilst de Wolfe's rise to celebrity was brisk, an Englishwoman with strong American links was establishing herself in London. Syrie Barnado, married and divorced from American pharmaceutical millionaire Henry Wellcome, later married author and playwright Somerset Maugham. Her career as an interior decorator started during the Maugham marriage when she employed the decorating department of Fortnum and Mason to redecorate her house, and became fascinated by the skills of their employees. After working and learning in the Fortnum's department she started her own business and in spite of divorce she would be known internationally as Syrie Maugham for the rest of her life.

Syrie's work was much more design-based than de Wolfe's; her decorating skills were considerably more eclectic and she was probably the most influential designer/decorator of her time, inspiring colleagues as distinguished as Jean Michel Franck, whose furniture she frequently commissioned. Her style was classic/contemporary, enhanced by her co-operation with Chicago architect David Adler and his sister, Frances Elkins. Both Syrie and Adler travelled constantly between England and Chicago, exchanging ideas and materials, and purchasing antique furniture and decorative items.

She shared with de Wolfe an appreciation of design concepts but had a particular flair for period styles complementing the products of contemporary designers. Her work was individual, and remains today an interesting study in fashion and inspiration, justifying her reputation as the most impressive British interior designer of the early 20th century. In America Frances Elkins was setting new but similar standards, a discriminate variety of style which relied on the value and contribution of each individual item selected for inclusion, rather than a slavish consideration of overall identity.

Elsie was more commercially cynical, defining her new profession as "… supplying objets d'art and giving advice regarding the decoration of their houses to wealthy persons who do not have the time, inclination or

Chapter 12

culture to do such work for themselves."

Syrie and Elsie had clients in Europe and America, Elsie because she hailed from the States but lived in Europe, and Syrie because, with her boundless energy, she and her secretary sailed to the States annually on one of the Cunard liners, carrying with them a collection of antiques for use and sale in New York or Chicago.

These women called themselves interior decorators without any effort at semantic discrimination. Martin Battersby must have had either or both in mind when he wrote that they had 'qualities of toughness that would have embarrassed Attila.' It was a quality much needed for any woman in that period attempting to set up a business. Both social and financial parameters were stacked against them and they had to fight a degree of patronisation that it is difficult for anyone of the 21st century to fully comprehend. American society was more accommodating but the view in England of any woman doing much more than secretarial work was considered to be slightly, if not wholly, ridiculous. This may well explain the degree of negative reporting that these early pioneers faced, at the time and in the later accounts of their careers.

The early years of the century saw a dramatic change in female status that was a result of women's role in the war. It was a period when women had proved themselves as competent, intelligent and hardworking in a variety of occupations, but even so it was not until 1928 that the English Parliament passed a bill granting enfranchisement to all women over 21.

The 1920s and 1930s threw up a number of talented women who perceived interior decoration as an interesting and financially viable career which accorded with their upbringing in a different era. Their education had included domestic skills, and their inclination coincided with the desire to marry, to found a family and to provide a family background, so that there was little objection to a pursuit that fitted in so naturally to circumstance and social strictures.

There is no doubt that whoever may have been the first interior decorator, both Syrie and Elsie were role models who not only understood the rigours of their profession but were also conscious of the value of marketing their skills and the demands of business management. Neither had any formal training but both were energised by a passion for style, an interest in travel and culture and the benefit of excellent social contacts.

Both were conscious of the importance of publicity; de Wolfe was at pains to court hungry journalists with a series of irresistible stories. She was said to be the first older woman to blue-rinse her hair, and it was reported that she stood on her head to defy age; of course it was all reported in the glossy magazines. In 1926 she married English diplomat

Sibyl Colefax

Sir Charles Mendl thus acquiring a title, established herself in a Paris flat and gave interviews in her glamorous bathroom. Wherever Elsie was, there was always a story and nearly always a headline. Elsie was the ultimate celebrity!

Syrie to some extent was defined by her relationship to Somerset Maugham, in spite of her own sparkling talent. Maugham was internationally famous and famously unpleasant, no doubt resenting the fact that his ex-wife was such a startling success. Towards the end of his life he instituted legal action to assert that their daughter was not his biological child and attempted to claw back his gifts as well as excluding her from his will in favour of his male secretary.

He went so far as to write a book along these bitchy lines, *Looking Back*, which was greeted with horror by Syrie's many friends. One of them, Beverley Nicholls, wrote a counter attack in her defence, calling his book *A case of Human Bondage* in mockery of Maugham's famous best seller.

Syrie was renowned for her constant use of white in her decorating schemes. When she travelled to India it prompted the waggish remark "Syrie has gone to India to paint the Black Hole white"! This predeliction was inspired by the white drawing room of a neighbour in the first years of her marriage to Maugham and whilst it may seem revolutionary it is worth recalling that white decoration was introduced at the turn of the 20th century in contrast to the heavy luxe, the vulgarity even, of the last days of empire. The disruption of 1914 intervened in the progress of fashion, so when Syrie picked up the theme in the 1920s it seemed more revolutionary than was true. This colour fashion coincided with the modernity of the period, with the diktats of the Bauhaus and perhaps also with the psychology of nations looking forward to a future, rather than a reference back to the past. Elsie was also keen on plenty of white paint, but on her first sight of the Parthenon anticipated Kelly Hoppen by remarking "It's beige – my colour!" James Amster, showing me his elegant New York apartment, pointed out that it was painted in 'Syrie's magnolia green' so she was not so boringly consistent as it is supposed. Colour is the most subjective of interior components, subject to fashion, circumstance, light and even temperament. It is unwise to give too much importance to Syrie's supposed preference although it is clear that she traded on the reputation and she certainly had a famous white room in her King's Road house which relied on lighting, texture and one of her famous mirror screens for interest, without the introduction of any colour at all.

A Business Balance

While Elkins and her brother David Adler were cherry picking Europe

Chapter 12

for beautiful objects, selecting them for their individual attraction and incorporating them into spaces which owed nothing to historic tradition, Syrie Maugham was searching the new world for new ideas. Meanwhile a significant number of well-heeled, well-educated and well-connected ladies were adopting the fashionable identity of 'lady decorator', among them Lady Astor, the American wife of an English peer, and Lady Colefax, the wife of lawyer, Sir Arthur Colefax.

The Colefaxes lived in Argyll House, a small mansion in the King's Road, where Sybil Colefax established a salon and entertained a potent mix of royalty, literature and art. Unhappily Sir Arthur died and Sybil, relying on her son's advice, lost a great deal of her capital in the financial crash of the early 1930s. Argyll House had to be abandoned and Lady Colefax was faced with earning her living. Since she was renowned for her style as well as for her glittering entertainments she turned to advising others and in due course had set herself up in business formally. The enterprise was so successful that she needed to enlarge her staff and it was at this moment that both Sybil Colefax and Syrie Maugham propositioned John Fowler in the hope that one of them could harness his talents to her own firm.

John Fowler

Fowler was a painter who had been employed at Peter Jones as head of the painted-furniture department, a fashion which flourished in the 1930s. He was a skilled colourist, and already an authority on the history and decorative details of English country house styles. Sybil was a well known hostess with an impressive circle of friends, which may well have influenced his choice. Certainly his talent and her connections took him into so many of the great English houses that his understanding and knowledge of the English style became encyclopaedic. Travel writer Rory Cameron, himself an aficionado of interior design, remarked that John considered Sybil would be easier to work with than Syrie and it seems this was probably the case. She was also a great deal less peripatetic than Syrie, the transatlantic traveller, in her search for clients.

When Sybil finally retired she sold the business to Nancy Lancaster who renamed the firm Sybil Colefax and John Fowler Limited. Thus was born one of the most iconic firms of decorators of the 20th century, still flourishing in its eightieth decade.

Another successful but later partnership was that of Mann and Fleming of Mount Street. In 1914 the eighteen-year-old Ronald Fleming enlisted in the Coldstream Guards and having survived the war went to Paris in order to study interior design and decoration. In 1931 he joined Keeble Limited, a firm which traced its origins back to the 17th century, said to have been founded in the wake of the Great Fire. He also published a book in the same year, *Talk on Decoration*, and moved on to be head of the very active Design Department of Fortnum and Mason. Finally he joined Mrs Mann in Mount Street and in 1948 became a director of Mann and Fleming. His work is not well known today, but in the 1950s Mann was a leading figure in the decoration world, specialising in the Regency period and actually recreating a Regency house for furniture historian Ralph Dutton, the original having been gutted by fire. Fleming was also an extremely successful antique dealer and epitomised the combination of dealer/collector/working designer as well as being unusual in that he had undertaken a period of formal training. There were many examples of women in the 1930s working with gay men who, in spite of their orientation, brought something of a male discipline to the partnership, thus balancing overt femininity.

The rise of the antique dealers at the turn of the 20th century in response to American demand established a retrospective craze for the past, in particular for the skills and products of the 18th century. One of the most remarkable dealers, Malletts of Bath, was started by the son of a jeweller who took over his father's firm and added furniture to the stock. After a successful foray into a London exhibition, Walter Mallett decided to take premises in Bond Street and whilst the firm did not undertake client projects, the relationship with designers had a profound effect on client taste and choice. By the time Michael and I were dealing in antiques in the 1950s, the elegant figure of Francis Egerton, chairman of Malletts, was a familiar one at the British Antique Dealers' annual exhibition and a fairly regular, if daunting visitor to our collection. He always knew exactly what he wanted and this clear opinion was the hallmark of successful antique dealing since it established artistic identity and forged specific relationships with both buyers and sellers. I recall buying a bureau plat at Christies one day and my neighbour, John Bly, looked surprised and asked me why I had done so. "Michael wants it, he told me to buy it" I replied, and John expressed surprise "I wouldn't have thought it was his taste" he commented. So John Bly had a clear image of Michael's preferences. In fact the bureau plat, Louis XV, was still in his apartment when he died. Michael's taste was eclectic and this is what made his work so interesting.

Partridges came later than Malletts, founded in 1904 by Frank Partridge who had already spent time in New York. They dealt in both English and French furniture, whilst Malletts were known for their specialisation in the great English cabinetmakers; and indeed the firm at one point made their own reproductions.

The styles of the 18th century became almost a fetish in the twenties and thirties, flourishing rather strangely alongside the determination of the Modern Movement to revolutionise not only architecture and design but the manner in which the public thought about those subjects. However, the antique dealers made their mark in the shaping of the interior designer and in the postwar years, with the English market almost saturated with wonderful antique furniture and objects, their businesses flourished as did their exports to the United States.

The role of the 'lady decorators' is too often dismissed as that of the amateur but in fact they were nerve-wrackingly efficient. Martin Battersby was not kind when he described them as 'Ruthless, often completely unscrupulous …. but all with an unshakeable belief in their own talents.' It was a belief that was frequently warranted, and it generated the passion which drove their careers and businesses forward. In retrospect it is evident that these highly-charged women played a major role in the formulation of the profession we know today as Interior Design, but it should be remembered that partnerships provided them with both support and talent. Colefax and Fowler, Mann and Fleming, the gay couple Elsie and Marbury, not to mention Elsie's gay minions, all flourished in relationships that were complementary and very successful.

Tony Duquette, set designer, protegée of Elsie de Wolfe, jewellery designer and competent self publicist, met de Wolfe in Paris and was immediately subsumed into her entourage. De Wolfe's reputation as the most important interior decorator deserves careful analysis in terms of her work but there is no doubt that she knew everyone and that she opened the doors of the rich and successful to her protegés, including Duquette. It is sobering to consider that Duquette's work was being produced at around the same time as Johnson's Glass House, and relevant to note that one of his several books was titled *More is More*, a defiant tilt at the great Mies van der Rohe, who stated that *'Less is More'*. Set design led to interior design and jewellery design, his first necklace commissioned for the Duchess of Windsor. He described the character of his interior design as neo-baroque, and the complexity of colour, pattern and applied art does indeed merit that description. There is no doubt that more, for Tony Duquette, was a very great deal more. Everything about his work is infused with a heightened sense of theatre and luxury so it is of little surprise that he forged such a close friendship with the thespian de Wolfe.

In 1951 he was invited to exhibit his work in the Pavilion de Marsan in the Louvre, the first American artist to be so honoured. It was perhaps evidence of the post-war depression in the art world that work as flamboyant, even as eccentric, could be seen as a desirable antidote to the greyness of Paris in 1951. Great events throw up an aftermath and Louise de Villeneuve reported that 'these works are dreams caught in the net of reality'. Perhaps Duquette was to Interior decorating what Warhol was to the world of art or perhaps Parisians were looking back wistfully to the glamorous days of the 1930s. Fashion is a demanding employer and easily bored.

Only Syrie seemed to work alone, relying on her stalwart secretary

Olive Cruickshank, who dared describe her employer as an adventuress! Nevertheless, even Syrie formed a close business relationship with Chicago architect David Adler and his sister, for whom she had great regard. Occasionally her passions erupted in the frustration of business. She and her team were based in a small Chelsea street, Paradise Row. "Sometimes", remarked her secretary, "it was hell in Paradise!"

The Magazines

In the second quarter of the 20th century the camera played a prime role, not so much in interior design itself but in interior design fashions. Photography developed the spread of visual knowledge and preference through magazines, which were increasingly cheap and therefore popular.

In 1901 a group of American architects had launched a magazine they called *House and Garden*, offering information and advice to the middle class regarding the manner in which they could themselves adapt their houses to suit the lifestyle of their families. The magazine further carried advertisements promoting furniture and products to support this advice so that a powerful form of education was established. In 1911 Condé Nast bought an interest and by 1915 was the sole owner of a publication that has been one of the greatest sources of influence in the interior design world.

The establishment of *Good Housekeeping* predates that of *House and Garden*. It was first issued in 1885, and was concerned directly with what became known as Womens' Interests.

These included cookery, family concerns and health with advice and information on household products. It was a time of increased interest in the role of women in society and although *Good Housekeeping* identified that role with the conservative view of marriage and motherhood, it nevertheless offered its readers a constructive and informed attitude which accorded dignity to a status which had hitherto been taken for granted. Such self-awareness moved easily into the aggravation that had spawned the suffragette movement, itself supported by the knowledge and experience of womens' war work in WWI.

Less controversial was the publication of *Country Life* in 1899, not least because it initially concentrated on golf and racing, both seen as mainly male interests. However, the personal preferences of its proprietor Edward Hudson, both an antiquarian and an historian, meant that his magazine, still prospering today, would prove to be one of the most important archival records of England's architecture, design and decoration. Inevitably, as magazine material took on a more balanced emphasis, *Country Life* with its famous photographers developed into a reference point for those living in such houses, or those interested in the development of style and decoration. These three publishing icons were all founded within two decades and provided a basis for the education of the purchasing public as well as encouraging the development of further publications which extended both knowledge and discrimination.

The presentation of design as an interest and a general possibility led into the burgeoning careers of the 'lady decorators' and initially caused a degree of mirth or outright hostility from the architectural profession. It was a time when many architects were struggling with the conservatism of natural evolution as opposed to the startling innovations of the Modern and International Movements. Nothing similar to that struggle had happened in the previous centuries. Architectural achievements had hitherto been dominated by an established life style and the building patterns that accommodated that style. These perspectives were shaken up by the dramatic social changes wrought by World War I, as well as by the 20th-century technologies newly available. Whilst some pioneers of modernity originated in Europe it was in the United States that they found both an audience and clients and so the famous names of early 20th-century architecture are forever associated with the young nation which offered such an enthusiastic welcome to European culture. It was in America that they designed and developed small houses for the professional classes, houses which reflected changing priorities and which would influence the future reality of how much of the world lives, or would like to live.

Seagram Building

Gropius and Mies van der Rohe were German architects who left their country during the Nazi regime, and established their practices in the US. In 1915 Walter Gropius had been appointed head of the Grand Ducal Saxon School of Arts and Crafts, an establishment that was founded in 1860 and which Gropius developed into the Bauhaus School, dedicated strangely to almost every art form except architecture. This was in spite of his own architectural training both in Munich and in the atelier of Peter Behrens where fellow students were Mies van der Rohe and Le Corbusier. As head of the school, Gropius committed the establishment to the quality of industrial design, following in the pioneering footsteps of the German Prince Consort, always so keen to make the best of design available to everyone.

In 1929 Gropius' colleague Mies, at the time still working in Germany, designed the German Pavilion for the International Exposition in Barcelona and in doing so attracted international applause, if not astonishment. The Pavilion was built of glass featuring not only exotic marbles but water. The result was an impression of continuous space and light, a floating arrangement of surfaces uninterrupted by extraneous decoration and furnished only with Barcelona chairs. The elegant style for which the architect is famous was established with his Pavilion, and

Philip Johnson's Glass House.

his philosophy was encapsulated in his assertion that "Less is more", a phrase that is constantly quoted and, in this age of consumerism, with good reason.

Whilst the Pavilion was being constructed, Mies met American Philip Johnson who, after studying at Harvard, had undertaken trips to Europe to visit the buildings made famous by the Grand Tourists of the 18th century. Apart from working together on the Seagram Building in 1958, the scholar and the architect formed a close collaboration which occasionally edged into competition.

In 1945 Mies was commissioned by Edith Farnsworth to build a small and elegant retreat. Her brief resulted in a building that had much in common with his German Pavilion. Known as the Farnsworth House it had considerable influence on Johnson's later Glass House, built in 1949. Although Johnson's Glass House can be described as derivative, it takes the original concept to the ultimate conclusion. It is a rectangular glass box, measuring 17 metres by 9.8 by 3.2 metres high. The only evidence of privacy lies in a circular brick construction which contains kitchen and bathroom facilities; otherwise the entire property is visible through all four 'walls'.

In the 1960s I was commissioned to interview six New York architects for the *Sunday Telegraph* and Johnson was one of them. When I asked permission to view the Glass House, the architect pointed out that it was unnecessary for me to have access – "you can see it all from outside" he remarked. When I questioned the matter of privacy and indeed its bedfellow, security, he had an irrefutable answer.

"The building is entirely surrounded by my own estate", he told me, "and at night I can light up the surroundings, and I can choose which trees to spotlight. The wallpaper is always changing, always fascinating."

Chapter 12

I was silenced, not least because this sentiment summed up what I was already considering as the ideal lifestyle.

The Glass House epitomises the relationship between domestic space and its verdant surroundings but in spite of its beauty there is no doubt that it is a demanding space in which to live. Indeed in Johnson's final years it was used for entertaining and I assume that when he wished to sleep there he did so in his equally demanding but fascinating guest house.

The guest house was constructed entirely underground, with air conditioning, and a sophisticated plan of concealed lighting. What strikes the visitor most forcibly however, is the stillness of the space. Even voice levels are dramatically reduced, the reason for this being that the walls are clad in carpet, making a startling adjustment to the acoustics. As a result the small house has an atmosphere of serenity and repose which is unmatched.

Frank Lloyd Wright's Falling Water.

I have since then often wondered about the psychological profile of Mr Johnson. A house that provides shelter only from the elements, with guests consigned to an underground apartment with an atmosphere that might be interpreted as luxurious confinement, certainly amounts to a project that defies and challenges any established form of living. Here there is theatre, fantasy and the freedom of finance that can make dreams possible. Whatever view is taken of the result, there is no doubt that this building was mind-changing.

Three centuries after Inigo Jones built his small house for the Danish Queen, American architect Frank Lloyd Wright devised an extraordinary building for Mrs Edgar J Kaufmann, also for occasional use, which he incorporated into the landscape of a waterfall. The design owes nothing to influence other than Lloyd Wright's inspiration in the interpretation of Mrs Kaufmann's instructions. The family had used the original buildings for weekends to enjoy the countryside and all that it offered; the architect designed a house that accommodated the spectacular inclusion of natural features, including the water falls, and appears so integral to the site that it conveys a suppleness unusual in a fixed building. Lloyd Wright was responsible for all the furniture and interior design.

Falling Water and the Glass House, among many other houses of the period, bring personal preferences and architectural talent into a sharper perspective than ever before and the fact that architects or designers were prepared to dream the impossible and take outrageous decisions was bound to offer a new freedom of thought to the general public, whether they were themselves talented, or needed to rely on others for the implementation of their requirements. The power of the media made all this universally available.

Meanwhile architecture was not the only source of inspiration.

The Camera

The development of camera techniques moved on to filming, and the fully-fledged establishment of film making, which created its own world and its own celebrities. The naïve fascination of early films quickly gave way to the ambitious productions of the 1920s and 1930s, offering an unending supply of wonder and adventure generated by the best contemporary authors, designers and actors that the Machiavellis controlling the studios could lure into contract.

Starlit names of the leading studios included Scott Fitzgerald, Dorothy Parker and one who combined the multiple talents of writing, acting and producing, Orson Welles.

In the 1930s the art of film entertainment reached an apogee of glamorous spectacle embodying drama, adventure, and romance. The stories by famous writers were brought to life, not only by beautiful and accomplished actors but by the talents of set designers and the skills of dress designers. Competition between studios, the considerable sums involved in production and the cut and thrust of marketing drove the industry to ever-greater perfectionism. Busby Berkeley, choreographer and director, reinvented the chorus line as an art form and films that included his spectaculars are famous for those features. The musicals for which Fred Astaire was famous were fairy tales devised to seduce the public with impossible notions of escapism and happy endings. No detail was overlooked not least because it was soon evident that the camera was unforgiving in the precision of its recording.

In 1941 Orson Welles was 26 when he co-wrote, produced, directed and acted in *Citizen Kane*, a film which some say is the greatest film ever made. His production director, responsible for set design, was Perry Ferguson, and his cinematographer was the brilliant Gregg Toland, a wizard in the manipulation of camera and lighting. The two worked closely together, Ferguson remarking that 'imaginative lighting (can) suggest a great deal more on the screen than actually exists on the stage'. There were said to be more than a hundred sets involved in this film, each carefully built to accommodate the camera, and Welles himself was involved in every detail of production. *Kane* was an extraordinary achievement in film history, and the precise skills required to convey a story onto celluloid were amply demonstrated. These achievements are far more extensive and indeed complicated than is perhaps generally appreciated and the endless developments in this competitive arena were bound to affect the principles and the fashions of interior design.

Lighting expert Toland, who died soon after the film's release, might have been surprised to read of Sydney Smith's attempt at economy in the 18th century. 'It was such a relief,' reported Smith's daughter, 'when we could afford candles to replace the bowls of mutton fat with which we lighted the rooms'. Candle light itself is both hot and unstable; argand lamps were an improvement as was gas, but it was not possible to manipulate light until the introduction of electricity and 20th-century cinematographers extended that possibility dramatically. In due course the interior designers took advantage of the ingenuity of these newly-skilled practitioners. Technology offered limitless opportunity which spilled over into both commercial and domestic interiors.

The work of designers like Gregg Toland and Perry Ferguson tend to be forgotten in the overall clamour of the film to which they contributed so much. Both were nominated for several Academy Awards, including one each for *Citizen Kane*, and it is regrettable that the star status of film production seems to be limited in the public mind to directors and actors.

The skills accelerated by the demands of film impacted on the photographers now required for the recording of fashionable interiors so much in demand by magazine publishers and the reading public.

In the 1960s my own house was featured in the new *Telegraph Magazine*. The young man who arrived to do the work was Michael Boys, well on his way to fame – indeed he made a preliminary visit to see if the project was of interest to him. He liked what he saw, explained that he did not use lighting and would arrive to work with the sunrise, using this subtle natural lighting to create the images. Having done quite a lot of photography work by that time, working with photographers using varying types of equipment and lights, I was surprised and when I saw the images I was more than impressed. As camera technology progressed, it became clear that the camera was a tool in its own right, subservient only to the operator, but also capable of distorting as well as enhancing interiors. Boys went on to produce a book of his images, demonstrating the effects of both morning and evening light, showing interiors of varying distinction but all sharing the subtle atmosphere that only natural light can bestow.

In the late 1950s Michael Inchbald had decorated the first rooms of a complete redecoration of the house in Milner Street, transforming the third floor space into a flat. Uninhibited by any particular requirement beyond practicality and appeal, he produced a bright, amusing space and *House and Garden* editor Anthony Hunt was delighted at the idea of featuring it in the magazine.

"I will send Anthony Denney, our best photographer" he promised, " but I warn you that he always changes things if he doesn't like them. Be careful how you react, he is not above walking off the site!" Michael too had that reputation!

In the event Denney arrived, moved nothing, took some enchanting shots and departed happy, although not as happy as Michael was to have his work featured in the leading design magazine.

William Pahlmann

Anthony Denney was an exceptionally stylish photographer who was also an interior designer, inspired decorator and painter. "My experience as a painter has facilitated my approach ... to colour photography" he commented, and his eye for design would have been heightened by his use of the camera, recording as it does the smallest detail of the image.

For a time Denney lived in a National Trust house, Rainham Hall, revelling in its retrospective Queen Anne enchantment and the fact that the interiors remained very much as they had been built in 1729 several years after the death of the Queen. Renovating this architectural beauty with care, he then filled it with contemporary art, interesting antique furniture and even more interesting artefacts. "I like to be surprised .. stunned even!", he noted. His work certainly had just that effect on his audience. Rainham remains as he left it, still in the care of the National Trust.

Denney took his eclectic views into marketing, although with mixed success. In the late 1950s, Gomme brothers, who owned G Plan Furniture, commissioned him to photograph their advertising campaign and he suggested that the pieces they designed could be shot in distinguished houses alongside the fine classic furniture of the original schemes, emphasising the integrity of contemporary furniture. Denney carried out this brief with great flair but it turned into an example of the manner in which advertisers can misread the market.

The owners of classic houses did not want modern furniture, and those who lived in more realistic spaces were put off by the fact that the imagery made the G Plan products appear too grand and thus beyond their budget. It was, nevertheless, an innovative way of presenting a well-made and elegant group of products and should have enjoyed success. Unhappily the project was consigned to history.

The English public were still incredibly conservative in their reactions, and it would take a long time for them to assimilate all that America had to offer in terms of ideas and design achievement.

Design Discipline

In the years between the wars, when Maugham and de Wolfe were rising stars, there was an increasing comprehension that interior design was not just a subject to be learned but that it qualified as a serious profession. The middle classes were flourishing, and in America they were mobile. When Americans changed their job it was likely that they might change their home; they wanted, and needed, houses that were at once attractive and practical and it was inevitable that there would be an increasing demand for the services of efficient professionals who could supply solutions.

One such was a Texan, William Pahlmann, who started his career with a correspondence course in Interior Design and by 1927 was attending the New York School of Fine and Decorative Arts. In 1929 he was awarded a scholarship to Ecole Parsons a Paris. In 1931 his work on an 18th-century house in Pennsylvania was featured in a magazine, resulting in a commission from Mrs Paley, the wife of the founder of CBS. Pahlmann's future was assured.

He was then employed by Lord and Taylor to run their decorating and home furnishing department where he initiated a new form of marketing by displaying products in room settings. The first of these shows was themed as 'Windows' and drew not only publicity but a satisfactory attendance in the showroom for which he was responsible. He then toured Peru for several weeks, returning with products and ideas which he transformed into yet another well-publicised show of model rooms, marketed as Pahlmann Peruvian. This exhibition attracted between 20,000 and 30,000 visitors a week and the system of marketing was taken up later on with great success by Bloomingdales. War interrupted his progress when he volunteered for the Army in 1942 and found himself Director of the Jefferson Barracks Camouflage School in Missouri. He met the fresh challenges with his usual élan.

"I built a 'fake' town in the South of France" he remembered "….. and with the pull of a string a whole house would collapse and reveal an anti-aircraft gun …. It was quite a show"

His post-war career was even more successful than his early years in the profession, including as it did a large volume of commercial as well as private commissions, and the Presidency of the New York Chapter of the Institute of Decorators. He believed fervently in education and the professionalism of his chosen career. He lectured constantly, in particular to his Alma Mater, Parsons School, and in 1955 wrote a comprehensive book aimed at the public, spelling out his principles of eclecticism, proportion and the properties of light, pattern and colour. *The Pahlmann Book of Interior Design* was a 1950's landmark on the subject of the domestic interior. When he was awarded the Elsie de Wolfe Award by the New York Chapter it was said that "…except for Elsie de Wolfe, no-one has influenced the American home more than Mr Pahlmann." It was a fitting accolade and there is no doubt that this distinguished American designer provided the template for the successful Interior Designer of the 20th century. The book he wrote may seem simplistic today but in 1951 he was addressing a new and still relatively uneducated audience in terms of practicality, rather than relying on the glamour of fashion.

No occupation can flourish professionally without the discipline of a regulatory body and accordingly in 1931 American decorators formed the first and then only board of governance of decorators, calling it the American Institute of Interior Decorators, AIID, just as Pahlmann himself was consolidating his future career. This move gave substance and official status to the young profession but the association was in its infancy and there would be changes of emphasis and educational qualifications in the years to come. The first adjustment was a name change in 1936 to AID, the American Institute of Decorators, the change possibly prompted by graphics.

By the 1950s the Institute had a number of chapters across America, the New York chapter being the most prominent. In 1957 this chapter elected to change its name to the National Society for Interior Designers (NSID) and to operate independently of the old Institute. The semantic shift was significant, the adjustment from Decorator to Designer underlining the new discussion as to the correct title for the Society's members. William Pahlmann was Chairman of the Board and first President of the Resource Council.

It is worth noting that during his relatively short Army career, Pahlmann had been elevated to the rank of Lt Colonel, indicating both leadership and management skills and it was this authority that marked him out among his peers as one of the most successful and inspiring of the New York designers.

In a later resolution of the developments, AID and NSID merged to form the American Society of Interior Designers (ASID), now the acknowledged governing body of the interior design profession in America, with some 25,000 members across the categories of qualification. Importantly the educational requirements have always been clear and since Parsons was well established in the early years of the Society's incarnation there was already in place a programme of required instruction that has formed the basis of design education ever since.

When I met William Pahlmann it was he who encouraged me to consider the establishment of both a School and a guiding body for the profession in England.

Pahlmann Peruvian epitomised the mix of cultures which had provided the real excitement in interior design for centuries, but he was one of the first to set about implementing style so deliberately, as part of his personal philosophy. As a furniture and spatial designer he enhanced his interiors with artefacts from other ages, cultures and nationalities, and in doing so he drew public attention to the individual beauty of any work of art, whatever its origin. His views were adopted and adapted by his own contemporaries, and eclecticism, appealing as it was to so many in both America and Europe, was soon identified as a distinctive style. He shared international interests with those pioneers, the so-called lady decorators, but he had early and formal training in both New York and Paris, had experienced the best of both cultural centres and a disciplined design talent was added to his flair for exciting spaces. Michael Inchbald in particular was a great admirer of his taste and his abilities and was himself influenced by the creative opportunities offered by such a diversity of interests. Syrie Maugham was not above taking a French chair and reproducing it with a contemporary look, or adapting classic plasterwork to suit a modern room, so Pahlmann was certainly not the only designer with this liberal approach but he crystallised the concept, not only in its artistic form but in his management work and marketing at Lord and Taylor, and in his writing.

The 1950s

The shock of the war years had totally inhibited the development of interior design in England, but Condé Nast's *House and Garden* started appearing in the UK after the cessation of conflict and young designers devoured the contents, admiring all that American design had to offer as well as the manner in which domestic comfort and domestic efficiency were prioritised.

Robsjohn-Gibbings

In the 1920s that was certainly the opinion of the young Robsjohn-Gibbings. Deprived by the financial rigours of WWI of the opportunity to study architecture and confined to the studio of one of the London decorating firms, he visited New York, was seduced by the American life style and opened his own business there in the 1930s, eventually applying for American citizenship. In spite of his extensive knowledge of the variety of historic English architecture and furniture "most of it sagging with centuries of elaboration", he adopted a lighter and crisper style that suited his demanding clients and had much in common with the sets devised by Carroll Clark for the Fred Astaire musicals. Although architecturally unqualified he designed some enchanting houses, which he also furnished and decorated, occasionally referring back to his youthful experience with a choice selection of antique furniture. Nevertheless this did not inhibit him from writing a satire on the influence of antique furnishings, entitled *Goodbye Mr Chippendale*. His architectural preference has been described as opulent simplicity, a design form that provides a sympathetic background for either modern or antique furniture, or indeed for an eclectic mix.

After years of designing furniture for the Widdicomb Furniture Company as well as for private clients, Robsjohn-Gibbings moved to Athens where he met the proprietors of the leading furniture firm, Saridis. In conjunction with Eleftherios and Susan Saridis, and his long term partner Carlton Pullin, he designed a collection of Greek furniture based on extensive research into the artefacts of classical Greece. His sources were archaeological sites, scholarly studies and above all the paintings which occur on every ancient Greek vase.

"On Greek vases I saw furniture that was young, untouched by time. Klismos chairs carved with the delicate grace of a new moon…..Vitality, surging through the human figures on the vases, surged through this furniture. I had wandered unsuspecting into a new world."

Gibbings died aged 71 in 1976. His furniture is now, ironically, prized in the same way as the antiques which he could not resist satirizing, and his designs are still made by Saridis. He was a landmark designer, but above all a classicist. In spite of his status in the 1940s and 1950s as one of the most significant of American interior designers, in spite of the fact that he wrote several popular books, it is interesting to note that his name is not nearly so well known as that of Elsie de Wolfe, the ultimate publicist, or Syrie Maugham the committed and efficient business woman. Whatever view the world took of these two ladies there is no doubt that between them they changed forever the nature and conduct of interior design and decoration and it must also be true that their reputations and capacity for personal promotion has to some extent overshadowed the achievements of other talented practitioners working at the same time.

The Profession Identified

In terms of the overall establishment of the interior design profession, there is no doubt that America led the way. There was educational progress in England but the use of the word 'design' had an industrial connotation. By the time that the Chase School had morphed into Parsons School of Design in the early 1930s, students were designated as future interior designers, and the educational programmes had the breadth and structure to achieve that end. Part of the reason for American superiority in this particular field lay in the fact that the still-new nation was building new homes as opposed to relying on existing housing stock. This in itself drove architectural ambitions and created a demand for qualified practitioners trained to cope with the challenges, both practical and cosmetic, that confronted an extensive business class.

It is understood today that the role of the designer is not one of domination, nor of artistic superiority. The designer takes instruction from the client, but may find the interpretation of that instruction challenging, perhaps because the client has neither the knowledge to convey their wishes in full, nor the vernacular in which to express them. Empathy is one of the required skills, the capacity to understand a limited brief, to analyse and expand it with deference to the lifestyle, taste and requirements of the client, without any degree of patronisation. "I pretty much know what I want" can be a very misleading statement and often takes no account of budget or possibility.

Interior design must take account of every product that is involved in the interior of a building, through plumbing to table decoration, and the tutors at Parsons understood and implemented this very diverse programme.

Contrary to the general perception, the purpose of the profession is not just about beautifying a house; it starts on the basics of the location, considers the form and construction of the space and creates an area which conforms to the clients brief.

The design solution thus achieved may well improve dramatically on that brief since the designer's knowledge will assist the client's comprehension.

The last Mr Crace complained bitterly about Employment Law; today he would have the added burden of Planning Law and Building Regulations so that it is now even more important that the creator of interiors should be fully cognisant of all that bureaucracy can throw at him. Further, the advance of technology has resulted in the necessity to understand IT installations, communication principles, and heating and lighting developments before any construction or cosmetic decisions are determined.

In semantic terms it seems to have taken a long time to accord the Interior Designer with a full and clear title, and the use of the word 'decorator' has confused the issue. The Craces started by calling themselves decorators but were quickly involved in the full responsibility of design. That swift reappraisal goes a long way to resolving the issues between the two words. Essentially design and decoration are part and parcel of the entire process of building or renovating a house. Impossible to apply decoration to a non-existent design or indeed to devise decorative schemes without full comprehension of the basic structure. In the years between the advent of the 'lady decorators' and the present state of the interior design world it was considered demeaning to refer to someone as a decorator, but given the character of work carried out in this mode by celebrated artists like Jean Bérain, perhaps it is acceptable to take the view that the two skills are, if not one and the same, so closely related as to be inter-changeable.

The English Style

In the years after the end of hostilities in 1945, it seemed that there was a general determination to carry life on from the date that England declared war in 1939. It was a mood of restoration, of an intense desire to go back in time and pick up the familiarities of urban or rural life as they had been in the 1920s and 1930s. In 1945 I was fourteen and about to leave school. For my generation, the Great Depression was a story unconnected to reality and the Great War, the one to end all the others, was a part of history. For those returning from active service and those who had been left in support of the country there was huge relief and a determination that life could be restored to normality. Few thought to consider the truth about normality in terms of the future. The good old days were a powerful memory.

By the time I was seventeen the country was reassembling itself. The detritus of bomb damage had been cleared away, fewer women were working in factories and on the farms and the London season had begun to resume a pattern of dances and parties that, given continuing rationing, seems amazing in retrospect. Even presentations at the Palace were resumed until they finally ceased in 1958, but Queen Charlotte's Ball soldiered on with its Birthday Cake and white clad debutantes until 1976.

Rationing did not only apply to food. Building materials were in short supply as were any domestic or decorative products. Industrial manufacture had been given over entirely to the war effort, to the production of planes, guns, ships, and ammunition; to the requirements for uniforms and boots and anything else that would contribute to final success. And of course the efforts of any designers left behind in England were dedicated to the creation of such products, large and small.

It was in this climate that I visited Michael Inchbald's exhibition at Peter Jones and was enchanted by his exploitation of antiques, the one form of furniture then in plentiful supply and at reasonable prices. He was the first designer to look creatively at historical styles and realize that here was an important market, not just for the rarefied client but for a much more practical public looking for tables and chairs and sofas. This success led him finally into several years of antique dealing which he enjoyed but which was eventually overtaken by the work of his studio.

At the outbreak of war interior design and decoration had come to an abrupt halt. Syrie Maugham, with American connections, continued to work but the partnership of Colefax and Fowler ceased for the duration, to be resuscitated after the war by Mrs Nancy Tree, later Nancy Lancaster, who purchased Sybil's firm and installed it in premises in Brook Street under the management of John Fowler. Still known as Colefax and Fowler, the list of mega clients was augmented by the Anglo-American contacts of Mrs Tree, whose own house, Haseley Court, was itself decorated by John and became something of an icon in the regeneration of the English country house. Extensive work of rejuvenation on many of the great English country houses turned John Fowler into an exceptional authority on the styles of architecture and decoration over the periods of the 17th and 18th century, but Georgian Britain was his true expertise, and in due course he was consulted frequently by the National Trust, remaining their advisor for many years after his retirement in 1975. John was one of the great decorators of his generation and enjoyed a partnership with a woman of equally great taste, Nancy Lancaster, although Lady Astor remarked of the pair that they were the "most unhappy unmarried couple in England." Be that as it may, between them they established a distinctive design and decoration philosophy, based largely on a shared devotion to all that was 18th century and to the notion that England was a treasure house.

The National Trust in these post-war years was also burgeoning. It was inundated with offers of beautiful buildings that owners could no longer afford to keep or quite simply could not use. The Trust's management adopted competent marketing methods and the number of visitors, both local and overseas, increased accordingly. The private work of John Fowler and his association with the Trust must surely have developed what became known as the English style. This was a form of elegant 18th-century furniture and fashions adapted to the smaller houses and apartments in which the clients now predominantly lived. This particular fashion referred, not so much to any single period, but to the rather odd development of style which goes on in large country houses; it was a series of make-overs by the generations, so that a Chippendale chair might be recovered, or discarded into a minor part of the house, even its legs reduced so that it could be used in a kitchen or in the servants' quarters. Queen Anne chests originally on stands are still found without the original stand; this is because, outdated, they were moved into a minor room where the ceiling height did not accommodate both sections and so the stand would be discarded. The pre-war English upper class didn't embark on re-decoration in the same way as in the 20th century. Their attention to the needs of their houses was on the whole much gentler or indeed more prudent and to some extent it was an attitude that had been cushioned by peace. Nor were the English a mobile population so that interiors tended to be added to rather than totally redesigned.

In the great houses in past days, servants were plentiful, everything was cared for, there was no technology to damage artefacts. The most vulnerable of the decorations were fabrics and even those were protected with summer covers, or dust covers in the family absences. Furniture was carefully and regularly polished, carpets were taken out and beaten, brass door furniture sparkled from constant attention, watercolours were kept in portfolios against the damage of the sun.

New brides might well bring in new fashions or new furniture, but it was less usual for an architect or designer to have the opportunity to do a complete renovation, and as a result these houses boasted wonderful furniture and furnishings from the past. The preferences of several generations were like a kaleidoscope of fashion and this was what John Fowler was so skilled at reproducing in more modest buildings than Haseley Court, and on balance with rather less money. The Fowler style became immensely popular and it is interesting to reflect that he was working successfully at the same time as Michael Inchbald and David Hicks, both brilliant but different, and the modernists Robin Day and Hugh Casson.

One of the most significant results of Fowler's work was the stimulus it accorded to the wide variety of skilled artisans who were called on to recreate or regenerate paint finishes, gilding, plasterwork, carving and many more detailed works that form part of what Thomas Hope referred to as "the decoration of houses".

However, given that the world was moving into the 21st century, this sentimental retrospection was surprising or was it still part of the post-war desire for what appeared to have been a better world? It degenerated into a strange affectation, a fashion called 'boho', an abbreviation of 'bohemian', which translates as unconventional but artistic. John's restorations drew attention to old fabrics irrevocably faded but still charming, the patina of woods that had been enhanced over generations by polish, and the finish of fine gilding now softened by age. 'Antique' is only a nuance away from 'shabby' and soon with a curious relationship to the Colefax and Fowler creed of sympathetic restoration, smart-scruffy became all the rage. Manufacturers produced linens and chintzes that deliberately appeared to be faded, polished surfaces were distressed, age of itself was suddenly fashionable.

It was a style that might be described as the 'cult of shabby chic', encouraging a lack of discipline that I have never comprehended.

A New Generation

The connotation of age was linked to aristocracy, a social convention that had survived history, and this in itself was appealing to the new and wider public purchasing power. The Fowler restoration of previous ages was a form of treasuring past glories and the fashion discovered plenty of minor but aged objects or buildings that could be imbued with what became a strange reverence. I recall a magazine giving a full colour page to a door, a cottage or stable door featuring layers of paint and years of wear and tear. I found this use of a full page to be extraordinary. It had no educational value, it really could not claim cosmetic attraction and if it had been shown in its own context it would have appeared as exactly what it was, a shabby door. What was the message of the editor to her readers? Was this an example of rural nonchalance, or an atavistic desire to be returned to the relaxed comfort of the nursery? This style was taken up enthusiasticlly by the media, I suspect because the media were desperate for a story and probably because shabby doors were very inexpensive!

Chapter 12

The 1920s and 1930s had seen a development of hedonism in interior design and decoration which seems incongruous alongside the architecture of the same period. This was so significant in its own identity that the architects were increasingly and naturally finishing their own buildings to the final detail. Destruction and deprivation may have prompted a psychological reaction to the war which resulted in John Fowler's purist restorations of houses which had, in their time, celebrated prosperity. There is no doubt that his firm was responsible for a surge of interest in the 18th and 19th centuries' artefacts and furniture as well as the lifestyle directed by opportunity. Nevertheless the influence of America, largely through film and magazine, was powerful and had great attraction.

Oliver Messel

The reasons for this are obvious. American interior designers were no longer primarily concerned with large houses, but with domestic dwellings with quite different priorities to those of the many turn-of-the-century palaces that had been built in the American 1900s. The middle classes in the US were increasingly short of servants, as were those in the UK, and America's design industry produced a myriad of comfort and convenience products that had immediate appeal in England. Heating was better, electrical products were superior, lighting was innovative and of course heavily influenced by the skills of the film makers. Further the American designers' constructive attitude of support to the work entailed in the running of a house was irresistible. Both designers and clients in England looked to the New World for the pattern of lifestyle that would develop in the post war years.

In 1950 Elsie de Wolfe died and Syrie followed her in 1955. Neither were officially working in their last years. Syrie sold her business to Fortnum and Mason, the firm that originally inspired her career, but her offices in Paradise Row had been destroyed in the London bombing.

Luminaries who were established in the 1930s included Oliver Messel, primarily a stage designer but like Inigo Jones very much an arbiter of fashion. Like Bill Pahlmann he worked in camouflage during the war, largely in the South West of England where he was able to indulge his fantasies by turning pill boxes variously into ruins or haystacks!

In 1953 he was commissioned to create the decoration of a suite in the Dorchester Hotel, a lavish affair to match the fantasy of any of the early Stuart masques or the inspirations of Tony Duquette. It was said to be Elizabeth Taylor's favourite residence in London and became a venue for publicity presentations. So well-known did it become that it was never referred to as the Dorchester suite, but always as the Oliver Messel Suite. Less well known is that the young John Siddeley also did a significant amount of work on this famous suite alongside Messel. Most of Messel's work was in the theatre so the OM Suite is one of the few commissions that survives apart from his work on villas in Mustique.

John Siddeley

Oliver Ford, who eventually had a Royal Warrant from the Queen Mother, was younger, born in 1925, so that his career as a designer was largely post-war and peaked with his commission to do the interiors of the Castle of Mey. He trained at the Arts University, Bournemouth where he studied Decorative Arts, going on to work at Lenygon and Morant, and later at Jansen in Paris under Stephane Boudin. His work was elegant but traditional. Indeed he purchased Lenygon and Morant, a firm that had started early in the 19th century, and Howard Chairs, a firm of upholsterers and cabinetmakers started in 1820, both of them firms of considerable distinction which he reinvigorated. As a designer he had an immensely successful career, including not only the Queen Mother amongst his clients but the Duke of Marlborough, both of them clients with substantial properties. He was known for his management abilities and it is entirely due to him that Howard Chairs still enjoys an impressive reputation. Howard designs were not, however, in any way innovative; they looked back to the early years of the 20th century when deeply comfortable armchairs were becoming popular and the relaxation in clothes fashions allowed for lounging! There were therefore distinct guidelines on how interior design might proceed. John Fowler's classicism was supported by the traditionalists like Oliver Ford whilst the fantasists like Messel and Duquette provided for an audience that liked to be startled into excitement; the new architecture of the 20th century was carving out a style of elegance, convenience and fresh perspectives that owed nothing to history.

It was against this background in the 1950s that Michael Inchbald, partly-trained architect, painter David Hicks, actor John Siddeley and concert pianist Australian Jon Bannenberg would venture into the world of English interior design. All four were interesting and challenging characters and together they made a very considerable impact on the 1950s and 1960s.

It is more than possible that these designers would have gone to an Interior Design School if one had been available. Michael, who was called up to serve in the war, could not have gone to Parsons anyhow, and it may not have been an option for Australian Jon Bannenberg who studied at the Sydney Conservatorium of Music.

Sometime in the late 1950s I met David Hicks and Michael and I went to dine with him and see the work he had done on his mother's house. The drawing room presented an air of vitality and youthful perspective. I do not recall any antiques, but I remember a collection of vivid paintings. David explained that they were his work but that he was now embarking on a career in interior design. With his painterly eye and his knowledge of hue, David broke every rule in the colour book with the greatest success. His work demonstrated a particular confidence in this respect, and in his use of pattern, so that surely even Anthony Denney would have been 'startled.'

Chapter 12

In designing his carpets and fabrics, David found a source in *The Grammar of Ornament*, a monumental work first published in 1856 by architect/designer Owen Jones, still in print. Jones was a close associate of Henry Cole of the V&A and a well-known design theorist during that vibrant century of design development. David went on to a spectacular career, his work always typified by his control and exploitation of colour and his appreciation of form and space. As a result of his outstanding talent, his client list was daunting including as it did the Queen, and Helena Rubinstein, queen of the cosmetic industry! In the mid 1950s he worked with Peter Evans of Eating House fame, who described him as a genius, largely on the basis of David's capacity to analyse a site and immediately produce a comprehensive scheme of ambience and design. Both Hicks and Evans worked with Patrick Garnett of Garnett, Cloughley, Blakemore, the architects of the Chelsea Drugstore, a building which helped to establish the reputation of the King's Road with its innumerable boutiques. Garnett was the founding member of GCB, a firm of architects who carried out a stream of interesting commissions until Tony Cloughley resigned on the basis, I was told by Patrick, that 'there was insufficient private patronage in England.' This was certainly true at that time. In fact he was also quoted as saying that he was fed up with the 'rat race of administration and the complexities of bureaucracy', something the last Mr Crace had long ago experienced.

Cloughley was a great loss to the English architectural scene, but before he left he had designed an enchanting pavilion in three sections for the chairman of Rank Hovis, the perfect small house for a busy executive and his wife.

Jon Bannenburg in his King's Road, Chelsea apartment.

Jon Bannenberg meanwhile had purchased a house in the same 18th-century Chelsea terrace as Argyll House, the erstwhile home of Sybil Colefax. Although Jon was an inspired contemporary designer, he treated the panelled interiors with sympathy and it was only when he moved to Carlyle Square that he really unleashed his talents for interior design. Jon was not only a design genius but had a dry sense of humour and boundless energy, a combination which took him to the very pinnacle of the career that he finally elected to pursue, designing and building many of the world's greatest and most beautiful yachts. For a time he was a very popular and challenging lecturer at Inchbald.

Before that he had premises in John Partridge's antique emporium in Bond Street, a felicitous arrangement combining as it did the very best of design talent and superlative antiques. While lecturing at Inchbald he met a charming Greek student, Chrysanthe, who suggested that he offer design services to a member of her family in Athens, and accordingly to Athens he went. It was in Greece that the love affair with yachts and the sea began, and Jon became the most iconic designer of the sailing world. In a holiday novel one day I read that the heroine had acquired "a Jon Bannenberg yacht" noted as a most significant achievement; this struck me as the ultimate in good publicity!

After Michael left school, Michael Inchbald's father had decided to send his son travelling in Europe with a classics tutor known to the family as "poor, dear Willie". Together they went to France, Italy and Greece and there is no doubt that poor, dear Willie's considerable erudition formed the cornerstone of Michael's own extensive command of the European styles of architecture and decoration.

On Michael's return from India he had resumed his education at the Architectural Association, joining a class which included students much younger than himself. He was still only 26 but had travelled the world in strange circumstances, and like many other military personnel who returned to education he was restless and anxious to get on with his life. In addition he was selected for a position as a set designer, a job which did not eventually materialise, but prompted him, nevertheless, to leave his studies. Selected by James Gardner to work on the Britain Can Make It Exhibition, he began to get private commissions, won awards for product design and finally was offered the position as head of the Peter Jones Interior Design Department. His design talents were brilliantly displayed there but his lack of interest in management was all too evident. However he was lucky to spend nearly two years in the department working with the experienced decorator who had been in charge for several years, from whom there is no doubt he learned a great deal. During this time he designed and decorated his apartment in 10 Milner Street, his study/bedroom in particular showing a strength of choice and style which would identify his work for the rest of his career and demonstrate a strong American influence.

Michael was a brilliant spatial designer, perhaps attributable to the fact that he was colour blind and thus insensitive to the distortions that colour and hue can create. His knowledge of style and his capacity to empathise with the designer's mind enabled his assembly of the fine collection of furniture and objects which filled the large drawing room he eventually created out of two of the main bedrooms of the house. His command of space made him an ideal designer to tackle public buildings and in the late 1950s he started extensive work for the Savoy Group, notably in the large ballroom and the private dining rooms. The ocean liner QEII, and the Berkeley Hotel followed among work for private clients impressed by the glamour of Michael's own house.

In 1961 the twenty-one-year old Mark Hampton met David Hicks in London. It was as a result of this relationship that Hampton would later open a Hicks office in New York, so it was clear that the two designers shared philosophies in common. There is no doubt that some of Hampton's finest work showed an influence, not just from Hicks himself but from the classic work of John Fowler. Hampton's interiors reflect the splendour of the English Country House but with a very American bias. There is nothing shabby here, and nothing remotely related to the pretence of ageing or fading. Hampton's interiors in this genre have all the elegance and sparkle that is associated not only with the American decorators but with the suppliers like Scalamandre, famous for their fabrics and passementerie, with whom Hampton himself worked. In London the Hicks studio was run by Inchbald graduate Stephen Ryan, who during his management years gave a new twist to the Hicks signature.

In 1962 David Mlnaric, then in his early twenties, joined the Inchbald Studio where he worked with Michael for a year after the Bartlett School of Architecture. In 1964 he opened his own studio in Bourne Street, Belgravia, initially doing classic/modern interiors but moving on to specialise in historic houses and extensive work for museums. His business was extended to Paris and contemporary designers joined the partnership to widen the style of the studio to an international level. Mlnaric himself began to specialise on the interiors of historic houses in the manner of John Fowler becoming, like Fowler, the accepted authority on the crafts and skills employed by the original workmen. The manner in which these interiors could be restored with integrity became a Mlnaric speciality.

David Mlnaric was born in 1939 ten years before John Pawson, who studied architecture after time spent in Japan, and became the leading exponent of minimalism in England. The marked difference in the styles of these two designers demonstrated the individuality of thought flourishing in the same generation.

These differences have occurred fairly consistently, defying the identification of fashion. On the one hand the purity of Classicism challenged by a burgeoning interest in the complexity of Gothick architecture; in another century Philip Johnson, designer of the improbable Glass House, was a contemporary of Elsie de Wolfe; and the elegance of Art Deco shared public enthusiasm with the style that cartoonist/architect Osbert Lancaster mocked as 'Vogue' Regency. Defining the art of interior design and decoration is no easy matter but Lancaster's book of cartoons, identifying and lampooning the styles of European design and decoration, is a sine qua non for any design library and a witty guide for students of the subject.

The Inchbald School

The Inchbald School was first established in our own large house in Chelsea in 1960, in spite of the fact that Michael did not consider it to be either a good or a sensible idea. The house at No. 10 Milner Street was very individual and had a curious history. It was built in 1849 by a youngish and successful building contractor for himself and his family. John Todd had previously lived in Cheyne Walk, in one of the elegant 18th-century houses on the river that would, in the mid-19th century, have been considered to be very old fashioned. At the time that he decided to move house to something grander he was employing some eighty workers so he was already a businessman of significance. He negotiated a land deal with the Trustees of the Dame Mary Milner Trust, effectively allowing him to build a given number of 'second-class houses' on a site in Chelsea adjoining the Hans Sloane estate, the Trust insisting that the houses should be completed within a stated period of time. Perhaps these parameters protected Dame Mary's interests against the possibility of the Todd enterprise failing, but there seemed to be no risk of that – Todd was a hardworking and ambitious man. He duly created a terrace of houses, Milner Street, to the stated level of second class. He also built a double-fronted house for himself, cleverly sited in the centre of the terrace so that the Northern aspect looked straight down the street opposite, giving maximum light to the interior of the building. This house was more than double the size of its neighbours, with a fashionably Italianate façade embellished with the latest in plate glass fenestration, a stucco rather than brick finish and an impressive conservatory at the end of the magnificent ground floor drawing room. Mr Todd called his new home Stanley House, presumably because it faced down Stanley Street, now better known as Ovington Street, the property of the Cadogan Estate.

Beyond the stable yard Todd installed a very large building works and created offices in the house next door which were accessed by a corridor from the first-floor landing of his own house. The resulting archway led to a large building yard which included the coach house, and stables for four horses, making 10 Milner Street the headquarters of Mr Todd's business.

His interior design thinking was unusual. Unlike most London houses, the drawing room, some thirty feet long, was on the ground floor and the whole of the first floor was comprised of four bedrooms. Todd's own dressing room was sited directly over the front door.

The top floor appears to have accommodated staff under a mansard roof which impacted on the rooms' proportions, a point which would not have concerned an ambitious mid-19th-century builder. Staff comfort was not then a priority.

Given the generous flight of the front door steps, the basement proportions were surprising; the rooms about ten feet high, with large windows providing ample light and air to a kitchen as large as the drawing room above, a servants' hall, a butlers' pantry and a larder.

By the time it was finished in 1851, Stanley House, with its cream stucco elevation and massive portico, had much in common with its fashionable neighbours in the newly-developing Belgravia of the Marquess of Westminster. Mr Todd was edging up the social ladder but the life of the family was overshadowed by the suicide of one of his daughters, said to have cut her throat with her father's razor in his dressing room. For sometime after this event the house was left empty with a reputation for being haunted.

Eventually it was let at a commensurate rent to the Vicar of St Luke's Chelsea and afterwards to one of the Fitzgeralds. In view of the tragic death of Todd's daughter both the vicar and the Catholic Fitzgeralds had the house exorcised. Finally, it was let to Mrs Arthur Ilbert, a still young and wealthy widow with two children, Courtenay and Rosemary Ilbert. At the end of the tenancy Mrs Ilbert and her son purchased the property and Stanley House remained in the family until the death of Rosemary's son, Michael Inchbald, in 2016 when it was put on the market.

The House had, however, enjoyed considerable significance during Courtenay Ilbert's tenure, during which time the drawing room was gradually emptied of furniture and filled, not so gradually, with Courtenay's collection of horology.

Initially Michael Inchbald had an apartment in the house, and a visit to the old Drawing Room, now the Clock Room, with his uncle Courtenay was something of a highlight. By the time I met him Courtenay had retired from professional work; now lacking a drawing room he used the dining room and at any given time he could be found sitting by the fire in a large 18th-century wing chair studying, or alternatively at his work table in the Clock Room, mending, adjusting or cleaning whatever item required attention. He was an expert in horological maintenance.

Horology is something of an abstruse hobby but nevertheless there are collectors and professionals all over the world and by the time Courtenay was in his sixties, his reputation was worldwide in spite of the fact that he sought neither publicity nor approbation. It was therefore no surprise when someone, announcing herself as Mr Wontner's secretary, asked if Mr Wontner could pay Mr Ilbert a visit. Courtenay was surprised but typically incurious and in due course a large car drew up and a man with an air of both distinction and authority was ushered in to the dining room. His grandfather, he said, was an amateur horologist and in his spare time he had made three watches. Since he was also a prison Governor, he decided not to sign them with his own name but to call himself RENTNOW, his name spelt in reverse. This captured Courtenay's attention but they were unable to take the matter very far. Before he left Mr Wontner inspected Michael's suite of rooms and was duly impressed. Mr Wontner was chairman of the Savoy Group and this felicitous visit led immediately to the start of Michael's extensive work for this leading London hotel.

When Michael and I married in 1955, Courtenay gave us the house as a wedding present. Quite soon afterward he expressed worry over the fate of the clock collection in the event of his death. I asked him which option he would prefer between selling the collection on the open market or letting it go to a museum.

"I would like my life's work to stay together – in a Museum" he replied "but I would be sorry to deny other collectors the pleasure I have had from collecting." No answer, only on the one hand or on the other. He died in 1956, and the most extensive collection of time measurement ever assembled went to the British Museum. We thought that, on balance, that is what he would have wanted and indeed that it would be a fitting memorial. The great Clock Room, shorn of its conservatory, was initially used to display the larger antiques we then had for sale.

By this time, I was doing a lot of the buying and came home one day with a 12-foot Chippendale mirror. The dealer, unable to accommodate its height in his showroom, sold it to me for £15 and when Michael saw it he remarked irritably "No wonder". We could just fit it into the height of the drawing room and it took builder Wally Wright and his father both time and considerable expertise to secure. As soon as it was hung an American dealer bought it and the Wrights had to return the next day to take it down again.

The mirror proved to be something of a catalyst.

It was clear that Michael's design talents were of greater importance than the antiques and I henceforth gave much thought to the promotion of his design studio.

Chapter 12

I was 27, pregnant, less ignorant and with a limited but very varied experience of work, both office and marketing. I am not clear who suggested, or why I decided, to find out about public relations. It was not an area about which I knew much, if anything, but whatever the reason I decided to go straight to the heart of the matter and contact whatever professional organization I could find and this I did. I was greeted with some surprise and perhaps a little confusion.

"You would like to promote an interior designer?" This appeared to be a baffling idea but I persisted and found myself talking to the chairman who suggested he might perhaps visit me to discuss the matter further. I had the feeling that he was as keen to promote his profession as I was keen to promote Michael's talent.

Accordingly, he came to Stanley House and I explained why I wanted promotion for my husband and the aims I wished to achieve for him. It seemed that this rather personal brief surprised him but he was intrigued, leaving me with three names to contact or, if I wished, to interview. One of the names belonged to a woman.

Geraldine Hill had been a well-known and very well-paid journalist, a *Times Magazine* correspondent; she was one of the brightest and most amusing people I have met and she became a good and very interesting friend. She tended to be prone to nervous strain and love affairs and I think it was the former that had prompted her to leave the rigours of journalism for the quieter province of working from home. She was also in love at the time and rearranging the pattern of her life.

She was incredibly easy to brief, very quick on the uptake and well informed about her own world and above all, those many women journalists who would prove to be such an incredible support to the new Inchbald enterprise in the future.

With Courtenay's death the clock collection had been gone to the British Museum and Michael was then free to start the reconstruction of the interior of the house, work that had been on his drawing board months before building actually started. His most important decision was to create a drawing room on the first floor, using two of the bedrooms to recreate the space provided previously on the ground floor.

This left the old drawing room empty.

Co-incidentally we had made contact with one or two of the great American designers featured in what became known colloquially as Condé Nast's *Yellow Book*, and were delighted to hear from them that on their way to raise funds for a Venice in some post-war distress, they proposed to stop in London on their journey to Italy. The antique market in London at this time was flourishing, flooded with the contents of the many hundreds of houses across the country being abandoned and destroyed in the rush to downsize, including many whose families had been among the great patrons of the past. The Americans were more than happy to have a contact in the heart of the city during their visit to London, as well as a guide to the best of the antique dealers. Among the group was William Pahlmann.

Bill was a big, handsome Texan with a huge enthusiasm for his profession and his work. He had trained as a designer at Parsons School, continuing his studies in their Paris faculty during the 1920s. It was hard work, he pointed out, 'and I used to drive a lorry to pay the fees, studying with my text book propped on the wheel.' It was an impressive if worrying image! He was astonished to hear that London had no dedicated interior design school and that the only source of tuition for a designer at the top level of the profession would still be Parsons. I had several conversations with him and received nothing but enthusiasm for the notion of a design school. The empty drawing room had already tempted my idea of organizing some kind of tuition programme and the encouragement of Bill, and interior designer Guy Roop from California was incredibly reassuring. The entrepreneurial energy of America was infectious, in spite of Michael's express disapproval. I suspect his reluctance was based on the understandable view that he preferred to concentrate on his glittering design talent and the interests of his studio. I was undeterred however, and was adamant that the two ventures could flourish side by side with benefit to both. Interestingly the Americans were even more persuasive that there should be a professional body in Britain to present the profession and lead it forward. Their enthusiasm and encouragement was to have a profound effect on the future development of interior design in England.

Reviewing the interior designer/decorators that I knew or knew of, I hesitated to think they might easily be led or indeed be enthusiastic about linking themselves to a professional organisation. England in this respect was still famous for gifted amateurs with the emphasis on talent and social skills rather than working ambition.

With Geraldine's skills and help, we achieved a lot of publicity for the developing interiors at No. 10, made so elegant by Michael. *House and Garden* featured Stanley House, printing posters with an image of the velvet-clad drawing room titled 'Is this the most beautiful room in London?' Unhappily they took so long to go to print that Michael unwittingly allowed *L'Oeil* to feature the room and its collection, enraging the Condé Nast editor, Robert Harling; he declared that he would never feature Michael again and he never did. It was childish, but I don't think it inhibited Michael's career. There are politics in every profession!

After the birth of my daughter Amanda in 1960, it seemed appropriate to pursue the idea that the profession of interior design in England should have the same educational support that it had long enjoyed in America.

Chapter 12

I asked Geraldine to help me but she was embarking on marriage and refused "You can do it yourself" she remarked. "I have taught you all I know". So I began to market and publicise and it proved to be much easier than I had anticipated. The fact was that, apart from Geraldine's tuition, everyone loved the story – it came at just the right moment.

The launch of the School was marketed via the personal advertisement columns in *Country Life*, a magazine popular with informed country and art lovers. By September 1960, the programmes were written, the lecturers assembled and with a week to go there were no students.

No applications – and no students at all.

In order to get this good idea off the ground and into some sort of educational programme I did require students and there was only one week to go before Michael's reservations would be justified!

I have never forgotten the first applicant who came for interview at the beginning of that week. She appeared on Monday, a pretty young woman from Ireland with dark hair and a charming smile. To my surprise she explained that she was a nurse, looking for a change of career. She was the precursor of many such changes-of career-students we have had, particularly in the last twenty years, but at that time her courage was a revelation to me. In the mid-20th century professionals settled into their chosen path, expecting to spend their lives pursuing promotion and finally a pension, without having peered beyond their chosen parameters. A girl who had decided and trained, to become a nurse, had surely made up her mind early in her teens that nursing was her aim. The courage now to give up the training and experience of one career to embark on another, at a time when the design profession was not officially established, seemed to me to be the very epitome of determination and independence.

So I explained that I needed a quorum to start on the following Monday, or I wonder if I really did do that? Whatever the case, I did not lose a night's sleep during the following week, demonstrating a striking lack of imagination. In those remaining days seven more students were enrolled and the first Inchbald term started on the appointed Monday.

I needed seven students simply to cover the costs involved in employing teaching staff, but for those budding entrepreneurs contemplating similar enterprises I have to say that since I was working in our own house I was spared the problems of rent, at least in the first three years, but I still had a lot to learn about budgets.

The following September I enrolled forty students, a number which proved there was both requirement and demand and this went a long way to justifying the decision to implement the original idea. The Inchbald School had started quietly and now it appeared to be moving forward successfully.

For the previous 7 or 8 years, I had worked with Michael and helped him to start first an antiques business and latterly a studio. Apart from learning a great deal about Interior design, it was evident that the decorative elements, fabrics, lighting, floor covering, were not only of great importance to the result, but that their qualities of manufacture needed to be clearly understood in the manner in which they were deployed, and knowledge of their use involved specific instruction.

The Inchbald antique business had been founded partly on my own experience of the antique world, but also on the fact that Michael, lacking design work, had spent time collecting antiques that he considered he could use in future commissions. He had also gone so far as to purchase fine quality but unusable pieces with a view to readapting them to a more contemporary purpose. Large 19th-century sideboards were a good example. He turned the end cupboards into sofa-end tables, or bedside tables, by separating them from the main body and giving them marble tops; the top of the sideboard became a coffee table, supported by the handsome feet of the original piece of furniture. Michael's knowledge and exploitation of historic style was extensive and it became part of his lifelong study of design. It was also an excellent introduction for students to the flexibility and interest of the designer's mind.

Meanwhile I was working very hard to build up the studio and with Geraldine's help we got a great deal of interest from the popular press. Private commissions were also multiplying, emphasising my interest in the myriad skills I was encountering.

I was quite clear as to the aim of the new programme and also the subjects that I wanted included in the curriculum. Interviewing lecturers was interesting and also inspiring so that gradually I formed a very comprehensive view of how to proceed, and one of the first issues that concerned me was the inclusion of the history of period styles in both art, architecture and furniture. The size of the project was daunting but by breaking it down into subjects rather than periods it became more acceptable.

The inclusion of paintings could perhaps have provoked surprise in an educator with more experience, but my view was that painting is one of the quickest and least expensive ways for an artist of any kind to convey the expression of thought and opinion. Canvas and paint are relatively cheap and mobile so the impact of the artist on the developing world of design, or fashion if you prefer, can flag up trends faster than does architecture which takes so much longer to realise. A very good example of the immediacy of such influence can be found in the work and spectacular rise of Andy Warhol, who in his short life and with media support, impacted on the perceptions of the art world as surely no other before him.

Chapter 12

On the other hand, the inclusion could not be labelled as tuition in Fine Art which is covered extensively by many Universities, is widely written about and is in itself very specific. My view was to identify the work of the painter as artistic expression, a personal opinion which is a different issue from artistic achievement.

Finding an expert to express this slightly radical view was not easy; furniture presented little problem because I knew several people who worked at the Victoria and Albert Museum, among them John Hayward who had a wide-ranging knowledge and experience. However, he was primarily a brilliant authority on silver and he very courteously suggested that his wife Helena might be able to help.

Stephen Garrett

I knew nothing about her, but we got on well and whilst she was fairly definite in her views on style, she was not only intrigued by the idea of a dedicated school but pleased to be able to put her expertise to useful effect. Her particular speciality was the 18th century in England, France and Austria but her knowledge was not limited to these countries and she was a dedicated and enthusiastic teacher. She remained a tutor at the School for many years and became a kind and helpful friend.

Architecture was covered by architect Stephen Garrett, whose interests were more contemporary, although later in his career he worked with Getty on the construction of the Getty Museum, a replica of the House of the Papyri at Pompeii. It was an enterprise which demonstrated his very open mind. He was a brilliant lecturer, engaging the students' attention and constantly challenging their standards and their opinions.

The real gaps lay in the skills of interior decoration which were then implemented by a diminishing group of skilled craftsmen and workshops and this vital area remained a serious challenge. Craftsmen are not renowned as lecturers or teachers. Too often they work alone or in small groups, dedicated to their personal achievements in a world of committed attention to quality and detail.

Historically the skills of the 18th and 19th century were passed on through a simplistic but most efficient pattern of apprenticeship, and in the wake of two world wars, the system was breaking down fast. Financial reward had not kept pace with the salaries young men could achieve in more prosaic occupations, and learning at the rate of apprenticeships did not compare with the immediacy of better money for occupations which were so much less demanding.

There was a cabinetmaker we used at the end of Ovington Street, who did indeed have such an apprentice, paid perhaps three pounds a week. Soon the young man left and when I inquired about him, his boss remarked drily "Gone to do spot welding, makes ten pounds a week – and in another twenty years he'll still be spot welding." It was perhaps an unfair view, but the new generation did seem to lack both patience and tolerance. The world was a different and much faster place in the 1940s and 1950s than it had been in the 1930s and everyone needed to get on with a new set of aspirations.

I did manage to persuade my upholsterer to give demonstrations, explaining the while about the varieties of material old and new, their possibilities and limitations, all of it a revelation to students who had never thought to enquire about the manner in which interior decorating effects were achieved. One day sometime in the third term, a visitor who insisted on seeing me turned out to be a teacher of curtain making at one of the polytechnics, and explained that she could teach these skills to my students. I welcomed her with very open arms – here was a woman, not only skilled but a teacher by training and her contribution was invaluable. She stayed with us until her retirement.

It struck me that I should consider taking students to workshops, to the Building and Design Centres and to the fabric and carpet merchants to see and feel for themselves rather than sit in an endless series of lectures. One famous workshop we visited was Jacksons in Fulham, the home of the *stuccadores*; here were all the moulds created and used by the Adam brothers and when the great house at Sledmere that Adam had built was damaged by fire, it was to Jacksons that the architects turned to recreate all the old interior details from the original moulds.

There was a sad footnote to the Jackson visit, which probably took place in 1960 or 1961. The manager was desperately anxious to engage the students' interest with a view to resuscitating the old successes of the firm, but unhappily the students could not really comprehend either the history of the firm or the immense possibilities of their products. The revival of what became known as the English Style was still a long way off. John Fowler was working hard but mainly on properties for private clients as well as for the National Trust. This did not resonate with the perceptions and aspirations of my students. It struck me, however, that many of the workshops we visited were, like Jacksons, anxious to revive their work and reengage the buying public. Modern efficiency and modern products ran counter to historically-established levels of quality and skill and this proved be another aspect which would engage my attention.

Writing the programmes, which were largely based not only on my experience with Michael but on my own assessment of the requirements, I began to share the apprehension that in the post-war quest for new products and fast delivery we were in danger of losing so much talent and brilliant craftsmanship and that it would be very difficult to turn this tide of apathy if it progressed much further.

It seemed to me vital that any educational programme I devised should include instruction about these skills and their development, in order to encourage interest in this fundamental part of design history, an

Chapter 12

area that had until now received a great deal less attention than was accorded to the great architectural and design names with which we are all familiar.

Inchbald was possibly the first educational establishment to take this view.

Design history I viewed as the grammar of the profession and thus I included it officially in the curriculum, following the example of Frank Parsons and his Paris atelier. Much later Sir Hugh Casson also advocated this area of learning when he was in charge of the Royal College of Art.

Jacqueline and Amanda Inchbald

As I sifted through the priorities and assembled the lecturers, slowly the programme began to take shape and I was amazed by the enthusiasm with which my project was greeted by the general public. Architect Stephen Garrett, who had rather mockingly agreed to lecture, now changed his view point. He came to see me and told me that, after all, he had to acknowledge that my idea was not only good but successful! However, he too was of the opinion that there should be a more disciplined approach to the structure and management of the school and if I wanted help, he would be very happy to act as 'a kind of consultant'. For this I was more than grateful. Stephen was extremely efficient and his architectural training filled a large gap in my own experience. He was also a man who looked beyond the present, anticipating not only success but possible failures in the system and I thought his contribution would be invaluable.

We agreed to meet regularly to review events, plan for the future and take into account student comments and student complaints. This was a relationship which proved invaluable to the progress of the school and made a great difference to the style of management. At every meeting Stephen arrived with a list of points he considered we needed to address and the result was a much greater understanding of the way forward and the professional expectation of students. It was the greatest support anyone could possibly have offered me.

Unhappily family matters were not going well and by 1962 Michael and I were discussing divorce. This was finalised in 1963 and whilst it was arranged that the school could stay temporarily at Milner Street, I was urgently looking for other premises to house a project which I now perceived as my future career.

Looking for premises for a school threw up multiple hurdles, even in 1963. Money was an obvious problem, as was location. Milner Street was very central in terms of the London geographic distribution. Mayfair, the heart of London for so long, was beginning to lose its lustre and there was great interest in Chelsea and the potential of both Sloane Street and the King's Road. This was where I wanted to be and prices were rising fast. The wide tracts of the Grosvenor estate were governed by a policy of leasehold properties and indeed many were still held on the last years of long leases granted in the 19th century. The Cadogan estate offered me a charming but grand house just off Cadogan Square, but the lease was short and it became evident that the reason for this was that the big estates were anxious to await developments in the area and thus were reluctant to cast their policies in stone.

Further to the financial worries, there was of course the issue of planning permission. Councils were now aware of the drawbacks of schools to traffic, student safety and the possible disruption to domestic urban life. Established schools had no problems but applying for new school planning was clearly going to be a different matter. I took some comfort from the fact that a mother with small children had formed a childrens' education group in a house in the Vale, Chelsea; this proved to be so successful that it had developed into a full-blown private school to which it appeared the Council had turned a blind eye. I could not, however, afford a house in the Vale!

Time dragged on, Stephen and I went to see several houses that might have been the answer, one in Lowndes Square, another wonderful property down the Fulham Road with a very large garden which my children would have loved. However, in 1963 the Fulham Road, now so fashionable, was almost in the next county. It was not well served by public transport, it was some way from the day schools my children attended, and although there were parking facilities I did not see my students making the journey willingly. In addition, it was a long way from the artistic centre dominated by the Victoria and Albert Museum and the Tate Gallery and access to these was important to the student's requirements.

Local agents knew that an eccentric lady was looking for premises for a so-called Interior Design school but it seemed an unlikely scenario vis-a-vis both money and planning and no-one seemed particularly hopeful. It is one of the reasons I have such sympathy with today's first-time buyers! But a door closes and there is always another ready to open.

My daughter Amanda was attending a school in Eaton Gate owned and run by an elderly lady, Miss Mitford Colmer, who decided to retire and put her house on the market. She had initially been anxious to profit by selling to a developer but the Grosvenor estate would not allow the division of the building. It was therefore on the market as a single building with the last twenty years of a hundred-year lease.

More importantly Miss Mitford Colmer had been running her school there since the 1920s and she had an unshakeable right to the appropriate planning legislation which she was in a position to pass on to any buyer. Luckily for me, few people felt the inclination to run schools in Eaton Gate, and certainly not schools for interior designers. So I inspected the premises, was not allowed into the top three floors where Miss Mitford Colmer lived (and nor was my surveyor) and sight unseen I purchased her lease.

Moving was relatively easy. The Inchbald School stock was no more than about fifty chairs, with some projectors and blackboards, three sewing machines for the curtain classes and a couple of desks for myself and my secretary. No 7 is a large house. I went into the old dining room; my secretary Jacqueline Smith went into the morning room and the students went into the very large first floor drawing room. There was a great deal of space left over and at one point I considered living there, but it was an impractical idea.

Henry Stephenson

Stephen was still running his architectural practice and was unable to take on further work in the school – indeed he probably did not wish to do so. I therefore engaged an extremely nice and formally-trained designer, William Graham, to take on the role of Senior Tutor. Students were now beginning to demand tuition in drawing plans and elevations so we purchased a quantity of drawing equipment and started classes to augment the curriculum. It soon became apparent that there was not sufficient time in the Ten Week Courses to accommodate these classes, and at the same time William tried very hard to convince me to extend the programmes with a year study course. It has to be said I was reluctant. I didn't think my educational background warranted such an ambitious project but William was firm and once again the students were enthusiastic. So, with his help and Stephen's support I launched the Year Course.

During the Milner Street period another young lecturer had started to teach. Henry Stephenson was a multi-talented designer, with brilliant skills in watercolour. He had done one or two perspectives for Michael's projects and when he joined the School it was evident that he was an inspired teacher. Accordingly, he continued to work at 7 Eaton Gate, involving himself more and more in work in the School until he took over the directorship of the Interior Design Faculty, a position he held until his retirement in 1993.

Around this time I was considering furnishing the duplex at the top of No 7 Eaton Gate as home; I sadly missed the days of antique dealing, and the many friends and contacts I had made and I was now seeking both furniture and pictures once again. One day I called on an old friend, Jeremy Maas, now establishing his own business under the name of the Maas Gallery. He and I had discovered a mutual appreciation of Victorian art, in particular the Pre-Raphaelites, but he had once admonished me to be careful: "There is a lot of ullage in this period Jacqueline"! He was of course, quite right – the 19th century developed a huge output of products under the multiple influences of a growing

Empire and on such a scale that there was bound to be development into mediocrity.

When I went to see Jeremy in his gallery, there in front of me was one of the most outstanding works by Lord Leighton – the wondrous drama of *Flaming June*. I was absolutely speechless. Whatever was Jeremy doing with Flaming June for sale? Selling it, of course, was the terse answer and he told me I could have it for £3,000!

Had I taken this incredible painting home to No. 10 Michael would not have been pleased – he disliked most things Victorian, and like a majority of people at that time, he did not like the Pre-Raphaelites. I was now engaged in divorce proceedings and thus newly independent, but I was also engaged in establishing my new venture and facing children's educational costs. Although I thought the price was risible in terms of real value, I was nervous about such an investment. Further I was very aware of the superb quality of the picture and felt that nothing I owned or would acquire could match it, and that it would therefore unbalance any scheme of design or decoration upon which I was about to embark. Jeremy was very persuasive but also honest to the effect that he had approached several dealers and encountered nothing but apathy, something I could hardly believe. In the event I heard that he had sold it to a South American museum, in spite of the fact that he had desperately wanted to keep it in England, Recently his son, Rupert, told me that the museum had got it for £2,000.! It was a great loss to our artistic heritage but hanging it in my drawing room would have been rather like floating the Queen Mary on a local lake. Sadly I resisted the temptation and got on with life's responsibilities.

By 1967 the team at Inchbald was made up of men and women not only competent in their particular fields, (although only one of them had received formal training), but also distinguished for their teaching ability.

None of them, however, was an interior designer to those clients in the rarefied area from which Inchbald, Hicks and Bannenberg were drawing their clients. And none of them knew much about the wide and general history of interior decoration and design. Finally, I found that I myself would have to fill this gap. My knowledge of the history was reasonably extensive but I also did a great deal of research into the period between 1800 and the 1960s on the development of styles, culminating as it did in the period after the depredations of the Second World War. My lectures benefited from my friendship with successful decorators but I was frustrated not to have met several of the great names that were pre-war but still flourishing in the 1950s.

There was outrage at the destruction of so many great houses in the economic chill of the 1950s. It had become a movement of national downsizing among the aristocratic and squirearchy owners, unable to find household staff or afford them, unable to heat the houses or install up-to-date heating and unable to do anything about the parlous state of buildings and interiors. Further to this distress, there was an inevitable temptation to cash in fine furniture and pictures which were all too frequently unappreciated but which also represented possible value. Unhappily the prices obtained were appreciated by collectors and museums but would not match their later worth. The cognoscenti began to object to the loss of fine paintings, among other artefacts, to overseas museums, in particular American ones.

The passage of art exports had been facilitated by Lord Duveen, the son of a Dutch/Jewish art dealer who took over his father's firm in 1906 and cashed in on the immense wealth created over the turn of the century by a flock of brilliant American entrepreneurs. These were people who, having achieved success, wished to display their wealth and had the money to underwrite their social ambitions.

The political and financial upheavals of the 1930s seem to have disrupted the trade and it is interesting to note that Duveen, perhaps the greatest antique dealer of all time, died in 1939 when the first part of the 20th century came to an abrupt halt and priorities, both social and financial, changed. Nevertheless, Duveen had identified the possible value of great artefacts and it is hardly surprising that owners, remembering this, and facing the social revolution of the 1940s and 1950s, would reach for support from the patronage of their ancestors. It must also be noted with sadness that both world wars had inevitably generated a very significant amount of payable estate duty which was an added burden to the estates of England whether large or modest.

In 1967, as Inchbald was bedding down in No. 7, it was announced that British Rail was to demolish the Deepdene, the Italianate country house designed and decorated by Thomas Hope. It was true that after 100 years of the Hope family's occupancy, the house had done time as an hotel and later as railway offices, so that it was certainly in a state of dilapidation. The geographical position was inconvenient for British Rail and the staff, whilst modern office design was taking off in contemporary terms. Whilst in itself the destruction of this house was certainly a deplorable decision it was, nevertheless, inevitable at that time. There was a small storm of protest but we had not yet got to the point when informed opinion could prompt a public outcry, as no doubt would happen today. However, the loss of the Deepdene proved in many ways to be a catalyst. The fact that the issue had been debated publicly gave pause to consider the fact that whilst Hope's house was a loss, it was only one of many such examples covering every style and century in the development of the English Country House.

This saga of destruction was finally halted by the energy and talents of a young man, Roy Strong, who had already invigorated the Portrait Gallery and now took over the directorship of the Victoria and Albert Museum, mounting a brilliant display of architectural tragedy called the Destruction of the English Country House. This was an exhibition that had unparalleled publicity and public attention, and it proved to be a vital turning point in the public vision of English heritage. These were events that reinforced my determination to encourage knowledge and understanding of the history of design and the myriad products of that history.

The Year Course opened in 1967, led by William, who also wrote the programme. In order to define the content of the Year Course I called it Architectural Interior Design, indicating that tuition in practical architectural alterations was included, as well as instruction in the production of working drawings and professional presentations. I also introduced 'real' clients who frequently offered quite different perspectives of taste, priority and requirement to those of the teaching staff or indeed the students. It was a way of broadening the imagination and opening it to new ventures.

Students on the Ten Week Course, meanwhile, were still anxious to learn drawing skills. I had long given up drawing myself, but recalled being asked to draw the front elevation of one of the early-19th-century Italianate villas in Weybridge, which was then a school. The experience of drawing buildings for the first time was captivating and very instructive, forcing me to remark and record every detail of the building's enrichment; it was clear that my students would benefit from this tuition, both practically and culturally. So Stephen set up a studio in his own offices which gave students the opportunity to understand the realities of live projects as well as offering professional insight into the planning of interiors and the concomitant planning laws. The school which I had started in some ignorance was moving forward into an emphasis on the professionalism and the requirements that a working design studio would demand of graduates.

William Graham meanwhile was doing private work for JP Getty and asked for architectural advice: I suggested that he consult Stephen. The two clearly got on well and more projects were commissioned, some in the tycoon's country house. One Saturday, as Stephen was preparing to leave a meeting, Getty turned to him and told him that he had something he would like to discuss further.

"I want to build a Museum," he announced, "to house my collection of antiquities and I want it to be a reproduction of the House of the Papyri." Stephen, whose education was not classical, was floored but not beaten. Careful and circuitous discussion elicited the fact that the House of the Papyri was a private mansion in Herculaneum, destroyed in the eruption of Vesuvius in AD 79, and excavated in 1750 through tunnelling. The work had been abandoned *c*.1755; this was helpful information but did not give much leeway for a fully-fledged discussion about the project.

"This is fascinating,' Stephen declared, "I was going to catch the last train back to London but I could go later if you can arrange a car?" He calculated (and perhaps prayed) that the reportedly tight-fisted client would agree and indeed that is what happened. Stephen caught the last train with the intention of spending Sunday researching in the Greek and Roman department of the British Museum, only to find the Department was closed! So, he contacted an erudite friend and found out the history and circumstances of the Herculaneum excavations. He was informed that the House of the Papyri was presently underneath a tomato farm!

Stephen was one of the most interesting and quirky people I have ever met, and it must surely be true to say that little deterred him, certainly not the prospect of such a challenging project and a move to California. Unhappily for the Inchbald School, he was off on this great adventure almost immediately, so the drawing school was closed almost overnight and we had to set up proper studios at No 7.

A second blow fell when William, married to a lady with properties in the South of France, explained to me that she wished to move there in order to develop them and he of course was going with her as the designer. He was not with the school for very long but he was charming and capable – I was sorry that he had to go but more importantly I was seriously challenged to find his replacement. The Head of Faculty had to have academic qualifications in order to ensure the professionalism of the programming, and indeed to lend gravitas to the School, which had now been running successfully for nearly ten years.

In spite of a great deal of serious publicity and thriving graduates, Inchbald was still looked on as something of a passing phase, a rather sophisticated finishing school full of charming girls on their way to marriage. This entrenched view was difficult to shake, but I fought this reputation with the greatest determination. Quite possibly the publicity itself, in the usual glossy magazines, promoted the impression of a passing fashion rather than the pathway to a serious career.

However, students themselves were becoming far more diverse. Quite soon after the initial year I had decided to impose an age limit; I accepted no-one under eighteen because it became clear that the lower age group had not had enough experience of the world and therefore had little to draw on in terms of stimuli outside their own social and domestic groups.

The years between 1945, the end of the War, and 1960, which marked the foundation of Inchbald, were the years of post-war recovery and they were harsh. When Michael and I married in 1955 we both had ration books athough food rationing was running down during 1954, nearly ten years after the War's end. Thus a sixteen-year-old student in 1960 would have been born in 1939, and would have only experienced the rigours of a country at war and recovering from that trauma. Luxury goods were still at a premium, secondhand upholstery was fetching surprising prices and the antique businesses were flourishing. There was, quite simply, a shortage of everything. In 1946 even bread was rationed for a couple of years.

An older student, Sylvia Mitchell on the Ten Week Course, asked so many questions, and offered so many opinions that I decided to invite her to lunch to find out whether she was enjoying the programme, and what she intended to do with her newly-gained knowledge.

Her story was interesting and something of a revelation. Her new husband, an architect, had recently injured his back in a serious car crash and was told by his doctors that it would be inadvisable to continually stand at a drawing board. He was depressed and she could not encourage him to move on.

"An architect"? I asked, "who can no longer manage to work at a drawing board – could he not come to teach at the school?"

John Odam reluctantly tried a little lecturing, moved on to tutoring in the studio and finally accepted the post of Director of the Architectural Design Course, an appointment he held with great distinction for many years. Sylvia joined him as a tutor specialising in sourcing, an invaluable subject for inexperienced students; working together they made a great contribution to the school's development.

An Association

When Bill Pahlmann and I were discussing design education, he also pointed out that there should be an English equivalent of the AID, the American Institute of Designers, to protect the status of the profession, ensure the quality of education and achievement and establish the integrity of the members.

Accordingly, sometime after the first year of the School and encouraged by the initial reception by the media, I invited David Hicks, John Siddeley and Jon Bannenberg to lunch at Milner Street with Michael and myself. It was on this occasion that I put forward the proposal that together we might plan some kind of association along the lines that Bill had explained to me. The initial reaction was astonishment, but gradually they began to see that it was not only sensible but would most certainly benefit the profession and give it the gravitas that it still lacked in the UK. Discussion was fairly wide, lingering over possible entrants, considering the methodology of qualification and touching on the matter of officers and president. It became clear to me that at least two of my guests thought they should be president but that neither would do the relevant work necessary to that office, and the other two could well be thought of as the junior partners but were capable of management. I remember wondering how it could be resolved when John Siddeley took the ball and ran with it. He suggested that a number of names should be approached with the date of a full meeting and that such a meeting could be held in his showroom in Henrietta Street. Agreement for the idea would be sought from this audience and it was hoped implementation would follow. Meanwhile I had a two-page letter from Jon Bannenberg.

Jacqueline at end-of-term Inchbald School presentations.

He was clearly concerned that I saw myself as taking over the whole project and instructed me, rather tartly, that I should not 'run for queen;" so I stayed away from the Siddeley meeting. When Michael returned he told me that everyone liked the idea but that no-one could decide on who to elect as President! Another meeting failed to resolve the problem and the concept of an association went into limbo until a man called Bonsack thought it would be to the benefit of his bathroom manufacturing firm to resuscitate the project. This he did with the aid of a charming previous employee of ours who called me to see if I would have any objection to his collaborating with Godfrey Bonsack. Even if I could have objected I would not have done so – I was anxious to see the establishment of a governing body put in place; but by this time I was so busy that I could not do more than support any efforts towards that aim.

In 1966 Bonsack had achieved a quorum of possible members, a company secretary and for reasons which were not clear to me, the lawyer, Victor Mishcon; they held a meeting in a house in Belgravia to which I was invited, and the association was established, but the subsequent story was not happy and it would be some time before an association of which the design world could be proud actually rose from the ashes of the first efforts.

Bonsack was entirely self-interested. He had already tried to secure the services of both David and Michael, explaining to them that he would promote their designs under his banner. Neither rose to the bait, both declaring separately that they did not trust him, so his plan came to nothing.

Late in 1964 an old friend, Dominic Elwes, came to see me with his idea for an annual Directory of Designers which he wanted me to edit. Briefly, each contributing designer would take a page (or more) which was paid for as advertising, the designer to supply images and text. My role was to find the designers and persuade them that this was an excellent idea "because you are the one person who knows them all", he told me winningly. I then had to edit all the texts to give uniformity to the content of the book.

I didn't know them all; I did know a lot of them and the success of the school had given me an identity in the design world, so I took this brief and started compiling a list of possible candidates for inclusion. There were three others in Dom's team, Hughie Millais the grandson of the Pre-Raphaelite artist, Nick Luard who had been associated with the team that wrote and produced Beyond the Fringe and graphic designer Ian Cameron. Alongside this sparky, if rather radical team, I must have identified as very conservative in both outlook and occupation. It was much harder work than I had envisaged but that was in no way unusual. The trouble was that Nick wanted to produce it for the Christmas market of 1965, so I really had to work hard juggling lectures with interviews. It very soon became obvious that there was another obstacle to progress and that was the delicate matter of selection. Both Dominic and I were of the opinion that there should be a high level of talent and professionalism in the presentations; unhappily there were successful decorators working at the time who did not come up to expectations but who were nevertheless well-known and presented a problem of diplomacy! One such I really had to include but to my relief she turned me down briskly so that was one problem solved. Alas, as we were going to press I had a telephone call from her "You are a clever girl", she told me sweetly, "everyone is going in so I can't be left out". The image submitted was not what I would have wished but Nick, aware of budget, was determined to include her.

ID&D '66 (Interior Design and Decoration), an annual specialising in the design profession, was duly launched in time for the Christmas market and in virtually a matter of weeks was sold out. Nick was delighted and announced that we would be going into a second edition and should start preparing for *ID&D67*, but publisher George Rainbird said No.

Rainbird had received a letter from the committee of the new Association (IDDA) expressing grave irritation at the publication of the first book, accusing us of using their name without permission and listing a number of faults they identified in the book.

At a meeting with Rainbird, who explained that unless he could obtain an apology and a refutation, he was unable to reprint or to embark on another book for 1967. When I next went to Nick's office, he told me that he was going to sue the committee and that I was to join suit. I was quite clear that I had no intention of taking any such action, whereupon he explained that he would subpoena me as a witness, which of course he had every right to do.

The relevant letter was sent on behalf of the committee and signed by the unfortunate Inchbald employee who was the Association secretary. It was, however, uncertain that it had been seen by all the committee members it purported to represent. Meanwhile the energetic Mr Bonsack had made an appointment with the executive of a leading broadsheet who was responsible for their publishing department. He presented the man with our book, explaining that he was President of the Association, that the book had been produced without the permission of the Association and was anyhow faulty.

He proposed that the newspaper should take up the idea and publish an annual directory along the same lines, but backed by IDDA. Unhappily for him, the executive to whom he made this proposal knew me, reported this questionable proposal to a mutual friend and no-one was better pleased than Nick when he instructed Counsel. The matter went to court, Nick won his case and was awarded both costs and damages, both of which involved significant sums. It was a shocking blow to the Association and an unpleasant example of how easy it is for self-centred ambition to dominate and take control.

Godfrey Bonsack resigned as President and his place was taken by Frederick Keeble, a safe pair of hands and a designer of long standing whose family had practised for many generations. The case was a terrible setback for the Association, which was revived under Fred's guidance and a small group of members who were determined that nothing would stand in the way of consolidating interior design as an interesting and challenging career. Today the British Institute of Interior Design stands proudly in support of the profession with six hundred full members, and 1200 student members to carry the torch into the next generation of talent.

On balance it was clearly a good idea and luckily it was salvaged.

In the spring of 1962 I thought it logical to build on the success of the Interior Design tuition and to open a similar School specialising in Garden Design specifically, as opposed to the skills of gardening. It seemed inevitable that these skills would have to be included to some degree but I was adamant that Inchbald's speciality was the commitment to design. With this in mind I contacted the Churchill Trust in the hope of persuading them to give me a grant towards the cost of a visit to Japan. The creative skills of Japan are legendary and their garden designs spectacular; I had seen a great many English and French gardens and I was very keen to see for myself the very different approach of this Far Eastern country. The Churchill Trust turned me down with great courtesy because my application was too late in the year, but I was invited to reapply in the autumn.

I gave this some thought but I wanted to start the school in the autumn so I decided to fund myself and bought a package tour from a fairly new travel agent, Steven Pettitt of Tonbridge, which involved travelling via Bangkok and Singapore to my final destinations in Japan. Time for a deep breath and a tidily written cheque!

Suddenly I found myself inundated with assurances from kind friends

Jacqueline on a business trip to Japan.

that they would give me local introductions, curiously everywhere except Japan. From the moment I disembarked in Bangkok I had messages and invitations that were repeated in Singapore so I had little time to worry over the risk I was taking in making impromptu decisions. I don't think I was much fun as a guest; I had real jet lag but was very grateful for the kindness shown to me everywhere. By the time I got to Japan I was suffering from a different kind of fatigue!

The Pettitt schedule included a week in Japan, during which time there was naturally quite a lot of travel and I worked very hard, visiting every garden that was available on the tour, taking photographs, making notes, wondering if I was more than a little arrogant in assuming that I could instruct others in a subject that was close to my interests but one in which I had no academic qualification. Nevertheless I had a very strong empathy with the personal requirements and reaction of students and the more I saw of the Japanese beauty and way of life, the more enthusiastic I felt about the possibilities of introducing these achievements to an English audience. It was very much a new perspective on both horticulture and the manner in which planting and design were presented and enjoyed. By the time I was heading for Tokyo I was very tired indeed and I had received a message from Colonel Peter Thwaites "Looking forward to seeing you in Singapore."

I remembered the Peter Thwaites introductions and indeed I use the plural because two or three friends had assured me that he enjoyed having visitors and would love to show me Singapore. But I was disinclined to tour Singapore or to stay with the Colonel and his family; I really wanted to rest, digest the recent experiences and get home. So I answered "I shall be in Singapore on Sunday for two days and this message will give you an excuse to be in the jungle". By the time I got to my hotel in Tokyo there was another message " You must be taking the 12.45pm – I will meet you", and instead of being grateful, I just thought "Oh no! Please not!" I sent back a message "It lands much too late – I will call you in the morning." Putting things off never works! I had committed myself to the courtesy of a telephone call and in due course I dialled the number.

"Well", barked a voice, "are you coming to stay here?"

That was a bit of a shock, though the tone of finality was not; after all that is what Colonels do is it not? I glanced round a boring hotel room and decided to being once again on my best behaviour for the Colonel, his wife and how many children? There was a further bark – "Do you like polo?" I admitted to occasional visits to Smith's Lawn and did not admit to a certain confusion as to the rules of the game.

"Very well", he said, "I will collect you at 12 o'clock, bring your luggage", and he was gone. Clearly once a senior officer has given a command he isn't too interested in further discussion!

In due course, packed, polished and appropriately dressed, I went down to the hall where there had assembled a startling number of people; I suppose it was the crowd for lunch.

Among the crowd I saw a man standing alone looking slightly perplexed. His clothes finished the story: slightly muddy white breeches, slightly muddied riding boots and an open neck shirt. "Colonel Thwaites?" I inquired. "Good God", he replied "how could you possibly know?"

John Brookes

Happily, my inward groan was inaudible!

So off we went down a long road which involved a passport check and it was at this point that I asked him tentatively whether his wife disliked polo. It transpired that he and his wife had been divorced for ten years. I pondered this information and thought to enquire after the children who, it turned out, were all elsewhere; one in Singapore and two in London. So here I was, somewhere in Malaya, with an acquaintance of some half an hour's length and here was the polo ground from which my companion was clearly drawing a refined form of spiritual oxygen. I was duly presented to the sultan and we settled in his stand for the afternoon. In due course we returned to Singapore as the sun was setting. As we drew up to the house night had fallen and I was surprised to see that the windows were all in darkness. It was at this point that I was told that the staff were out but would be back in the morning; so no wife, no children and now no staff, but that was not the end of this adventure.

'I am not sure what we have in the fridge' was the introduction to dinner. In the event we had some yoghurt and a cup of tea, the Colonel did not suggest he show me to my room; his interpretation of this very ordinary suggestion was startling. "Let me show you how to go to bed", he invited! I followed him thoughtfully into the bedroom to discover him grappling with some kind of mosquito preventive lamp. He shook me courteously by the hand and bade me a good night.

Colonel Thwaites was certainly the most charming officer.

By the time I arrived back in London the summer was already in full flower but I managed to put together a programme for the new Garden School with the help of Patrick Matthews. It was a small class but I noticed that, unlike the background of the Interior designers, the garden students on the whole tended to arrive at Inchbald with a lot of horticultural knowledge. This arose from the fact that they were either from country families, or had been captivated as so many children are, by the fascination of growing plants. Patrick was quite soon joined by a young occasional lecturer, John Brookes, who was making waves in

Brigadier and Mrs Thwaites.

the horticultural world with outspoken views and much personal talent. John was an articulate speaker and a very gifted teacher, skills which do not necessarily accompany natural expertise. When Patrick retired he urged me to make John Brookes the Director of the Garden School and he did indeed prove to be a great success. He had a particular capacity to draw out talent and to encourage the most diffident of students. From the time he joined the school we built up a close and rewarding friendship which continued until his sadly early death in 2018.

Quite soon Colonel Thwaites reappeared, back from Singapore to a new posting in London and I found myself quite frequently at Smith's Lawn. His brother and my Inchbald brother-in-law, Tony, had both been killed in Italy in the war in Peter's regiment, the Grenadier Guards. Eventually I came to terms with his sense of humour and about a year after we met we married. Had I waited for the Churchill Award to come through it is unlikely that I would ever have met my beloved husband and I might never have learnt how to go to bed!

The Manor House, Ayot St Lawrence, a happy home for many years.

Soon after the establishment of the Garden School Peter was put on gardening leave in anticipation of his next appointment and promoted to Brigadier. It was during this time that he was approached by the representative of the Sultan of Oman, Tim Landon, both of them known well to him from his time in the Omani campaign, to offer him a very good job in Muscat. However he confessed that his ambition was to be an 'English General' so he hung about for over a year in the hope of a more senior job in the British Army. He turned down an appointment in Ireland during this time. The Military Secretary had a job lined up but the incumbent did not want to leave and the negotiations dragged on to the limit of Peter's patience so he called Tim Landon, then the Sultan's representative, and said he would indeed like to return to Oman and serve the young Sultan as Chairman of his Joint Staff. I noted to myself that commuting to Oman was going to be tricky but there is no point searching for problems in daily life; they tend to surface at all times with incredible ease.

In due course Peter left for Oman and I found myself checking the times that I could cope with absences from the School and the now-Brigadier. The Sultan financed travel which was a great help, and quite often gave either of us places on his private plane. So life took on a different rhythm; Peter came back frequently for meetings in England and I arranged my absences around his appointments. I was more than lucky in that John Brookes was now very much in charge of the Garden Students and Henry Stephenson had taken over the overall direction of the Interior Designers.

Henry had been teaching at the School from the early years. He was an accomplished artist, musician and designer. His capacity to engage his students' interest and develop their natural talent was unmatched

Chapter 12

and, allied to the natural sweetness of his temperament, made him an outstanding leader in the hierarchy of the Inchbald School. His students benefited from his skills and his generous temperament and during the four years of Peter's deployment in Oman when I was absent for three week intervals three times a year, my confidence in his guidance of the School was absolute.

Amanda Inchbald and Allegra Thwaites

However, I was still running the School and indeed lecturing regularly; thus the Omani absences were an increasing burden on the staff and in addition Peter, who had a deteriorating kidney condition not helped by the Muscat heat, needed to return to England for medical support.

At this point I was approached by a representative of the Shah of Persia (now Iran) with a request that I open the Inchbald School of Design in Tehran.

The Shah was a charismatic figure on the international scene, and Persia, with its long and inspiring cultural history, was still an evocative centre for the world of art. I wrote back in the affirmative, asking for timetable and finance details and meanwhile tried to identify a member of staff who was both talented and competent and who would value spending time in Tehran, a major capital city. This was surely a great opportunity and something of an unusual adventure and I assumed there might be two or three applicants. My assumption was totally incorrect, no-one wanted the job! Since John Brookes was now working full time in the Garden School I saw quite a lot of him and I expressed my surprise at this lack of enterprise. To my further surprise he came to me one day and asked if he could take up the appointment himself. I pointed out that his qualifications did not include those of the normal interior designer and he argued that the two disciplines shared a rule book, a statement with which I was bound to agree. So I wrote a programme, supplied notes for lectures, put together a case of relevant slides for each session and saw John off to Iran. I had some misgivings in spite of his reassurances; he had none.

Meanwhile, still in Oman in a position of considerable authority, Peter was urging me to abandon the enterprise but was unable to justify his worries because his knowledge was strictly confidential.

John set off in the summer of 1978. Premises were waiting for him, with a flat, and his first problem was to find an assistant. The autumn term started almost immediately and his class had already been enrolled. I spoke to him often and he was very happy, but politics were creeping up on the Shah himself and I remembered Peter's warnings and was worried for John's security. Christmas came and went and Henry Stephenson was due to pay John a supportive visit in the new year. For no reason that I can remember we gave Henry a fresh salmon to take with him for John and he was about to leave for the airport when revolution erupted in

Andrew Duff

Tehran and all flights were cancelled. And there was Henry, patient as ever, with his suitcase and his salmon. He rang me "What shall I do with the salmon" he asked. "Eat it" I replied. It seemed logical!

There were a number of calls to John; I begged him to come home and finally told him that I could no longer insure him because cover had been suspended. He was unimpressed.

"Jacqueline" he said, "I am sitting on my balcony with a glass of cool Persian wine, gazing at the sun-sparkled snow on the distant mountains! It is wonderful here." I had nothing further to say and John saw the year out with his students. At the end of the summer term the Inchbald School in Tehran closed and John travelled home via Muscat where Peter was beginning to wind up his responsibilities prior to retirement. John constantly returned to the school as a guest lecturer and he and I remained close friends until he died in 2018.

In 1980 Peter followed him back to the UK. After a long and successful career in the Grenadier Guards, he now became a Director of the Inchbald School and was appointed Chairman of the Hurlingham Polo Association, the governing body of the game, a position he held with great success until his death from kidney disease in 1991.

In 1984 Peter took me to see the Birthday Parade because it was the turn of the Grenadiers to Troop their Colour. This magnificent spectacle involves all seven Regiments of the Household Division on parade in celebration of the Monarch's birthday, and has been held annually since the reign of Charles II. Some 1000 soldiers of the Household Division are there on Horseguards Parade, under the overall command of the Field Officer, drawn from the regiment whose Colour is being trooped. Some half-way through the programme, Peter's enthusiasm was evident. "This is the best Parade I have ever seen, and the Field Officer is doing it brilliantly!" he remarked. Peering down at an immaculate figure on horseback, I asked who was the Field Officer. "It is Andrew Duncan, and he is doing it magnificently" was the answer. Andrew was, at that time, in command of the Regiment as The Lieutenant Colonel so I knew of him but had never met him.

Three years after Peter died in 1991, we met and embarked on thirty years of very happy marriage. In his retirement he took on the Administration of ISD as Director, and proved unsurprisingly to be at once totally committed to the school and its reputation. Military discipline is closely related to the essential discipline of the design world and thus he carved out another successful career for himself, earning love and respect from everyone at Inchbald.

Of that famous Parade he once told me that a friend had congratulated him directly afterward, remarking thoughtfully "… and I don't think your arse ever left the saddle!"

Chapter 12

When John retired from Inchbald his place was filled with by Tim Rees. Tim was succeeded by Andrew Wilson who left to run his own study group. Julia Fogg held the fort for the next four years until Andrew Duff took the helm of the Garden School in 2005.

Soon after Peter came home from Oman I was approached by Mrs Rajaa Moumena, who wished to start a school in Saudi Arabia, her own country. She already had an establishment called the Future Centre for Ladies and wished to set up an Inchbald Course within this centre. Accordingly I flew out to see her and discuss how we could develop a programme that conformed to Inchbald standards and suited Rajaa's potential students. It was not difficult, and the Future centre for Ladies accordingly came under the Inchbald umbrella, interrupted only by the shock of the pandemic which engulfed the Western world in 2020.

Alan Hughes

In 1999 Inchbald had started initial negotiations with the University of Wales with a view to validating the school's curricula, the first course to be approved being the development of the MA in 2000.

Quite soon Alan Hughes was drafted in as no one involved in the initial negotiations had an MA, and he oversaw the introduction of the University's preferred modular system.

The University of Wales was very impressed with the professionalism and depth of the courses as they stood, and they were keen to get us to collaborate with them. Alan felt strongly that the academic parity with universities was justifiable, and we were all confident (and Wales had confirmed) that our current courses were at the right level to convert to Postgraduate study. This would provide a valuable distinction from other private schools who had no validations at this stage; Wales wanted a connection to a successful professional course and they recognized that Inchbald provided the required level.

We attracted distinguished tutors and external examiners, and the hunger for qualifications was strong from both students and the profession; it was clear this interest would gain pace. In the first few years Alan had double figures for the ID MA (the current BA has become more popular since) and he was also tutoring the GD students as regards Research and Design Methodology. Graduates at Masters level went to work for Zaha Hadid, Fosters and similar leading studios. Further academic success was to follow with the introduction of the BA.

The University generated strict regulations and disciplines; in 2020 as a result of management error Inchbald was found to have failed regulations and we lost our visa allocations, which was disastrous. On the heels of this problem we were engulfed by the Covid pandemic and the accompanying national chaos. Travel between European countries was curtailed, English social structure was impacted by the illness to a far greater degree than had been anticipated, and successful businesses

Jacqueline c.1990.
© All rights reserved

were failing on a daily basis as a result. I had no option but to close 32 Eccleston Square and concentrate the student body once again at No. 7 Eaton Gate. Unhappily the top floor of No. 32 was my own flat and the sale of the building left me without the London base from which I directed the school, making life very difficult. However, we managed to survive some three years of reduced student intake, together with all the problems caused by the pandemic that we shared as a nation.

During the course of my career at Inchbald I did a certain amount of public service. This emanated from a genuine interest in both national and local affairs and included service on the Monopolies Commission, the Copyright Committee, the Westminster City Council and latterly some twenty years as a J.P. This work brought me into contact with different personalities and new perspectives, experiences which I found invaluable in my dealings with my students who came from all over the world and many different cultures.

There are two primary factors that have served to identify the designer of today, and they are of course the twin pillars of education, and professional status, the latter defined by the disciplines of an Association. In terms of the interior designer/decorator, these two factors were established in America by Parsons School, and by those designers who inaugurated the American Institute of Interior Decorators in 1931.

Frank Parsons was the Pygmalion who informed and refined the identity of that 20th-century professional initially described as an Interior Decorator. His concern about every aspect of design as it occurred in the lives of ordinary people extended from space to fashion and his students were encouraged to address these subjects from every viewpoint. Parsons was concerned with the wide canvas of life and his students learned to see themselves not as arbiters of taste, but of lifestyle, whilst their inspirational tutor was a democrat committed to improving and beautifying the lives of people rather than patrons.

The identification of a profession that catered to a general requirement for help and advice in private living spaces did not come to real fruition until the 20th century. Indeed the remark made by Elsie de Wolfe to the effect that her job was to advise people who lacked the time, inclination or culture to do for themselves what she undertook to do for them, cast a shadow on professional integrity and was at once damning and arrogant. It was the kind of attitude that presented interior decoration as something of a raffish exercise undertaken by gifted amateurs at the expense of foolish and wealthy clients. This impression was prevalent when I met Michael in 1948.

Fads and fashion permeate design in every age and in all its mutations; it is fashion that links design thought and design products, from architecture through to flower arrangement and it was this overall view of the interior designer's role that was advocated so clearly by Frank Parsons. Practical considerations are the basis of good interior design and afterwards comes the flowering of the imagination, pushing the boundaries of fashion and indeed sometimes of good taste. As the profession established in America, designers felt that the word 'decoration' did not fully indicate the serious and constructive aspects of their work. Accordingly as late as 1961 it was agreed that the American Institute of Interior Decorators should henceforth be changed to 'Interior Designers", a decision which probably precipitated the constant discussion about the differentials between the two nouns and the argument as to who is, and who is not, a designer.

Andrew and Jacqueline Duncan c.2015.

Reviewing the developments in lifestyle as they occurred through history, together with the swings and foibles of fashion, it is evident that no single group of people have determined the character of the contemporary interior designer. Instead it is a potent mix of privileged talent, dedicated skills and the magical element of imagination that has formed this blend of artistry and management ability. It has been a long journey from the relationship between monarchy and the thespian skills of interior design, and it has also been equally difficult to establish this occupation as a profession of gravitas, requiring extensive and sophisticated training in order to create the quality of private and public interiors which today we take for granted.

There is another factor whose influence is too easily forgotten and that is the Client. The client/designer relationship is only as successful as the designer's capacity to empathise, not only with the client's taste but importantly with the life style which becomes the subject of manipulation by a stranger. This is true of private spaces but it is also relevant where public commissions are concerned. Practicality, suitability and visual appeal are all vital to the completed work. But without real understanding of client motivation, the emotional extra that allows insight into the reasons that help has been sought, the finished design must lack the vitality that captivated Robsjohn-Gibbings on the Greek vases that were his inspiration.

INTERIOR DESIGN

The skill of an interior designer is to absorb and reflect a client's priorities and lifestyle, including their sense of humour.

HENRIETTA SPENCER-CHURCHILL

Henrietta Spencer-Churchill studied Art History in Italy and France before enrolling at the Inchbald School of Design in London. She started her Interior Design business Woodstock Designs in 1981 having worked for 3 years with Diana Hanbury and Jean Monro.

She specializes in the restoration and refurbishment of period and listed buildings with emphasis placed on conserving their historic value and features whilst bringing them into the 21st century. Many of her commissions are abroad which involves the challenges of learning about and incorporating local cultures and trends.

She also has a company in the USA Spencer-Churchill Designs Inc and has worked on many new build houses in the Georgian Style as well as restoration projects in NYC, Atlanta, Dallas and Connecticut.

As well as her Interior Design business much of her time is dedicated to the overseeing of the restorations of her family home Blenheim Palace, the running of the Blenheim Foundation and organizing special and fund-raising events for local charities.

She is the author of 11 books and has carried out many lectures and TV appearances for historic documentaries and restoration programmes. Her 12th book was published in September 2024: Blenheim – 300 years of Life in a Palace.

Interior Design

Interior Design

INCHBALD

HARRIET ANSTRUTHER

An award-winning, British designer, writer and art director, Harriet's book REVEAL; Interior design as a Reflection of Who We Are, *gives insight into her central interest in the psychology and haptics of design in all its disciplines.*

With a background living in London and New York, and over thirty years of experience working in textiles, film, fashion and the arts, Harriet launched her interior design studio HAS in 2012. Past colletions of her silk scarves (which now form part of the permanent collection of the V&A Museum), retailed worldwide through stores including Browns, Harrods, Harvey Nichols, Saks Fifth Avenue and Barneys' New York.

Latest collaborators include Plain English *and* InnovationRCA.

"Harriet Anstruther knows how to rhyme a room, in a way. She listens to spaces and objects and people, coaxing from them the stories they most want to tell – personal stories, timeless stories, clever or irreverent or wicked stories. Their singular, resonant truths, the things they were most meant to say. The results, inevitably wrought from feeling and memory and affection, are their very best version of themselves. Harriet is an artist and a poet and a magician and a dreamer and a rascal – and she is extraordinary."
Private client, USA.

Interior Design

Interior Design

ZEYNEP FADILLIOĞLU

Zeynep Fadıllıoğlu was born in 1955 in Istanbul, Turkey, and grew up in a waterfront yalı – an Italian inspired palazzo on the Bosphorus. She began her academic journey at the University of Sussex, continued her computer science studies at Control Data Institute in London and refined her artistic eye with her studies in Art History and Design at The Inchbald School of Design, London.

Her design career began with over twenty restaurants and clubs for her husband, Metin Fadıllıoğlu, a pioneer of Istanbul's artistic dining culture. In 1995, she founded her own studio, Zeynep Fadıllıoğlu Design and Architecture, promoting an interdisciplinary approach.

The studio has since created luxury residences, yachts, hotels, shops, and cultural spaces in over a dozen countries including the UAE, Kuwait, UK, France, Germany, the U.S., India, Qatar, Saudi Arabia, Oman.

Zeynep is widely recognized as the first woman to design a mosque–the Şakirin Mosque in Istanbul (2009)–a landmark project nominated for the Aga Khan Award for Architecture. She also taught Design Management and Culture at Istanbul Bilgi University for a decade.

Her work has been featured annually in the Andrew Martin Design Review for 17 years where she was named International Designer of the Year in 2002. That same year, she was invited to design a show bedroom for the Daily Telegraph/House & Garden Fair. *In 2005, she won Modern Designer of the Year at the London Design & Decoration Awards and received the WIFTS International Visionary Award in 2011.*

In 2012, she launched the Zeynep Fadıllıoğlu Product Range and, in 2013, debuted a furniture collection at Paris Maison&Objet, combining contemporary design with Turkey's rich cultural heritage and handcrafting traditions.

Interior Design

INCHBALD

JOHN McCALL

Born 1954
Inchbald 1972-1973
Worked as Interior Designer and Director of CVP Designs, London 1973-86.
Formed John McCall Ltd, Interior Design 1986.
The company continues to work on residential and commercial projects in the UK and internationally. Projects have been completed in USA, France, Portugal, Greece, The Bahamas, Monaco, the Republic of Ireland and the Middle East.

Selected Projects: Christie's London, White's Club, The Grand Penthouse of the Millenium Tower Boston, A new build house in the Bahamas awarded the finest new house in the Caribbean 2019.

Interior Design

STEPHEN RYAN

Stephen Ryan graduated from the Inchbald School of Design (ISD) in 1980, with Distinction. He was offered a position with John Siddeley (Lord Kenilworth) but accepted a position of Assistant Junior Designer at Bill Bennette Design, where he crafted his position over three years.

He was headhunted by Robin Guild (Homeworks), a trendy designer with a glorious Pimlico showroom. Very shortly after this tenure, he was again headhunted, by David Hicks (DHI) to become their Chief Designer.

This was a dream job, having devoured his books (the only interior design ones available in the day, in the local library) as a 13 year old, and later writing to David Hicks as a teenager (without a response), having been totally inspired by the great designer's repertoire.

At 27, a huge responsibility with a 20 strong project team of designers, and the joy of also working alongside the David Hicks International product design team, Ryan relished all the creative challenges, and exciting interior design projects, worldwide.

Ryan decided to set up Stephen Ryan Design & Decoration in 1993, after a short interlude, having once again been headhunted by Colefax & Fowler. After various design studio/offices Stephen Ryan Design & Decoration opened a retail showroom and design studio in Holland Park, London.

Maintaining a small practice, by design, it personally handled UK and worldwide projects including residential, hotels and private boats, retaining a style coined classic contemporary undertaking both traditional and modern aesthetics.

Interior Design

SIMONE SUSS

Founded by award-winning interior designer, Simone Suss, Studio Suss creates amazing spaces that never compromise on comfort, functionality and style.

Recognised as one of the World's Top 100 Interior Designers, *we work with clients who share our vision of contemporary, timeless, and sustainable interiors. We use natural materials wherever we can and employ cutting-edge industry practices.*

Our projects range from new-build private residences for high-net-worth individuals across the world, to commercial developments and branded office and retail spaces for companies. Simone trained at Central St Martin's College of Art and Design, the Chelsea School of Art and Design, and the Inchbald School of Design and is a regular guest lecturer at several design schools. She is an alumna of the University of Cambridge Institute for Sustainability Leadership and sits on the Professional Practice and Sustainability committee of the British Institute of Interior Design (BIID) whom she represents on the Construction Industry Council Climate Change Committee. She is a founding signatory of Interior Design Declares whom she represents on the Built Environment Declares Steering Group, collaborating with colleagues to set the interior design industry's sustainability agenda and long-term strategy.

Simone has spoken at all the major industry events including Decorex, Focus, Surface Design Show, Future Build, Clerkenwell Design Week, Design London. She is on the Decorex Sustainability Task Force and features in the Documentary Sustainability: A Broken Record. Simone is now studying an MA in Regenerative Design.

Interior Design

INCHBALD

TOLLGARD STUDIO

Tollgard Studio is a creative and collaborative interior and product design studio and a respected curator of international contemporary design.

Born out of a shared passion for design, Tollgard is run by Inchbald-educated, design and life partners, Staffan and Monique Tollgård. Hailing from Sweden and South Africa respectively, with previous careers in film and documentary-making, their nuanced understanding of culture and a love of storytelling through design have been consistently recognised by the world's leading design publications.

Their education at Inchbald laid the firm foundations of their design journey: first their eponymous design studio, then three design stores and later a dedicated contracts team to add value at every stage of the design process. A new path has now been forged into product design, allowing them to tell the story of the piece rather than the story of the space.

For twenty years, through three-hundred and fifty projects, Tollgard Studio has crystallised its design ethos into a signature principle: the search for the project's distinctive 'röda tråden'. The red thread is a northern European concept used across all creative endeavors to describe the creative DNA that makes a work distinct. For Tollgard, the red thread is found in the unique intersection between environment, architecture, and identity: the choice of this *place*, this *dwelling*, by this *individual* and this *family*. Whether a family oasis buffering city life; a biophilic headquarters; or a sand-dune sanctuary on the Danish coast: places shape people.

As storytellers and place-makers, Tollgard is set apart by the value they place on empathy, communication and collaboration, and their strongly held belief that good design makes people's lives better.

Interior Design

Interior Design

INCHBALD

GRAÇA VITERBO

Graça Viterbo's love for Art and Design is the result of a distinguished, international and awarded career in Interiors, spanning over six decades.

As Portugal's most notable Decorator, Graça studied at the Inchbald School in 1967 – those days were about swinging London but also the very beginning of an industry set to flourish in the decades to follow. Graça Viterbo's pioneering studio in Portugal in the seventies expanded dramatically to luxury residences and retail, with a penchant for designing memorable hotels such as the most recent ventures Estoril Vintage Hotel and Bela Vista Hotel & SPA in Portugal.

She set up the Portugal Chapter for IIDA- International Interior Design Association in the nineties and her children followed suit at the Inchbald in London, setting off successful design careers in their own right in New York and Singapore. She is immensely proud of her legacy and is a die-hard believer in the power of classicism. Her passion for fabric saw her innovate in the eighties and nineties in great style with Pierre Frey and Manuel Canovas. She would argue there is no perfect drawing room without a very British chintz or the touch of a Portuguese tile and to this day she goes by the use of mirror and screens as the greatest trick in Interior Design.

She is a proud alumna of the Inchbald School, supportive of Jacqueline's vision in how design can be a powerful business when run professionally, making people's lives more beautiful. She would love to see her grandchildren study there one day. Graca is yet to design a sailing yacht, but that currently sits at the top of her to-do-list.

Interior Design

INCHBALD

VSP INTERIORS

VSP Interiors was founded in 2000 and is led by Creative Director Henriette von Stockhausen. Henriette loves combining rich colours, prints and antiques to create layered interiors with lots of interest and warm lived-in comfort. This approach enables Henriette and her dynamic team to specialise in designing authentic interiors for listed buildings and homes of architectural interest. Working in the UK and overseas, they undertake projects of all sizes, providing a highly bespoke and dedicated service.

Henriette studied at City & Guild's of London Art School and gained a Master's Degree at Sotheby's Institute where she honed her appreciation and love of antique furniture and decorative design from the 17th Century through to the 20th Century. She was also involved in country house sales which fed her appetite for beautiful architecture of historical interest.

Henriette credits Inchbald for bringing together all the elements she previously had learned about, both in life and from art school. Having completed her degree at Inchbald, she reflects,

"Jacqueline Duncan remains a massive inspiration, and I feel honoured to have attended the very institute she founded over 60 years ago!"

"When planning the interiors of period properties, we believe in preserving quality craftsmanship and architectural features while introducing contemporary elements through the use of colour, texture and modern art. The juxtaposition of the new with the old creates an evolved and collected interior."

Interior Design

GARDEN DESIGN

The garden designer works with God's palette which is at once challenging and rewarding.

JONATHAN CRAGGS

Janathan Craggs is a graduate of the Inchbald School of Design in London, England (Distinction 1993) and he studied horticulture at the Royal Horticultural Society's garden, Wisley, in Surrey, England.

He has a diverse portfolio of projects with a focus on high-end residential and estate gardens. Since 1993 he has completed many projects throughout southern Vancouver Island and the Greater Vancouver area, as well as projects in Northern B.C. the Okanagan, Alberta, California, the Caribbean and Europe.

Completed projects range from formally structured classic and contemporary layouts, to naturalistic landscapes that blend seamlessly with native environments.

Drawing inspiration from cultural sources and from landscape style from around the world, Jonathan's skill in revealing and enhancing the unique qualities inherent in each site, results in landscapes that are at once peaceful, stimulating and timeless in nature.

Garden Design

Garden Design

INCHBALD

LUCIANO GIUBBILEI

Luciano Giubbilei began his career in gardens when he moved from his birthplace, Siena, to London in 1994. By 1997, he had completed his studies at the Inchbald School of Design and established his own practice.

The studio is recognised for the understated elegance and serenity found in the gardens it creates, defined by light and influenced by the classical Italian design heritage of proportion and balance. The gardens evolve through an exploration of spacing, rhythm, and the repetition of single elements.

As a practice, great emphasis is placed on exploring and nurturing a sustained dialogue with artists, architects, plantsmen, and craftsmen. This commitment to collaboration is essential to expanding and challenging the creative process, enabling the studio to move beyond the limitations of a familiar language.

The motivation is to create timeless spaces—multi-layered environments where culture and nature are in close communication. The approach continually evolves, shaped by the individuality of each client and the unique characteristics of every site. The studio strives to forge an emotional connection between place and people, valuing local materials and expressing a desire to connect people to nature, not merely through plants and flowers but through spatial composition and beauty.

Garden Design

INCHBALD

JONATHAN SNOW

We love to create inviting outdoor spaces that people want to spend time in, in the countryside or in town. We specialise in working with discerning clients with an interest in investing in their garden for the long term, and an appreciation for aesthetics, quality of finish, and beautiful planting throughout the year. We enjoy collaborating with architects and interior designers, and teaming up with skilled garden builders and the best tree and plant nurseries in the country, and we work with gardeners to ensure that each garden that we design matures and reaches its full potential over the coming years.

Jonathan has over 15 years' experience of designing gardens. A graduate of The Inchbald School of Design, he worked for Arne Maynard, and then Tom Stuart-Smith, before setting up his own practice. He has exhibited on Main Avenue at the Chelsea Flower Show three times, most recently picking up a much coveted Gold Medal, and the award for Best Construction, for his Himalayan garden, in 2021. As evidenced by his gardens at Chelsea, a passion for botany, and studying how plants grow in the wild all over the world underpins much of his planting design. Jonathan is a member of the International Dendrology Society, a pre-registered member of the Society of Garden Designers, and a regular speaker at Inchbald.

Garden Design

Garden Design

Garden Design

Acknowledgements

Throughout the 65 years during which I have been running the school, I have been privileged to have amazing and unstinting support from friends and colleagues. Initially, and without that support, the school might never have come to fruition. The great Bill Pahlman's enthusiasm for an idea that I thought he might well consider to be risible was a wonderful encouragement to me to develop the ambitious project!

Architect Stephen Garrett's kind and unpompous offer of support and encouragement was matchless, exactly what I so needed to help me shape the format and discipline required for a programme of teaching in a subject in which I had no formal education. "Just call me the old consultant" he said and quite soon he opened his own studio to those students who wished to learn the skills of architectural drawing. It worked well and thus we continued until his commissions from Paul Getty involved a move to America and another adventure.

I had discussed the possibility of a Year Course with Stephen before he left and with his departure, I was lucky to find a kind and efficient Director of Design in William Graham, a qualified designer who set up the Course and ran it for several years. When he retired, his place was taken by architect John Odam, who supplied brilliantly all the gaps in my own education; he brought with him his wife, Sylvia. Sylvia Mitchell had taken the 10 Week Course and spent sometime telling me where the gaps were! Explaining that her husband had hurt his back and could no longer stand at a drawing board, they embarked on the running of the Year, John as Director and Sylvia, who was a brilliant Sourcer, specialising in that very subject. They were hugely popular with their students and there are many successful interior designers out there who are more than indebted to them.

During the quite early years I had retained a brilliant young illustrator to help students with drawing skills. Highly intelligent and very charming, Henry Stephenson had been with the school for years when John Odam retired, and his appointment as the Course Director was inevitable and hugely successful. Nothing required by either staff or students was ever too much for him and he was a wondrous colleague when Exhibitions came along. When John decided that his back could no longer cope with the demands of a very concentrated workload, I turned to Henry who had been at the School for many years.

Acknowledgements

Henry Stephenson's appointment concerned me slightly – he was above all else an artist, and indeed a musician, but I had no idea about his managerial skills. I should not have worried. This Man of all Skills ran the Inchbald Year Course with a perfect and charming authority, constantly exploring new ideas, quick to listen to his colleagues' or students' new ideas and endlessly alert to the shifts in the professional world of design. He was succeeded in running the Year Course by Jill Georgalakis, an architect who had run the Ten Week Course with great skill, and made the transition to the Year Course very successfully.

In 1972, in concert with John Brookes, I started the Inchbald School of Garden Design after an inspiring tour of Japanese gardens. John was an inspirational tutor and a major player in this new venture, which he continued to oversee with huge enthusiasm until his own workload became too great; accordingly he handed over direction to Tim Rees and thereafter to Andrew Wilson who continued to direct the Course. He was followed by Julia Fogg who spent four years as director until the leadership was taken over by another colleague of John Brookes, Andrew Duff. Andrew has now directed the Garden School for some twenty years with great success and is the Managing Director of ISD Ltd.

Alan Hughes first came to Inchbald as a part-time tutor in the mid-nineties, gradually increasing his commitment to Inchbald over the years until he took over the Leadership of the Year and University Courses in 2000, he is now Principal of Inchbald and Director of the Interior Design Faculty. He works in concert with Tony Taliadoros and with Piers Northam, an Inchbald graduate from the 1989/90 intake who took over the direction of the Ten Week Course from Nico Springman, also a graduate of the School, with outstanding success in 2015.

The support team at the School includes a secretarial staff, an IT Manager and an accountant, backed up by a group of visiting lecturers and tutors. Everyone at the Inchbald School of Design is concerned with the wellbeing of the students, the successful progress of their studies and the vital outcome of their launch on a career in the design subject of their choice.

Over more than half a century, Inchbald has trained starry generations of successful designers, a record of which we are understandably very proud.

Jacqueline Duncan OBE FIDDA
Dean

Index

Page numbers in *italic* font refer to illustrations. Places are in London unless stated otherwise.

A

Adam, Robert 77–8, *77*
Adam Style 77–8
Adelphi 78
Adler, David 104
Aiton, William Townsend 91
Albert, Prince 55, 92, 97, 98
Albrighton Hall, Shropshire 11, *12*, 13
Aldermaston, Berkshire 30
Alletson, Mary 16, 30
Amberley Castle, Sussex 39–40, *40*
American architecture 112–13
American Institute of Decorators 117–18
American Red Cross 23–4, 30
American Society of Interior Designers 118
Amster, James 106
Anne, Queen 69, 72
Anne of Denmark, Queen 64
architects 64, 73–4, 77, 81, 82–3, 93, 111–13, 127
Architectural Association 47, 48
Ascot, Berkshire 29–30
associations of interior designers see American Society of Interior Designers; Interior Decorators and Designers Association (IDDA)

B

Bannenberg, Jon 126, *127*, 128, 146–7
Banqueting House 64
Barbon, Nicholas 78
Bath, Somerset 78
Battersby, Martin 105, 109
Bauhaus 111–12
Beauchamp Place 49, 50
Beckford, William 82–4
Belvedere, Naples 88–9
Bérain, Jean 70–1
Black, Misha 56
Blathwaite, Justin 35
Blessington, Charles Gardiner, 1st Earl of 88–9
Blessington, Marguerite Gardiner, Countess of 88–9, 95, 9
Bonsack, Godfrey 147, 148–9
Bower, Elizabeth 22

Bower, Henrietta (née Strickland) 19, 21
Bower, Commander Robert 21, 22
Bowles, Thomas Gibson 101
Bowring, Diana 29–30
Boys, Michael 115
Brighton Pavilion, Sussex 92–3, *93*
Britain Can Make It (1946) 56
British design 55–6, 58–9, 125–7, 129
    see also English Style; Inchbald, Michael
British East India Company 68, 80–1
British Institute of Interior Design 149
British Museum 53
Bromley, John 3, 4, 6–7
Brookes, John 151–2, 153–4, *151*
Buckingham Palace 92
Burlington House 73, 98
Burlington, Richard Boyle, 3rd Earl of *72*, 73–4

C

Cameron, Ian 148
Cameron, Rory 107
camouflage, war-time 56, 117, 125
Campbell, Colen 73
Campbell, Davida 10, 17, 19, 37
career changes 135
Carlton House 91
carriages 90
cartoons 102
Catterick, North Yorkshire 31
Charles I, King 64–5
Charles II, King 65–6, 68
Chase, William Merritt 99
Chelsea 140
    see also King's Road, Chelsea
'Chinoiserie' 71
Chippendale, Thomas 79–80
Chiswick House 73–4, *74*
Citizen Kane 114, 115
Civil War period 65
client/designer relationship 157
Clive, Robert, 1st Baron (Clive of India) 80–1
Cloughley, Tony 127
Clutton, Mother (nun) 18, 25
Clyne, Phyl (b. Frances, née Pentney) 2, 23–4, 28
Clyne, Ted 28
coaches 90
Cockerell, Charles 81
Cockerell, Samuel Pepys 81
Colbert, Jean Baptiste 70
Cole, Henry 98–9

Colefax & Fowler 107, 122
Colefax, Sibyl *106*, 107, 122, 127
Collins, Mrs 29
Collins, Arthur iii, 44–5
Colony Club, New York 103
colour 106, 127
Commonwealth period 65
Coole, horologist 49–50
Coppins, Buckinghamshire 32
Council of Industrial Design 56
Country Life 110–11
court, presentation at 41–2
Covid-19 pandemic 155
Cowper, William 88
Crace & Co. 90, 94–5, *94*
Crace, Frederick 90, 94
Crace, John 90, 94
Crace, John Diblee 94, 95
Crace, John Gregory 94
Cruickshank, Olive 109–10

D

Daguerre, Dominique 91
Dale family 17
Daniell, Thomas 81
d'Arcy family 13
Davis, Miss (school teacher) 4, 5, 11, 12
Day, Robin 56, *57*
Daylesford, Gloucestershire 81
De Wolfe, Elsie iv–v, 102–4, *102*, 105–6, 109, 125, 156
Deepdene, Surrey 87, 143
Denney, Anthony 115–16
Design Council 55
design education 59
directory of designers 147–8
Donaldson family 2–3, 9
Dorchester Hotel 125
Drivers Jonas 31, 32, 34–5
Duchess Street 86, 87
Duff, Andrew 155, *154*
Duncan, Andrew 154, *157*
Duncan, Jacqueline (née Pentney)
  appearance 30, 34, *44*, 53, *62*, *139*, *147*, *150*, *156–157*
  birth and early years 1, 2, 3
  coming out 41–3
  design and
    association of interior designers 146–7
    directory of designers 147–8
    interest in 57, 58
    promotion of Michael Inchbald 133
  design schools *see* Inchbald School of Design
  education
    pre-war, Lodge at Yapton 4–7, 9–10, 11
    Sacred Heart Convent, Hove 8–9, *8–9*, 10–12, 28–9
    Sacred Heart Convent, Lutwyche Hall 14–19, *14–15*, 25, 90
    Les Dames de St Maur, Oatlands Park 37–8
    House of Citizenship 37–8, 39
  employment
    General Trading Company 44
    KLM 45–6
    Withers 44–5
  evacuation 12–13
  family background 1–2, 2–3, 9
  interests
    antiques iv, 44, *44*, 50–1, 59, 132
    art and architecture 18, 25, 142
    gardening 5
    Ilbert Collection and 53
  marriages
    Andrew Duncan 154
    Michael Inchbald 47, 50–1, 52, *53*, 132–3, 139
    Peter Thwaites 150–1, 152, *152*, 153, 154
  public service 156
  skills
    bath oil mixing 44
    cricket 16
    drawing 144
    office management 45, 46
    riding 17, 22, 27
    secretarial skills 37, 44
    sewing 27, 29
Duquette, Tony 109
Dutch influence 68–9
Duveen, Sir Joseph 101, 143

E

East India Companies 68–9, 80–1
East Indies 68–9
Eaton Gate (No. 7) 140–1, 156
Ecclestone Square (No. 32) 156
Egerton, Francis 108
Elkins, Frances 104
Elwes, Dominic 147
Emmet, Anne 38–9, *39*, 41
Emmet, Evelyn 39, 40

English Style 123–4, 125
estates 34–5, 44
   see also country houses
exhibitions 55–6

F

Fairhurst, Margaret iii–iv, 44–5
Fallingwater, Pennsylvania 113, *113*
Farnsworth House, Illinois 112
fashion and design 156–7
Ferguson, Perry 114, 115
Festival of Britain 55–6
Ffoulkes ('Fookie', horologist) 49–50
First World War 2, 101
Fleming, Ronald 107–8
Fogg, Julia 155
Fonthill Abbey, Wiltshire 82–4
Fonthill Splendens, Wiltshire 82, 84
Forbes, Mother (nun) 11, 13, 16, 19
Ford, Oliver 126
Fouquet, Nicholas 66
400 Club, Leicester Square 41, 43–4
Fowler, John 81, 107, *107*, 122–3, 123–4, 125, 129
France
   furniture from 104
   influence of 66–8, 70–1, 88
   post-Revolution period 83–4, 90–1
Frick, Henry J. v, 103
furniture 56–7, 104, 116, 126
   see also cabinetmakers

G

G Plan furniture 116
gardening 5
gardens 91–2
Gardiner, Malcolm 49, 50
Gardner, James 56, *56*, 128
Garnett, Cloughley, Blakemore (GCB) 127
Garnett, Patrick 127
Garrett, Stephen 137, *137*, 139, 141, 144–5
General Trading Company 44
George, Prince, Duke of Kent 32
George I, King 72–3
George IV, King 91, 92
George VI, King 7, 42
Georgian period 72–84
Getty Museum, Los Angeles 144–5
Glass House, Connecticut 112–13, *112*
Gobelins Factory, Paris 70

Good Housekeeping 110
Gore House, Kensington 95
Gothic Revival 75–7, 91
Government School of Design 98, 99
Graham, William 141, 144, 145
Grand Tours 63, 73, 77, 85–6, 88, 89
Grand Trianon, France 67
Grant, Sally 12–13
Great Exhibition (1851) 55, *96*, 97, 98
Greece, inspiration from 119–20
Gropius, Walter 111
'grotesque' style 71

H

Hampton, Mark 129
Harling, Robert 134
Hastings, Warren 81
Hayward, Helena 137
Henri IV, King of France 78
Hepplewhite, George 79–80
Hereford Square 36
Hicks, David 51, *51*, 126–7, 129, 146–7
Hill, Geraldine 133, 134, 135
Holland, Henry 90, 92
Holocaust 28
Hope, Thomas 83, 85–8
House and Garden 58–9, 110, 115, 134
House of Citizenship iii, 37–8, 39
Howard Chairs 126
Howell, James 95
Howell James & Co. 95, 97
Hudson, Edward 110
Hughes, Alan 155, *155*
Hunt, Mrs, 4, 5
Hurlingham Club, Fulham 39

I

Ilbert Collection 48–9, 52–4, 132
Ilbert, Courtenay iv, 48–50, *49*, 51–2, 131–2
Inchbald, Amanda *139*, 140, 153
Inchbald, Jacqueline *see* Duncan, Jacqueline
Inchbald, Michael
   antique business iv, 50–1, 59, 136
   association of interior designers 146–7
   background 47–8
   career 128–9
   colour blindness 51, 129
   designs and commissions
      Milner Street *60–1*, 128–9, 131, 133, 134
      Peter Jones 57, 122

Index

Savoy Hotel 52
education 128
Jacqueline
  children 52, *53*
  divorce 139
  first meeting 47
  marriages 50–1
  portraits *vii*
Inchbald, Rosemary 48
Inchbald School of Design
  creation of 59, 62, 134–5
  curriculum and lecturers 136–9, 141, 142, 144, 145, 146, 152–3, 155
  garden design school 149, 151–2
  pandemic, impact of 155
  premises in Eaton Gate 139–41
  Saudi Arabia and 155
  students 135, 145–6
  Teheran/Tehran Inchbald School 153–4
  validation of 155
India 68–9, 80–1
Interior Decorators and Designers Association (IDDA) 146–7, 148–9
Interior Design and Decoration 147–8
interior design as a profession 120–1, 156–7
'interior design', use of term 80
Iran 153–4
Iver, Buckinghamshire 32

J

Jackson, George & Sons 138
Jamaica 82
James VI and I, King 64, 65
James, Isaac 95
Japan 69, 149–50, *150*
Jebb, Philip 81
Johnson, Philip 112–13, *112*
Jones, Inigo 63–4, *64*
Jones, Owen 127
Josephine, Empress 88

K

Kaufmann, Mrs. Edgar J. 113
Keeble, Frederick 149
Kent, George, Prince, Duke of 32
Kent, William 73, *73*, 74
Kenya 4
King's Road, Chelsea *127*, 128
KLM 45–6

L

'lady decorators' 107, 109
Lancaster, Nancy 122–3
Lancaster, Osbert 130
land agents 31, 32, 34–5
Landon, Tim 152
Le Vau, Louis 66, 67
Leigh, Owen 5, 10
Leighton, Sir Frederic, *Flaming June* 142
Les Dames de St Maur, Oatlands Park, Surrey 37, 38
Levens Hall, Cumbria 19–20, *20*, 21
lighting 114–15
Lillie, Mother (nun) 10, 14, 15, 16
London, Second World War 19, 29
Louis XIV, King of France 66–7, 72
Louis XVI, King of France 91
Luard, Nick 148, 149
Lutwyche Hall, Shropshire 14–19, *14–15*, 24, 28, 90

M

Maas, Jeremy 51, 141–2
magazines 58–9, 101–2, 110–11
Mallett, Walter 108
Malletts of Bath 108
Mann & Fleming 107–8
Marble Hill House 75
Marbury, Elisabeth 103
Marie Antoinette, Queen of France 91
Marot, Daniel 69–70, 71
Mary II, Queen 68, 71, 72
Mary of Teck, Queen 48
masques 64
Matthews, Charles 89
Matthews, Patrick 151–2
Maugham, Somerset 106
Maugham, Syrie v, *103*, 104–5, 106, 107, 109–10, 125
Messel, Oliver 125, *125*
Mies van der Rohe, Ludwig 111–12
Millais, Hughie 148
Milner Street (No. 10) 48–50, *60–1*, 128–9, 130–2, 134
minimalism 129
Mishcon, Victor 147
Mitchell, Sylvia 146
Mitford Colmer, Miss 140–1
Mlinaric, David 59, 129

Modern movement 111
Money-Coutts, Anne *see* Emmet, Anne
Montagu, Elizabeth 88
Montague House 88
Morris, Roger 75
Morrison, Herbert 55–6
Moumena, Rajaa 155
Mughal style 81, *82*
Museum of Ornamental Art 98

N

Naples 88–9
Nash, John 93
Nast, Condé 58, 59
National Society for Interior Designers 118
National Trust 123
Netherlands, influence of 68–9
Neville-Rolfe, Dorothy iii, 38
New York 99–100
New York School of Art 99
news media 85
    see also magazines
Nicholls, Beverley 106

O

Oatlands Park, Surrey 37, 38
O'Brien, Maureen 43
Odam, John 146
Odom, William 100
Oman 152
Orsay, Alfred d', count 88, 89, 95, 97

P

Pahlmann, William v–vi, *116*, 117, 118–19, 134
Palladianism 73, 75
Palladio, Andrea 73
Paris, France 70, 78, 100, 109
Parsons, Frank 99, *99*, 156
Parsons Paris Atelier 100
Parsons School of Design 100, *100*
Partridge, Frank 109
Partridge, John 108
Pawson, John 129
Pentney, Beatrice (née Morris, grandmother) 1, 2
Pentney, James (grandfather) 1–2
Pentney, Phyllis (b. Frances, m. Clyne) 2, 23–4, 28
Pentney, Sonia (b. Phyllis; m. Bromley, Whitaker; mother)
appearance 2, 3, 6, 23, 25

children, ideas about dressing 30, 34
employment 2, 23–4
family background 1, 2
houses and 33, 34, 35–6
Jacqueline
control of 38, 39, 41, 42, 43–4, 45
marriages
Donald Whitaker 24, 29
John Bromley 3–4, 6–7, 23
personality 7, 30
Second World War 6–7, 23–4, 30
Persia 153–4
Peter Jones 48, 57, 122, 128
Pettit, Stephen 149
photography 114–16
Place Royale (Place des Vosges), Paris 78
Pope, Alexander 75
Portman Square 88
Portsmouth, Hampshire 1–2
Pre-Raphaelite artists 142
prisoners of war 10, 28, 37
prostitutes 33, 34
Pudlicote, Oxfordshire 24, 25–7, *26*

Q

Queen Anne style 69
Queen's House, Greenwich 64, 65

R

Rainbird, George 148
Rainbow Corner 23
Rainham Hall, Havering 116
Rees, Tim 155
Reilly, Sir Paul 58, *58*, 59
Repton, Humphry 91–2
Restoration period 65
Robsjohn-Gibbings, T. H. 119–20, *119*
Room Outside 20
Roop, Guy 134
Rothermere, Esmond Harmsworth, 2nd Viscount 81
Royal Academy of Arts 97–8
Royal College of Art 98, 99
Royal Family 42
Royal Society of the Arts 78
Ryan, Stephen 129

S

Sacred Heart Convent, Hove 8–9, *8–9*, 10–12, 28–9

see also Lutwyche Hall, Shropshire
Saudi Arabia 155
Savoy Hotel 52
Second World War
   American Red Cross 23–4, 30
   camouflage 56, 117, 125
   design, impact on 58
   end of 28, 55, 121–2
   evacuation 12–13
   London during 19, 29
   Michael Inchbald and 47–8
   outbreak of 6–7
   prisoners of war 10, 28, 37
   Sonia Pentney during 30
Sezincote, Gloucestershire 81, *82*
shabby chic 124
Shepherd Street, Mayfair 33, 34
Shepherd's Market, Mayfair 33
Sheraton, Thomas 79–80
Shrewsbury, Shropshire 12–13
Shropshire 25
Siam 71
Siddeley, John 125, *126*, 146–7
Sizergh Castle, Cumbria 19, *19*, 20–2
Somerset House 98
South Kensington Museum 98–9
Southampton, Hampshire 24
Spanish Club, Beauchamp Place 49
Spy cartoons 102
Stanley House *see* Milner Street (No. 10)
Stephenson, Henry 141, *141*, 152–3, 154
Strawberry Hill 75–7
Strickland family 21
Strong, Sir Roy 143–4
Stuart period 63–5, 68–9, 71–2
Suffolk, Henrietta Howard, Countess of 75

T

Tehran Inchbald School 153–4
Tennyson d'Eyncourt, Mrs 36
Thornton Smith, Ernest v
Thwaites, Peter 150–1, 152, *152*, 153, 154
Todd, John 130–1
Toland, Gregg 114, 115
topiary gardens 20, *20*
training for interior designers v
Trianon de Porcelaine, France 67
Twickenham 75

U

University of Wales 155
upholsterers 94
upholstery 69–70

V

Vanity Fair 101–2
Vaux-le-Vicomte, France 66
Versailles, France 66–7, 91
Victoria & Albert Museum 56, 144
Victoria, Queen 92
Villeneuve, Louise de 109

W

Walpole, Horace 75–7, 86, 91
Walton Street 43, 45, 51
Ward, Leslie ('Spy', cartoonist) 102
Warilow, Mother (nun) 19–20, 21
Weld, Jo (Colonel Sir Joseph Weld OBE TD) 45
Welles, Orson 114
West, Benjamin 83
West Indies 82
Wharton, Edith 103
Whitaker family 27
Whitaker, Bernard 26–7
Whitaker, Donald 24, 29, 30–1, 32–3, 34–5, 41–2
Whitaker, Mabel 27
white decoration 106
White, Stanford 103
William III, King 71, 72
Wilson, Andrew 155
Withers iii–iv, 44–5
women decorators 102–7, 109
women's professional development iii–iv
Wontner, Sir Hugh 50, 51–2, *52*, 132
Wood, John 78
World War I 2, 101
World War II *see* Second World War
Wright, Frank Lloyd 113, *113*
Wright, W. and Son 34
Wyatt, James 82–3, 89

XYZ

Yapton, The Lodge, Sussex 4–7, 9–10, 11, 12

Illustration Credits

All images from the archives of the Inchbald School of Design unless otherwise stated.

8 © J.Middleton
9 Royal Pavilion & Museums, Brighton & Hove
12 Photo © Terry Robinson/www.geograph.org.uk
14, 15 Historic England Archive
19 Robert Harding/Alamy Stock Photo
20 Look and Learn/Bridgeman Images
26 Photo © Paul Massey
38 Greg Balfour Evans/Alamy Stock Photo
51 Pictorial Press Ltd/Alamy Stock Photo
52 © Keystone Pictures USA/Zumapress.com/Mary Evans
56 Design Council Archive, University of Brighton Design Archives (DCA-30-1-POR-G-4-1)
57 Trinity Mirror/Mirrorpix/Alamy Stock Photo
59 Everett Collection/Bridgeman Images
64 Look and Learn/Elgar Collection/Bridgeman Images
72 Reproduced by permission of Chatsworth Settlement Trustees/Bridgeman Images
73 Photo John Bethell. All rights reserved 2025/Bridgeman Images
74 Leklek73/Dreamstime.com (274550394)
77 Look and Learn/Bridgeman Images
81 Impress/Alamy Stock Photo
82 Stuart Black/Alamy Stock Photo
85 Getty Research Institute
91 Cooper Hewitt, Smithsonian Design Museum. Museum purchase through gift of Mrs. John Innes Kane (1948-40-103)
93 *left* Granger Historical Picture Archive/Alamy Stock Photo
right Howard Taylor/Alamy Stock Photo
95 Private collection
94 Cooper Hewitt, Smithsonian Design Museum. Museum purchase through gift of Mrs. John Innes Kane (1948-40-99)
96 *above*, 96 *below* Smithsonian Libraries and Archives
99 Parsons School of Design Alumni Association records, The New School Archives and Special Collections, The New School, New York, N.Y. Photo Fotoform News/World Events in Pictures/1819 Broadway, New York City
100 Parsons School of Design Alumni Association records, The New School Archives and Special Collections, The New School, New York, N.Y. (box 6, folder 25)
102 Christie's Images/Bridgeman Images
103 Chronicle/Alamy Stock Photo
106 Cecil Beaton, Vogue © Condé Nast
107 Sibyl Colefax & John Fowler, Sibylcolefax.com
111 Angelo Hornak/Alamy Stock Photo
112 Alpha Stock/Alamy Stock Photo
113 Daniel Wilson/Alamy Stock Photo
116 Piemags/LCB/Alamy Stock Photo
119 Loomis Dean/The LIFE Picture Collection/Shutterstock
125 Chroma Collection/Alamy Stock Photo
127 Walter Brown/ANL/Shutterstock

Alumni: Photographer Credits

164-167 Henry Bourne
168 (top) Brian McKee, (bottom) Ahmet Ertuğ
169 (top) Emre Dörter,
(bottom) Fritz Von Der Schulenburg
170-171 Alexander James
174-175 Philip Vile
176-179 Richard Gooding,
179 (bottom) Daniella Cesarei
180 Salvador Colaço
181 Antonio Moutinho
182 Hayley Kelsing
183 (top) Antonio Moutinho
183 (bottom) Francisco Nogueira
184-185 Paul Massey
186 Steven Wooster
188-193 Jonathan Craggs
194 (top) Steven Wooster
(middle) Steven Wooster
(bottom) Allan Pollok-Morris
195 (top) Allan Pollok-Morris
(bottom) Carl Bengtsson
196-201 Russell Hogg